The Street Where I Live

The Street Where I Live

A MEMOIR

ALAN JAY LERNER

Foreword by John Lahr

W • W • NORTON & COMPANY

INDEPENDENT PUBLISHERS SINCE 1923

NEW YORK | LONDON

To Fritz,

without whom this would have been

an address book.

Contents

Foreword

Alan Jay Lerner described his job this way: "I write musicals—every word spoken or sung from curtain up to curtain down." But Lerner's songs, not his stories, are what live after him. In the late 1940s, when Lerner hit his stride as a lyricist, America was enjoying the greatest rise in per-capita income in the history of Western civilization. Between 1945 and 1955, individual wealth nearly tripled. Lerner's lyrics were part of the luster of this Golden Age; his witty eloquence made the high times sparkle. In such memorable musicals as *Brigadoon, Paint Your Wagon, My Fair Lady, Gigi,* and *Camelot,* Lerner whipped up verbal soufflés to accompany the buoyant melodies of Frederick Loewe and put before the American public a glamorous sense of its own well-being. Lerner insisted on joy; he even incarnated it in the "happily-ever-aftering" of "Camelot," an Eden where "the climate must be perfect all the year." To our sour age, in which frivolity has been more or less banished, such fantasies may seem antique. But if the fifties and early sixties were "the *belle époque* of American musical theatre," as Lerner claims in his memoir, then he was one of the most radiant belles of the ball.

Lerner was a Park Avenue princeling; he exuded the optimism of his privilege. Although Lerner lived in many deluxe homes through the decades—a Manhattan townhouse, a villa in the South of France, a colonial farmhouse in Rockland County—his permanent residence was in the Superbia of his imagination. His father, Joseph, owned a successful chain of women's specialty stores; Lerner's emporium was Broadway. He imposed on his lyrics and on his troubled life the shellac of charm. "I can never find it in my heart to despise glamour," Lerner said. His particular lyrical line was longing, not loss. "As a rule, it is not sadness that brings tears to my eyes but a longing fulfilled," he said. His impeccably crafted lyrics—the title song for *On a Clear Day You Can See Forever*, for instance, took ninety-one drafts and nearly a year to complete—made an exhibition of perfect equipoise.

Lerner grew up his father's favorite of three boys in a fractious family. "My Pappy was rich and my Ma was good-lookin' but by the time I was born my father no longer thought so," he writes in his memoir. "Their life together was a familiar symphony in three movements: arguing, separating, reuniting." Lerner identified more with his high-rolling father than with his roly-poly mother, Edie, who once slapped him because he looked like her husband. "I adored him," Lerner said of his misogynistic old man. (Of Edie, he observed, "My mother didn't start really loving me until after the success of *Brigadoon*.") Lerner regularly accompanied Joseph to boxing matches and, from the age of five, to musicals. (He had been named after the insolent Hearst drama critic Alan Hale.) His obsession with language and its meticulous deployment also began with his father. Joseph dispatched his children to Bedales, the exclusive British boarding school, to acquire proper use of their mother tongue. "I never sent him a letter that he did not return to me with notes in the margin suggesting more interesting ways of saying the same sentence," Lerner recalled.

Lerner carried his father's preoccupations (musicals, language, boxing, philandering) and his high expectations into adult life. In the mid-fifties, Joseph, at the hospital for his fiftieth operation for throat cancer, which had left him unable to speak, scribbled his son a note and pressed it into his hand as he was wheeled into the operating theater. "I suppose you're wondering why I want to live?" he wrote. "Because I want to see what happens to you."

Lerner's lyrics were exercises in seduction, a way of recapturing the adoration in Joseph's defining gaze. Lerner, who had lost an eye while boxing at Harvard, literally had an eye for the ladies. He was a courtly lover. He married eight times. "Alan was a broken man inside," his third wife, the Academy Award–winning actress Nancy Olson, whose marriage to Lerner spanned his most creative period (1950–57), told me. "The only way he could feel whole was when the eyes of another were on him." Another of his ex-wives quipped, "Marriage was Alan's way of saying goodbye." The glow of idealization was the intoxication of courtship— "almost like being in love," as Lerner famously admitted in song. About the affairs of his restless heart, his memoir is weasel-worded. "The heart may have its reasons of which the reason knows nothing; but reason all too often has no heart," he wrote. Elsewhere, however, he confessed, "I wanted the thrill of love, not its disappointments."

Lerner also had trouble being faithful to his collaborator Fritz Loewe, which became an issue between them. When they formed their partnership, in 1942, after a chance meeting at the Lamb's Club, Lerner was an eager beaver of twenty-four; Loewe, at forty-one, was a veteran of disappointment. Lerner was fast-talking, fast-thinking, fast-moving—in other words, American. Loewe, who was Austrian and whose father had been a star of Viennese operetta, was cultured and sardonic. He had been a child prodigy, had made his solo piano debut with the Berlin Philharmonic at fourteen and, at fifteen, wrote "Kathrin (The Girl with the Best Legs in Berlin)," the sheet music for which sold two million copies. Perhaps because he'd struggled so hard and so long to find a theatrical foothold in America, Loewe was given to loudly proclaiming his genius. ("He was the single most conceited man I ever knew," said André Previn, who was the musical director of *Gigi*, and for whom Loewe wrote some of his lushest melodies.)

Lerner's roots were on 42nd Street, Loewe's were in operetta. According to Lerner, Loewe could musically characterize any period or locale, "providing it is not contemporary," he said. "Alan felt there was something a little dated about [Loewe's] composing. Somewhere he always felt that he should be writing with Richard Rodgers or a more current 'with it' composer," Nancy Olson writes in her unpublished memoir, *A Front Row Seat*. "I never was really a songwriter," Loewe insisted. "I always considered myself a dramatic composer . . . someone that can illustrate in music any emotion."

Lerner could work without Loewe, but Loewe couldn't really work without Lerner. (Of Loewe's six musicals, five were written with Lerner.) In 1947, after their breakthrough success, *Brigadoon*, Lerner jilted Loewe to collaborate with another diminutive émigré, Kurt Weill, on *Love Life* (1948). After their second success, *Paint Your Wagon*, in 1951, Lerner left Loewe again for a fling in Hollywood with Burton Lane and Arthur Schwartz. As early as 1952, Lerner and Loewe had flirted with the idea of adapting George Bernard Shaw's *Pygmalion*, but, like many composing teams before them, they could not crack the play's structure to make it singable. In 1954, when the property became free again, the American musical was undergoing a mutation. "It no longer seemed essential that a musical have a subplot, nor that there be an ever-present ensemble filling the air with high C's and flying limbs," Lerner said. Even more important, Lerner had hit upon the key to musicalizing *Pygmalion*: he made the lyrics an extension of Shaw's dialogue. There was only one problem: he and Loewe were not on speaking terms.

In the two years since they'd been in touch, Lerner's Hollywood projects had collapsed and his mooted stage musical based on Al Capp's *Li'l Abner* had stalled. Olson remembers Lerner in tears at the edge of their bed, feeling washed up, and stymied about the Shaw project. "He said Fritz was the only composer that could possibly do it, but of course Fritz was no longer talking to him," Olson recalled. "I sat up in bed and handed Alan a Kleenex, put my arms around him, and said, 'Don't you understand that Fritz is sitting by his telephone waiting for your call?' Alan said that was nonsense, he doubted that Fritz would answer the phone. I said, 'I'll prove it to you.' I picked up the phone and dialed Fritz's home. The minute he heard my voice he said, 'Nance!'—pronounced *Naahnce*—'How are you?' I explained that Alan had an idea for a new work and there was only one person in the entire world who could compose the music and that was him. Could he possibly join us for lunch tomorrow? He asked, 'What time?'"

By the end of lunch, the pair had begun work. Loewe rented a house near Lerner's, in Rockland County. "For one year Fritz sat at our dining-room table for breakfast, lunch, and dinner," Olson writes. Two false starts and thirty songs later, Lerner and Loewe had made their masterpiece, a show that changed their lives and the shape of musical storytelling. Lerner, who had never adapted a story, was at his most brilliant; almost all of the show's fifteen songs became standards. The Broadway opening of *My Fair Lady*, in 1956, was one of the most memorable in history. "A great night for envy," Oscar Levant called it. Lerner and Loewe owned thirty percent of the show. By the mid-sixties, when the revenues from the various productions, recordings, and the movie were calculated, the show had grossed just over six billion dollars in today's money.

As a partnership, Lerner and Loewe were a study in contradictions: one was workaholic, the other a bon vivant. One preferred gambling on the roulette wheels of the Riviera; the other's flutter was marriage. "You are a funny little boy," Loewe told Lerner. "You build a nest and then shit in it." To the end of his days, Loewe, who had tried marriage once, preferred to play the field. Both were roués of the Rialto. "It's a melancholy fact that between the two of us we have supported more women than Playtex," Loewe said. Lerner liked to socialize with the Great and the Good, counting as friends his Choate classmate John F. Kennedy and his Harvard collaborator Leonard Bernstein, with whom he'd written a Hasty Pudding Club show. By contrast, Loewe preferred to keep to himself. "What's the point of seeing people: those poor sad faces with all their heartbreaking troubles?" he asked.

Almost all their songs were first inspired by Loewe's improvisations at the piano, usually in his underpants, the "Byronesque costume in which he always works," Lerner writes. ("I couldn't write a note with clothes on," Loewe told a reporter after *Brigadoon* became a hit. "That is why I usually work in the morning before I'm dressed.") At the piano, Loewe lost himself in the music, sometimes for hours; Lerner listened, scribbling ideas, biting his cuticles until they bled so badly that in public he wore surgical gloves. Once a melody caught Lerner's fancy, Loewe was in the habit of saying, "The poor little boy. I've knocked him up!" At that point, Loewe would leave Lerner alone to write, weighing in only when the song was done. "Fritz never regarded the music as finished until the lyric was finished," Lerner writes. "He refused to play anyone a naked melody. He never kept a bar of music that I didn't like and I've never kept a word he didn't like."

Every Broadway hit is some kind of mystery. Lerner's witty memoir *The Street Where I Live* charts the exhausting, sometimes hilarious roller-coaster ride of this luminous body of work. In the wings of this lively account of a show-biz life are Lerner's romantic entanglements, his mounting alimony payments, his tax evasion, and finally, his discovery of the notorious Max Jacobson—"Dr. Feelgood"—whose shots of amphetamines, laced with steroids, painkillers, and animal hormones lifted his spirits, along with those of many other depressed celebrities from Tennessee Williams and Marilyn Monroe to JFK. Jacobson, who was known as "Uncle Max" to Lerner's children, became a fixture in Lerner's life, administering his pick-me-up jabs as often as three times a day. "Maybe those shots will destroy me but they make me see life in a good light," Lerner said, at the divorce proceedings with Wife No. 4 in 1964.

After the hard slog to mount *Camelot*, in 1960, at age sixty Loewe retired from the partnership. "There were no formal farewells, no goodbyes, nothing to mark the end of the long voyage we had been on together," Lerner writes, leaving the reader to decode Loewe's loud silence after a decade of sensational success.

The arrival of rock and roll also contributed to the shift in Lerner's luck. "Youth has many glories, but judgment is not one of them. No amount of electronic amplification can turn a belch into an aria," he writes. Vietnam abroad and assassination at home unmoored both the musical and Lerner. He, and his lyrical idiom, were suddenly passé, overtaken by history and the wah-wah pedal. As he put it so brilliantly, in "What Did I Have That I Don't Have Now," from *On a Clear Day You Can See Forever*, which was written with Burton Lane and premiered on Broadway in 1965:

I'M JUST A VICTIM OF TIME,
OBSOLETE IN MY PRIME!

The Street Where I Live focuses exclusively on Lerner's collaboration with Loewe, but his career didn't end there. He went on to write nine more musicals with other outstanding composers, André Previn, Leonard Bernstein, and Charles Strouse among them. He never had another hit. However, he had high hopes for a show with Andrew Lloyd Webber. "Who would have thought it," he wrote to Lloyd Webber from his hospital bed, where he died of lung cancer on June 14, 1986, at the age of sixty-seven. "Instead of writing 'Phantom of the Opera,' I ended up looking like him."

—John Lahr

Note

Lyrics, no less than music, are written to be heard. A lyric without its musical clothes is a scrawny creature and should never be allowed to parade naked across the printed page. Nevertheless, for purposes of reference, that is precisely what I am heartlessly allowing mine to do.

Should the reader be interested in reading any of the lyrics discussed in the following pages, he will find them shivering in toto at the end of the book.

I am grateful to Stephanie Lyall
for her irrepressible assistance

and to Judy Insel,
a cricket on my hearth.

The Street Where I Live

Overture

This is the story of climaxes and endings and the sundown of a decade that blazed with joy, excitement, and triumph: so much, in fact, that as I look back I am haunted by the fear that perhaps I drank the wine too fast to taste it and instead of slowing down to enjoy the scenery, kept my foot on the accelerator and my eyes on the road ahead, gazing only occasionally from side to side and waiting far too long to glance at the rear-view mirror.

The decade was roughly from the early fifties to the early sixties when the "belle epoque" of the musical theatre that had begun with *Oklahoma* in 1943 reached its zenith. It was the decade when Metro-Goldwyn-Mayer, the creator of the modern screen musical, made its last Academy Award-winning gasp and within a year closed its musical doors forever. It was the decade that ended with a musical play that became, in a way, the twilight of the gods—the last musical score for Broadway by Frederick Loewe who retired, the last costumes ever designed by Adrian who died after he had completed the initial sketches, the last production of the famous English producer, Jack Hylton, who died shortly after it opened at Drury Lane, the last contribution to Broadway of the great Moss Hart who died of a heart attack within a year after it opened, and a musical that became the symbol of John F. Kennedy's all too "brief shining moment."

In short, this is the story of *My Fair Lady, Gigi,* and *Camelot.* And in order to explain the part that I, myself, played I shall have to begin with the biographical sketch that usually appears at the back of the program.

ALAN JAY LERNER (*librettist*). Born: New York City, August 31, 1918. Educated: Columbia Grammar School, New York City; Bedales, Hampshire, England; The Choate School; Harvard '40. Parents:

My Pappy was rich and my Ma was good lookin', but by the time I was born my father no longer thought so. As far back as I can remember, their life together was a familiar symphony in three movements: arguing, separating, reuniting. They played it over and over again but each time the second movement became longer and the third shorter, until finally, one day, it stopped after the second movement. This was how it happened.

Every Friday night my father went to the prize fights at Madison Square Garden. The boxing profession in the late twenties and thirties was populated with some of the great names in pugilistic history: Bennie Leonard, Jimmy MacLaren, Maxie Rosenbloom, Mickey Walker, Max Baer, Henry Armstrong, Louis, Schmelling, Tony Canzoneri, who, incidentally, knocked out Fritz Loewe in one round and jabbed him back to the keyboard. The list is endless and explains why Friday night at Madison Square Garden was the Philharmonic of sport. Like the Philharmonic, the patrons had season tickets and the ringside was always sprinkled with the faces of the great and famous.

When I said that my father went every Friday night, I should have said almost every Friday night, for on many occasions his taste for combat drew him to other, more quilted arenas.

In those days people worked on Saturdays and one Saturday

morning, my father later told me, as he was preparing to go to the office, two things happened that had never happened before during his entire married life. The first was that while he was dressing my mother woke up. The second was that as she opened her eyes she said: "Who won the fight?" Alas, that Friday happened to have been one of the nights that my father's ringside seat was empty. I do not remember who fought in the main bout, but will call them Smith and Jones. My father, taking a chance, said: "Smith." My mother turned over and went back to sleep. My father went into the dining room and opened the *New York Times* to the sports page. Jones had won.

He methodically finished his breakfast and went downtown to his office. Once there he called the house. There was one maid specifically assigned to looking after his clothes. He told her to pack everything and the chauffeur would call for his luggage shortly. By the time my mother fully awakened, my father and all that was his were gone. As he later explained to me, it seemed the only sensible thing to do. He realized that it deprived my mother of her innings, but it avoided a great deal of noise and he would have ended up at the Waldorf anyhow.

I was one of three sons, the middle one. I was my father's favorite and I adored him. However, he made things very difficult for me at home by never attempting to conceal his partiality. At least once a week he would call the house and leave word that the car would call for me to take me to have dinner with him and spend the evening. Sometimes we would go to Madison Square Garden, and so I grew up wanting to box. He also loved the musical theatre and from the time I was five years old there was hardly a musical on Broadway that he did not take me to see.

By the age of twelve I had only one ambition and that was to be involved, someday, somehow, in the musical theatre. I had studied the piano from the age of five and began writing "songs" in my early teens. To all of that, my father paid no attention. He was not one of those who believed in encouraging children, nor may I add, many years later when he saw I was serious, did he ever discourage me. Fundamentally, I suppose, he simply hoped I would not embarrass him.

Besides his enjoyment of boxing and his interest in music, he was passionate about the English language which was the reason my brothers and I were all shipped off to school in England, i.e., to learn the language. Until I graduated from college, I never sent him a letter that he did not return to me with notes in the margin suggesting more interesting ways of saying the same sentence. In my twenties, even after I had won a Drama Critics' Award for *Brigadoon*, he said to me one weekend—I should say he wrote to me, for by this time he had been stricken with cancer and his tongue had been removed—"Alan, I have counted the words you have used this weekend and you have an active vocabulary of 297 words. I don't see how you can make a career as a writer with an active vocabulary of 297 words. However, I believe you have talent and if you would like to return to school and study, I would be more than happy to subsidise you."

I feel I should mention that neither boxing, nor music, nor the English language were in any way related to his actual occupation. A Philadelphian by birth, he had started life as a dentist of all things. While still in his twenties, he had the good sense to realize that among his many talents, dentistry was not one of them and before World War I he became the founder of a highly successful chain of stores that still bears his name, although it is twenty-five years since there has been any family connection.

His influence on me was indelible and my love for him as alive as it was the day he died in 1954, but there were many issues where we parted company. Principally they were politics and women. He was a dedicated Republican, as had been his father before him, and was permanently but silently irritated when he discovered I was a liberal Democrat.

As far as his attitude toward women was concerned, he never fully emerged from the Victorian era and regarded women as inferior men. He believed, and it is a belief that still exists today, that the hallmark of maturity was the absence of a committed, romantic passion. It so happens that I am firmly convinced that one of the greatest myths perpetrated by the post-Freudian age is the notion that there is such a thing as a mature person in the first place. Experienced? Yes. Wise? Yes. Mature? Perhaps in one area or another, but that is all. I have never known anyone who consistently placed empathy ahead of ego. I have seen corporation presidents behave in the most adolescent, petulant fashion, sometimes treating subordinates with the cruelty of a child. I have seen distinguished professors possessed of enough vanity to fill three theatres, and the wisest and most stable of politicians lose all perspective under the impact of applause. I have also known many men who have never been in love, never been possessive, never been jealous, never been wounded by imaginary arrows, never known the agonies of self-doubt nor the often paranoic fears of inadequacy. But, immature as the whole romantic kit-and-caboodle may seem to be, to go through life in a permanent state of self-protection, incapable of giving because of the fear of exposure is not my idea of maturity. The heart may have its reasons of which the reason knows nothing; but reason all too often has no heart.

My father said to me one day when I was about eighteen: "Let me tell you something about women, son. You will have your troubles with them. We all do. There will be arguments; a marriage may not work; there may be times when you get into bed and not be able to function. But *always* remember this. No matter what happens, it's her fault." I stared at him in disbelief. "The proof of it is," he went on "that you will go to bed with one woman on Monday and it will be a failure and another on Tuesday and it will be successful. You are the same person. Only the woman has changed. Therefore, whose fault is it? Hers."

The extraordinary part is that he truly believed it and viewed the romantic streak in my nature as a child's disease that I would outgrow, or so he hoped. I did not. And whatever I have written clearly indicates it.

If I seem to have slighted my mother, it is not because of lack of affection on my part or lack of interest in the musical theatre on hers. In fact, when she was in her teens she studied singing in that semi-serious way dowagers' nieces did at the turn of the century. Her accompanist, incidentally, was Richard Rodgers' mother. Neither lady, I may add, was motivated by financial need. No, I have devoted more time to my father because this book concerns the theatre and these introductory words are to explain who lit the fire in me, and there is no question that it was he. My mother's contribution was more that of a guide, who took me on educational sightseeing tours ranging from concert hall to museum, from ancient ruin to European cathedral. But directly or indirectly, by intention or accident, by admiration, rebellion or resistance, it was my father who created the child who became the father of the man.

He was almost a handsome man, firmly built, of medium height, brownish-blonde hair that grayed early at the temples, a ruddy complexion, and very large sky blue eyes. He possessed great charm and was impeccably dressed always. He spoke four languages fluently, loved the gay life, especially dancing, and was more popular with his fellow-men than they were with him.

He had no use for organized religion and consequently we had no religious training. He claimed to have faith in God but I doubt if he trusted Him. He substituted resolve for prayer and accepted his aloneness as he accepted being a Jew with neither defiance, self-pity, pride, or resentment. Nor did he, during all the years of his agony, ever recant or weaken. Two days before his death, he looked up from his hospital bed and wrote to my younger brother, Bob: "What religion are your children?" Bob replied good humoredly: "I don't know. Whatever church is on the corner I'll send them to." My father nodded approvingly and wrote: "It's all a lot of apple sauce."

During the seventeen years he was in and out of the Memorial Hospital in New York, he became friends with Cardinal Spellman. I believe they met through Damon Runyon who was in the next room. Spellman used to visit him at least once a week. I could understand his fondness for my father. After all, it is part of the duty of every religious leader to win as many rich souls to the cause as possible. I could not understand my father, however. One day I asked him what he and the cardinal could possibly have in common. He wrote back, with a twinkle in his eyes: "We have a great deal in common. We're both in the chain store business."

But neither the cardinal nor anyone else ever convinced him that the life of the spirit did not coincide with the life of the body. One day, when my years could still be counted on two hands, I asked him where we go when we die. Without a moment's hesitation he answered: "Nowhere. And if anyone ever tells you differently, he's lying to you." I was horrified, but of course did not show it. He might have thought I was questioning his word. "You go to sleep," he went on, "and never wake up."

That was the last good night's sleep I had for a long time to come. I was afraid to close my eyes for fear they would not open again, and in the summer I constantly searched the sky for some sign—I have no idea what—that my father was wrong. One night I saw a huge cloud formation that resembled a man's head, and for one moment my hopes rose. But then a gust of wind came along and blew "God's" face away and my hopes with it. When I was twelve, in school in England, it was part of the curriculum that every Sunday we had to read the *London Times*. I was a great Sherlock Holmes fan and one day an item in the paper caught my eye. It said that in three weeks, Sir Arthur Conan-Doyle would be addressing the British Psychic Society on the nature and existence of God. Oh boy! I thought. At last! Sherlock Holmes has found God and my father is wrong. I could not wait to read the *London Times* three weeks hence. When the great day came, I picked up the newspaper and read to my dismay that that week Sir Arthur Conan-Doyle had died. Well, I reasoned, that proves it; Sherlock Holmes solved the mystery, but God did not want him to tell anyone. Nevertheless, I found the address of the British Psychic Society in the London telephone directory and wrote them a letter, asking if anyone had a copy of the speech Sir Arthur had intended to deliver. A few days later I received a reply, thanking me for my letter but telling me that no one at the Society had seen the speech and, therefore, no copy was available. They asked if I would be interested in joining their organization and I wrote back that I would. From then on, I began to receive literature from the Society, most of which to my twelve-year-old eyes might as well have been written in ancient Mayan. But now and then I would understand a sentence or two—enough, at least, to make me realize that all the answers were not in.

They say the difference between the Oriental and the Occidental is that the Occidental is afraid of the mystery and the Oriental glories in it. Some Asian gene must have wandered far from home and gotten mixed up with mine, because ever since that day in the library of the Bedales School in Petersfield, Hampshire, until this very moment, nothing, outside of the theatre, has intrigued me and sustained my unflagging interest more than the occult, extrasensory perception, reincarnation and all that is called metaphysical (until it is understood and becomes physical). Undoubtedly it is responsible for my penchant for fantasy as subject matter, and in

1965 I even wrote a musical about parapsychology and reincarnation called *On a Clear Day You Can See Forever.*

Needless to say I did not communicate any of this budding interest to my father. It was not because of fear that he would think I had gone quite mad. He knew everyone in the world did not agree with him. But his children were different. They were supposed to.

I seldom discussed any part of my life with him that was not within his own intellectual orbit, including my theatrical career. He responded in kind by rarely commenting. In fact, he never even seemed pleased. But he never fooled me for a moment.

When *Brigadoon* opened and was enthusiastically received, a neighbor came up to him on the beach in Florida, where he lived in the winter, and said to him: "I just read the reviews of *Brigadoon.* Your son is certainly a lucky boy." My father took out the pad and pencil he always carried with him and wrote: "Yes, it's a funny thing about Alan. The harder he works the luckier he gets." I know the story is true because the man sent me the slip of paper.

On another occasion I was nominated for an Academy Award for the screenplay of *An American in Paris.* I was not present at the ceremony because my father was being operated on the same day for the forty-ninth time. (I remember the number clearly because when he signed the official form giving permission for the operation and saw on it: "Number of operations: 49," he wrote underneath: "When it gets to fifty, sell.") Although he never said so, I knew he liked me being there before an operation. Besides, in all honesty, I never thought I would win. No screenplay for a musical ever had before. After his operation he was, of course, heavily sedated and not expected to regain consciousness until the morning. The Academy Awards were being broadcast at eleven o'clock, New York time. To my astonishment I won. On the way home, I stopped by the hospital and told his nurse that when he awakened, would she please tell him the news. "Oh," she said, "he knows." I was bewildered. "How?" I asked. "Well, she said, "at five minutes to eleven he came out of his coma, reached over, and turned on the radio." After he heard that I had won, she told me, he turned it off and lapsed back into unconsciousness. The next day, however, when I went to see him he never mentioned the incident nor congratulated me.

But one day when I was pushing his bed into the elevator to take him to the operating room, he wrote to me: "I suppose you're wondering why I want to live." It was precisely what I was thinking and I nodded. He wrote another note and just before the nurses took him away, he tore it from the pad and stuffed it into my hand. The operation he had before him was a brute, and there was a strong possibility he would not survive it. So for a few minutes I did not think to read his note. Downstairs in his room, I suddenly remembered it was in my hand and I opened it. It read: "Because I want to see what happens to you."

He died a month before I began to write *My Fair Lady*. I know how much it would have meant to him and I know how much his absence meant to me.

As I indicated in the "program notes," I am a librettist. However, whenever I fill out a form which asks that I identify my profession I do not say I am a librettist. I say I am a "playwright-lyricist." I write every word that is spoken or sung from curtain up to curtain down. If it be an adaptation, varying amounts of the original dialogue may be retained. In the case of *My Fair Lady* more than half was by Bernard Shaw. Less than half was by me, the playwright-lyricist. Until a few years ago it was not even proper to say "lyricist" because there was no such word in the dictionary. A man who wrote words for a song was officially called a lyrist. Popular usage finally defeated tradition and lyricist became accepted. Amen.

One of the reasons I dislike the word librettist is best illustrated by a famous Mrs. Malaprop of New York who years ago, when asked where she had been the night before, said: "To the opera." Asked what she had seen, she replied: "It was some Italian opera called 'Libretto'." (She was the same lady, incidentally, who shrewdly observed one night that "mirages are not what they seem.") A librettist has always seemed to me someone associated with opera and operetta and who specialized in unintelligibility and anonymity. Nevertheless, that is what I am. A librettist.

I became a professional librettist because of a cigarette on a golf course, a left hook to the side of the head and a wrong turn on the way to the men's room.

The cigarette I lit was on the golf course of The Choate School in Connecticut. It was a few months before graduation and the following year I was to go to the Sorbonne (for French), then to a university in Spain (for Spanish), then to Italy, and finally to the foreign service school at Georgetown in Washington, D.C. Despite my passion for the theatre and to be a writer, my father decided that what I wanted was a diplomatic career. He did not place much stock in the opinion of adolescents and, in general, ruled his children very much as the British ruled India. Every Indian was guaranteed a fair trial by jury, but in the entire history of the British mandate no Indian was ever found innocent. My father also ruled in absentia.

It so happened that at Choate in those days smoking was verboten. A butt in the mouth was automatically followed by a train ticket in one hand and your suitcase in the other. That is, if you were caught. I was caught. This flagrant act of disobedience so enraged my father that he cancelled my diplomatic career and sentenced me to four years of hard labor at an American university, which was a little like punishing a prisoner by kicking him out of jail. Thus it was that in September, 1936, instead of living la vie de boheme along the Boulevard St. Germain, I found myself more provincially ensconced at Harvard University, Cambridge, Massachusetts, twenty-eight hundred miles closer to Times Square.

At Harvard I contributed to the Hasty Pudding shows, the annual undergraduate musical romp, saw the Boston tryout of every play and musical en route to Broadway, took flying lessons so that if war came I could join the air corps and, naturally, went out for the boxing team. One day in the boxing ring my mind wandered, my guard dropped, and a left hook to the side of the head removed all sense from my expression. For the next two weeks New England's clear, winter days grew murkier and murkier . . . but only to me. My vision had been seriously impaired. Upon examination it was discovered I had lost the retina of my left eye and was in danger of losing the sight in the other as well. One operation and several blindfolded months later, I was back at school with all exercise forbidden for five years and a stern warning that sneezing or bending over could make me a candidate for a cane and dog. But I had one good eye with which to see and shortly after graduation it saw my brothers and friends go off to war.

Anguished and ashamed that I was not with them, I deserted "the old familiar places" and faces of my youth and moved from the East Seventies to West Forty-fourth Street. First to the Lambs Club, the famous old theatrical establishment, now extinct, where I met the first man who ever encouraged me to believe that I might have a future as a lyric writer. He also happened to be one of the great lyric writers of our time—Lorenz (Larry) Hart of Rodgers and. During the three years before he died we became good friends, not because he found me particularly fascinating but because he was so terrifyingly lonely, and I worshipped him so that I made myself available to join him at any hour of the day or night, usually for gin rummy which I played badly because I was not interested, and he played badly because he was usually drunk. I do not know his actual height, but I imagine he was about four feet and ten inches. It is inconceivable that his stature was not a major contributor to his perpetual torment. His education was vast; he spoke German fluently and was a blood descendant of Heinrich Heine. I believe he was also a literary descendant. There is a bittersweet quality in so many of Larry's lyrics that seem redolent of Heine. Because of his size the opposite sex was denied him and he was forced to find relief in the only other sex left. But all this I only heard about from others and never saw a sign of myself. He was kind, endearing, sad, infuriating, and funny, but, at the time that I knew him, in a devastating state of emotional disarray.

When Dick Rodgers turned to Oscar Hammerstein as a collaborator and their first effort became the greatest success Dick had ever had, namely *Oklahoma,* Larry's pain must have been unbearable. One of the saddest moments I can remember happened a few months after the musical opened. We were in Fritz Loewe's living room. There was a blackout and the room was pitch dark. The only light came from Larry's cigar. Fritz turned on the radio and an orchestra was playing something from *Oklahoma.* The end of the cigar flashed brighter and brighter with accelerated puffs. Fritz immediately switched to another station. Again someone was playing a song from *Oklahoma.* And Larry's cigar grew brighter and the puffs became faster. It happened three times and then Fritz turned off the radio. The glow from the cigar subsided and the breathing so slow the cigar almost went out. The whole incident probably took less than two minutes and during it not a word was said, but I wept for him in the dark. The moment the lights came on Larry continued the conversation that had been interrupted by the blackout without a trace of what had happened in his voice or on his face.

He died the following year at the age of forty-seven and I believe Fritz was the last one to see him alive. Larry had a cousin who was a close friend of Fritz and late one night he called Fritz, worried because he could not find Larry. It was about three in the morning and raining heavily. Fritz went out looking for him. He found him sitting in the gutter outside a bar on Eighth Avenue, drunk and drenched to the skin. He put him in a cab and took him to Delmonico's where Larry was staying at the time. He made Larry promise he would go upstairs and go to bed and stayed in the cab until he saw him enter the hotel. Then he went home. Larry, true to his promise, went up to his room and got into bed. When he fell asleep he never awakened. He had contracted pneumonia and was gone by noon the next day. Life had ended for him much earlier and death was but a formality.

The word genius, like most superlatives these days, has grown feeble from overwork, but if lyric writing is worthy of a genius it had one in Larry.

From the Lambs I moved to the Hotel Royalton, also on Forty-fourth Street, whose most famous resident at the time was the famous critic, George Jean Nathan, who lived in a room without ventilation and so thick with smoke that the elevator man, who used to double as a bellboy, told me that when he brought Mr. Nathan his coffee in the morning he could never find him.

A few years later when *Brigadoon* opened to a unanimously enthusiastic press, Nathan developed a high-school crush on the leading lady, invited her frequently to supper, and sent her all his books, each inscribed with an adolescent expression of endearment. One weekend he called to ask her out and discovered she was visiting me in the country, not for artistic reasons. This so enraged him that he devoted his entire next week's column to how I had stolen the plot of *Brigadoon* and *The Day Before Spring*, Fritz Loewe's and my effort of the year before. His attacks continued for three weeks with such venom that the *New York Times* called and offered me space to answer him, which I did, labeling the whole accusation as rubbish and documenting the developments of each play into the final product. Nathan took my article, deleted a sentence here and a word there until it seemed as if I had confessed to plagiarism, and then published it in his annual year book of the theatre.

The critics knew the whole story and when *Brigadoon* won the award for the best musical of the year, Brooks Atkinson in his Sunday column in the *New York Times* reported that the main opposition to *Brigadoon* was Mr. Nathan, who claimed it had been pilfered from some ancient Icelandic legend that only Mr. Nathan was old enough to remember. Nevertheless, to this day chroniclers of the musical theatre invariably state that *Brigadoon* was based on a folk tale and give Nathan as their authority.

So much for the accuracy of theatrical historians. As Voltaire said: "History is a collection of agreed upon lies."

After a year and a half at the Royalton, I moved across the street to that most illustrious and legend-filled theatrical hotel, the Algonquin.

During this period, instead of flying through the air as I had planned, I was filling it with words. Immediately upon graduation from college I became a radio writer, on the theory that anything I wrote in the morning of my twenties was bound to teach me something. And it did. It taught me never to be afraid of a deadline. In future years when I was on the road with a play, no matter how much work may have been demanded, in no matter how short a period, I never panicked or doubted I would do it. The quality one can never vouch for under any circumstances, but that it would be written I have always been certain.

At one point I was writing five daytime shows a week, comedy for Victor Borge, twenty minutes of comedic material for a Tuesday night show called "The Raleigh Room," and a one hour program on Sunday called "The Philco Hall Of Fame." I was also writing a play (unproduced) and the only way I could make the schedule work was not to sleep on Monday night.

Once a year I also wrote lyrics for the Lambs Gambols, the annual show. One day late in August of 1942, I was having lunch in the grill when a short, well-built, tightly strung man with a large head and hands and immensely dark circles under his eyes strode to a few feet from my table and stopped short. His destination was the men's room and he had gone the wrong way. He turned to get back on the right road and suddenly saw me. He stared for a moment. I knew who he was. His name was Frederick Loewe, Fritz to the membership, a Viennese-born, ex-concert pianist and a talented, struggling composer. He came to my table and sat down. "You're Lerner, aren't you?" he asked. I could not deny it. "You write lyrics, don't you?" he continued. "I try," I replied. "Well," he said "would you like to write with me?" I immediately said, "Yes." And we went to work.

And thus, with a cigarette, a left hook, and a wrong turn to the men's room I became a professional librettist. Such are the capricious winds of chance that either bring you closer to home or farther and forever out to sea.

Fritz Loewe and I worked together for a total of eighteen consecutive years, then once again ten years after that for another two years. We began in Detroit in 1942 working in a stock company, rewriting old plays, and adding a few songs. When I say old plays I exaggerate. The stock company closed after one old play. We returned to New York and our first production on Broadway was an ill-advised, little effort called *What's Up?* which was, oddly enough, directed by George Balanchine. It lasted about a week. In 1945 came *The Day Before Spring,* and in 1947 we "arrived" with *Brigadoon,* which won the Drama Critics' Award for the best musical of the year. Our next joint work was *Paint Your Wagon* in 1951, which was a success but not a hit. By that I mean the reviews were mixed and the backers eventually made a small profit.

Then came *My Fair Lady, Gigi,* and *Camelot* which are the subjects of this book.

FREDERICK LOEWE (*composer*). Born: Berlin, June 11, 1901, of Viennese parents. Student of Busoni and Eugene d'Albert. Made his concert debut at the age of fourteen with Berlin Philharmonic and won the Amsterdam Medal for the best young concert pianist in Europe at the age of sixteen. Son of Edmund Loewe, a celebrated singing actor who created the role of Prince Danilo in the Berlin production of *The Merry Widow.* Mr. and Mrs. Loewe and son came to America in 1923 at the invitation of David Belasco, the famous theatrical impresario and part-time author. While in rehearsal Mr. Loewe died, leaving son Frederick (Fritz) and mother stranded and penniless—Mr. Loewe having been an inveterate gambler, a trait inherited by his son, thus proving the Lysenkian theory that an acquired instinct can be inherited. Being addicted to eating and in order to provide funds for both himself and his mother, Fritz became at various times a cowboy, a professional boxer, a pianist in a German beer garden in New York City, and the rehearsal pianist for the Broadway production of *Die Fledermaus,* called *Champagne Sec* starring Kitty Carlisle, possessor of a beautiful voice, a beautiful face, hailed by the critics for her beautiful legs and later the possessor of Moss Hart and vice versa.

In 1937, Fritz composed the music for *Great Lady* and in 1943, in the Lambs Club, while on his way to the men's room . . .

My Fair Lady

I n the early spring of 1952 I was in Hollywood doing the screenplay for *Brigadoon*. Producer Arthur Freed had persuaded MGM to acquire the film rights. I use the word "persuaded" precisely. The studio did not mind that *Brigadoon* was about Scotland, but it was unhappy that Scotland was not populated by the Irish because of the large Irish audience in the United States. Arthur convinced them that it was simply too late to make the change.

One day I received a phone call from a man called Gabriel Pascal. I knew who he was. Many years earlier he had astonished the motion picture world by acquiring the rights to several of Bernard Shaw's plays. There are many versions of how he accomplished this extraordinary feat, but the one he told me went something like this: One day he appeared at the door of Shaw's cottage in Ayot St. Lawrence and rang the doorbell. The maid (or secretary) answered it. He said he wished to see Mr. Shaw. The maid said, "May I ask who sent you?" "Yes," he said, "Fate sent me." Shaw, who was on the stairs, heard this announcement and came to the door himself. "Who are you?" he asked. Pascal answered, "I am Gabriel Pascal. I am [a] motion picture producer and I wish to bring your works of genius to [the] screen." "How much money do you have?" asked Shaw. Pascal reached in his pocket and took out a few shillings. "Twelve shillings," he replied. "Come in," said Shaw.

"You're the first honest film producer I've ever met." When Pascal left the house he had a paper in his pocket giving him the rights to several of the great man's works, including *Pygmalion*.

He was in Hollywood at the time converting *Androcles and the Lion* into a film. He invited me—nay, ordered me—to have lunch with him at a popular restaurant of the time called Lucy's, and two days later we met.

Pascal was a Rumanian who claimed to be Hungarian and looked like a Himalayan. Architecturally he was circular and his voice had the timbre of a 78 record played at 33. His accent defied any known place of national origin, and his conversation consisted of a medley of simple, declarative sentences without articles. "You will come to restaurant." "Tonight I go to theatre," etc.

Seating himself in a buddha-like squat at the table, he ordered four plates of spaghetti, one for me and three for himself, and four raw eggs. "I will show you," he said "only way to eat spaghetti." He cracked one raw egg and split the contents over my spaghetti and used the other three for himself. To my surprise it was quite good. As he swooshed the spaghetti into his mouth he said, "I want to make musical of *Pygmalion*. I want you to write music." I hastened to explain to him that I did not write music. "Who writes music?" he asked. "The composer," I replied. "Fritz Loewe." "Good," he said. "We will meet again and you will bring man who writes music." I told him Fritz was in New York. "Good," he said. "You will tell him to come out here."

The rest of the meal he devoted to Bernard Shaw's sex life which, he claimed, was nonexistent. "The Irish Pope," he said "died a virgin." An opinion, I might add, shared by many Shavian authorities. Having disposed of Shaw's celibacy, he then proceeded to the subject of Mahatma Gandhi who, according to Pascal, was licentiously just the opposite, a man with a voracious sexual appetite. "I am thinking," he said "of making motion picture about

Gandhi because it was his sex life that freed India." As he continued to swirl the spaghetti around his fork, snapping up the loose ends like an anteater, he told me how Gandhi not only had an insatiable appetite for the ladies, but primarily for the wives of his friends. "I suppose," said Pascal "sitting around in loin cloth does that to you." But, each time he bedded a friend's wife his guilt mounted. Finally he made an irrevocable vow of chastity. But, alas, one day the wife of an English officer aroused him to such uncontrollable paroxysms of desire that he broke his vow. Stricken with remorse, he decided to seek penance in the total abstention from food. According to Pascal, when the British Home Office heard Gandhi was on another hunger strike, they moaned: "Oh Christ, there he goes again . . ." and freed India.

I asked Pascal who was going to write this great epic for him. He said, "There is only one man, Aldous Huxley." "Has he agreed to do it?" I enquired. "No," said Pascal, "he does not know. Next week I will go tell him." I said that I was certain Huxley would leap at it and unquestionably Gaby had a real winner there.

After lunch we joined the crowd outside who was waiting for the parking attendants to fetch their cars. While we stood there, without so much as a pause in his conversation, his hands moved toward the reproductive area and he opened his fly, extracted the contents, and proceeded to relieve himself. Everyone stared, but no one moved or said anything, including me, because no one could believe his eyes. The splashing ended as his car drew up. He tucked himself in, zipped himself up, did not say goodbye, got into his car, and drove off.

I have not been able to be embarrassed since.

It so happened that Fritz had intended to come to California anyhow to begin discussions about our next venture for the theatre. The great difference, and it is a great and deep difference, between a permanent collaboration and a collaboration that comes into existence because someone, either a producer or an author, has an idea for a musical, is that in the latter case it is the project that creates the reality. With a permanent collaboration the collaboration itself is the reality. Fritz and I knew that whenever we sat down to write a show, eventually we would settle on a project. To a large degree it is the collaboration that accounts for the immense productivity of Rodgers and Hart, Rodgers and Hammerstein, Gilbert and Sullivan, and the Gershwins, among others. Fritz and I figured one day that from the time we said: "Let's go to work" until the curtain rose out of town, it invariably took two years. Consequently, except for one period, every two years we had a play ready for Broadway.

Because a musical is a collaborative art form, there is no question that this kind of partnership is the most ideal way to function. You not only grow, but you grow together, in every sense of the word. It also serves as a frame. A painter once told me that the first problem he had to solve before he began to work was the size of the picture. The frame in a collaboration is determined by the style and creative inclinations of both collaborators. Fritz and I, for instance, could no more have written *St. Louis Blues* than W. C. Handy could have written *Camelot*. Fritz is a dramatic composer who can musically characterize a period or a locale, providing it is not contemporary, without losing his individuality and, at the same time, make it contemporary. For him *Pygmalion* was ideal material.

My own taste has always run toward the romantic (meaning larger than life, not operetta). I have no gift for satire and I instinctively look for humor in the antics of personality. I like to write stories that move me, with the implicit hope that they will move others, too. This does not necessarily mean love stories, but it usually does. As a rule it is not sadness that brings tears to my eyes, but a longing fulfilled. Both *Brigadoon* and *Camelot* contained miracles, but if my father were here he would have no need to worry. I do not believe in miracles. I have seen too many.

When Fritz and I began our collaboration I had a precise, lyrical goal in view. Larry Hart, brilliant as he was, was not a dramatic lyric writer, nor was there any reason for him to be. A musical in the twenties and thirties had no dramatic or emotional validity and the wit was the lyric writer's, never the character's. Oscar Hammerstein, on the other hand, was very much a dramatic lyric writer and with *Oklahoma* he and Dick Rodgers radically changed the course of the musical theatre. The musical comedy became a musical play.

With all the fears and confidence of youth I set out to try to combine the dramatic lyrics of Hammerstein with the wit and tenderness of Larry. In other words, to write musical plays in which the songs would be witty and tender because the characters were witty and tender, and dramatize, musically and lyrically, legitimate situations.

Fritz's and my first major attempt was along those lines. It was a musical play called *The Day Before Spring*. With critics and public alike it was an "almost." The sort of play George Kaufman used to call a "succes d'estime," i.e., a success that runs out of steam. But then I got off the track. Both *Brigadoon* and *Paint Your Wagon* were much more along the *Oklahoma* road than the one I had set out on, and I was determined somehow to find my way back. So I, too, was as drawn to *Pygmalion* as Fritz was. After all, where could one find wittier characters than those invented by GBS?

When Fritz arrived in Hollywood we had several lunches with Gaby at the house he had rented in Westwood. Los Angeles is often described as a collection of suburbs in search of a city and Westwood is one of those suburbs.

The great man's house was inevitable. It had been the residence of a famous star of the silent films named Milton Sills and it was

one of those enormous, neo-Spanish haciendas that had success-
fully extracted from Spanish architecture all that was ugly and
depressing. Gaby, not content with leaving bad enough alone, had
furnished it with a collection of pseudo-Italian renaissance furniture of such visual horror that when I crossed the living room
toward the terrace, where we always had lunch, I invariably closed
my one good eye.

The grounds had obviously not been touched since the days
of Milton Sills and the jungle had been moving closer and closer
toward the manse. It was only a matter of time before the trees
would enter the house and it would become a Hollywood version
of one of those lost Mayan temples that are constantly being discovered in the jungles of Guatemala. From time to time during our
conversations, overripe oranges would plop on to the terrace like
decaying hot-water bottles, which seemed to bother Gaby not at
all. He had a most charming wife who usually had lunch with us
and one small, worn out maid, named Maria, I believe, who was
constantly running back and forth from the table to the kitchen—
which was located somewhere in Nevada.

Gaby told us that we were the only people who could possibly
realize his dream of a musical *Pygmalion*. We agreed with him and
never mentioned the fact that we knew he had previously offered it
to Rodgers and Hammerstein. We told him that we were most definitely interested, that we had no idea how to do it and would return
to New York where we lived and begin mulling it over. We also told
him that we hoped he was aware of the fact that he was not a theatrical producer and our interest depended upon his aligning himself with a proper New York manager. "Good," he said "I will get
manager." We agreed to meet again in New York in a few weeks.

After our last lunch I looked around for Maria to give her some
small token of our appreciation for her incredible long distance
service. She was nowhere to be seen. Reaching into my pocket, I

said to Gaby: "Where's Maria? I would like to thank her." He stared at me. "Are you mad?" he retorted. "That's my mother-in-law."

In 1952 I was living upstate New York, Rockland County to be exact, in a unique community with an all-star cast consisting of playwright Maxwell Anderson; Burgess Meredith and his wife, then Paulette Goddard (she is still Paulette Goddard but no longer his wife); the well-known painter Henry Varnum Poor and his wife novelist Bessie Breuer; cartoonists Bill Mauldin and Milton Caniff, creator of *Terry and the Pirates* and *Steve Canyon*; Lotte Lenya, recently widowed by the sudden death of her great husband Kurt Weill; a few miles away in Nyack, Helen Hayes and her husband Charles MacArthur—and several other "featured players." I was married, not for the first time and not for the last, to screen actress Nancy Olson, and we had an infant daughter, Liza. Fritz, now separated from his wife, lived in the Algonquin Hotel where all good theatre people go when they leave home.

We began, as we always did, meeting regularly, either in town or country, and talking, talking, talking. The more we talked the more insoluble the problems seemed to become because, unfortunately, the characters in Shaw's play also kept talking, talking, and talking. *Pygmalion* is a drawing-room comedy and no matter how hard we tried, we did not seem to be able to tear down the walls of the drawing room and allow the play to unfold in a setting and atmosphere that suggested music.

There were certain rules for the construction of a musical that the play seemed incapable of obeying. The first was: Who would be the ensemble? Where would it come from? For a while we thought of locating the play at Oxford where Henry Higgins would be a professor of phonetics. The ensemble would be the undergraduates. That not only seemed obvious, but clumsily uninspired and useless. Then, what about a secondary love story, a subplot? A proper musical at that time demanded a subplot to provide musical variety. For example, in Rodgers and Hammerstein's *South Pacific* the main story was the middle-aged planter and the young nurse. The secondary plot was the young Lieutenant and the Polynesian girl. *Brigadoon* was not only the story of a town that disappeared in the Highland mist and returned one day every one hundred years, but besides the main love story of the American boy and the Scottish girl, there were two secondary subplots involving two other sets of opposite sexes. *Pygmalion,* however, had one story and one story only. It was a superb one, but the only one, and any author who thinks he can add characters to a play by Shaw is exhibiting behavioral evidence of the first signs of acute paranoia. Also, *Pygmalion,* although Shaw called it a romance, is a non-love story.

Unlike the original legend of Pygmalion and Galatea in which Pygmalion brought his statue to life because of his love for her, in Shaw's play Pygmalion brings Galatea to life by *not* loving her. Even though all through the last act Higgins rants and raves like a man in love, the play ends with Eliza leaving and Higgins supposedly delighted with himself because he has created a human being capable of standing on her own two feet. To make certain there was no doubt about his intentions, Shaw added an epilogue in which he states that Eliza eventually marries Freddie Eynsford-Hill.

Mrs. Patrick Campbell, for whom Shaw wrote the play, refused to play it as Shaw had written it, and on the opening night in London, much to Shaw's horror, added her own last line. In the closing moments when Eliza is saying farewell, Higgins imperiously tells her to stop off and buy him some Stilton cheese and a pair of gloves. Ignoring his order she exits with finality. Higgins breaks into gales of enigmatic laughter and the play ends. On the opening night, however, Mrs. Campbell returned to the stage and said: "What size?" And the curtain fell, along with Shaw's jaw.

However, no matter how the play ended, until the last scene it was most definitely a non-love story and how, may I ask, does one write a non-love song? These were but a few of the stumbling blocks Fritz and I encountered as we worked on it during those summer months.

Gaby, true to his word—an event in itself—did indeed come East and made a co-production agreement with the Theatre Guild. The Guild, which ran the Westport Playhouse in Connecticut, decided it would help all of us if we could see *Pygmalion* again on the stage and included a production of it during the summer season. It was a joy to see it again, but the joy only increased our frustration.

During that summer my concentration on *Pygmalion* was interrupted by the presidential election. Adlai Stevenson was running against Eisenhower and the country was at the height of that most shameful period in our history—until Watergate—known as the McCarthy era. Since Roosevelt, the performing and creative arts have always been predominantly Democratic. More than predominantly, Republicans in our profession are rare. Also, ever since Roosevelt, actors, singers, comedians, and writers have "come to the aid of the Party" and given freely of their time and talents. In this heinous year of 1952, however, McCarthy's slander, aided and abetted by a Republican press desperate for a Republican president and by the silent cowardice of too many of our elected representatives, had so permeated the nation that a Democratic performer was automatically suspect of being subversive. An actor or writer who wore a Stevenson button into the hallowed halls of NBC and CBS did so at the risk of inviting unemployment. Bill Mauldin and I had never been active politically and were too young to have been members of any of the organizations labeled by McCarthy as pro-Communist. We found ourselves perpetually foaming at the mouth. One day we could stand it no longer and we boarded a plane and flew to Springfield, Illinois, the headquarters of the Stevenson campaign, to volunteer our services. For the next two months only half my time was spent on *Pygmalion,* while the rest was devoted to arranging Democratic rallies in the New York area.

It was the Democratic tradition in those days for the last rally before the election to take place at Madison Square Garden in New York City. Among those present at the Garden willing to put their names and reputations on the line was Oscar Hammerstein. On the night of the rally while we were chatting together, he asked me how Fritz and I were getting along with *Pygmalion.* "Slowly," I answered. Oscar shook his head hopelessly. "It can't be done," he said. "Dick and I worked on it for over a year and gave it up." He enumerated all the problems they had encountered. They coincided exactly with the difficulties Fritz and I had been having.

The next day I related all this to Fritz and it reinforced our own thinking. Two or three weeks later we abandoned the project.

End of Act One.

Act Two.

In the summer of 1954 Gabriel Pascal gave up the ghost and became one. During the intervening years almost every mobile composer and lyricist on Broadway had been approached to do *Pygmalion* and had turned it down. It was also during that same period that I, slowly but irretrievably, began to feel myself sinking into a stagnant sea of self-doubt. I was thirty-four years old, I had won a Drama Critics' Award in 1947 and an Academy Award in 1952 and yet, for reasons perhaps logical, perhaps illogical, I had begun to feel an ever-widening separation between myself and the times in which I lived. Although the musical theatre is a popular art form one cannot write to please an audience. One writes to please oneself. The self-doubt is born out of the fear that you may be the only one. I sensed something changing around me, but not in me. I did not know what to write. With no faith in myself, how could I have faith in any idea? To make matters worse, I looked back over what I had written and felt dissatisfied with the best of it.

In retrospect I undoubtedly should have tried to work it out with Fritz. But I did not. Instead we separated and he began writing a new musical with Harold Rome. I floundered and fretted and searched for a bridge with such intensity that after a year I developed brain fever, medically known as encephalitis. The brain fever developed into spinal meningitis. After a spell of delirium and several weeks in hospital with a paralyzed left leg, I returned to work and almost desperately decided to try to make a sort of *Good Soldier Schweik* out of Al Capp's popular cartoon *L'il Abner*. I approached Burton Lane to do the music. He was interested and sat by impatiently while I struggled for months, trying to radiate optimism and yet knowing in the dark hours of the morning that I was munching on "alien corn."

As time dragged on, Al Capp became restless and I turned to a good friend of his, Herman Levin, for help. I asked him to produce it, if "it" ever happened. Herman had recently produced *Gentlemen Prefer Blondes* and *Call Me Mister* and was a seasoned veteran. The plan was for him to keep Capp in good spirits while I continued to bang my head against my self-constructed stone wall.

At the time of Gaby's death, Herman was out of the country having accepted an invitation from the eminent film producer, Sam Spiegel, to cruise the Mediterranean on his yacht. When Gaby's name appeared in the obituary columns, I suddenly found myself thinking about *Pygmalion* again. I called Fritz and we had lunch together. It was like going home. As we began to discuss it I saw, for the first time in two years, the thin line of a distant dawn on the horizon. I felt like a long distance runner slowly catching up with the herd.

We discovered to our amazement that many of the selfsame reasons that made the project seem impossible two years earlier were now in its favor. During those two years since we had abandoned it, I began to realize that the "rules," for some of us, had begun to change and by the time lunch was over we were both blazing with excitement. To understand what I mean by the "rules," I had best begin at the beginning.

The American musical began when the American theatre began, roughly at the end of World War I. Until then, the national musical staple was essentially old Vienna in English (English?!) and the operettas of Stolz, Kalman, Lehar, and lesser versions of them flourished. Storyville, the redlight district of New Orleans, which got its colorful name not from some imaginative satisfied customer, but from Judge Story who first roped it off, had been filling the night air with Dixieland music since before the turn of the century; but as far as Broadway was concerned Storyville and the beat of jazz did not exist.

When the Provincetown Theatre presented Eugene O'Neill's *Beyond the Horizon,* the American theatre stopped reaching across the ocean and started reaching into its own soul. Shortly thereafter, at the Princess Theatre in New York, composer Jerome Kern, lyricist P. G. Wodehouse (the father of "Jeeves"), and book writer Guy Bolton began creating a series of smallish musicals that became known, rather logically, as the Princess Theatre shows. Even though Bolton and Wodehouse were both English, those smallish musicals inaugurated the American musical. They were American because the music was American. Kern was writing genuine, eighteen karat American popular theatre music, and elegantly, discreetly but distinctly the music had a beat.

Operetta lyrics which generally consisted of "thee" "thou," "be mine," and "ah" had been tolerated because most of the sopranos, and baritones in those early pre-war days were either foreign born and could not be understood, or, if they were of native stock, had been carefully tutored in the art of singing in code. It was not necessary to instruct coloraturas because coloraturas speak no known language and sing so high anyhow that only the dogs in the audience can hear them. Fritz used to say that coloratura is not a voice, it is a disease. Sigmund Romberg, the famous operetta composer, was once brought a lyric by Oscar Hammerstein. He placed it on the piano and played and sang it through, looked up at Oscar and said: "It fits." And that was just about all operetta lyrics were supposed to do: fit.

The Princess Theatre shows changed all that. The books were light and amusing and the music in the popular voice range, and Wodehouse wrote lyrics that were appropriate to both: clever, graceful, and wittily rhymed. Picking up the light verse tradition of W. S. Gilbert, he became the pathfinder for Larry Hart, Cole Porter, Ira Gershwin, and everyone else who followed ("My Bill" from Kern and Hammerstein's *Show Boat* was actually a leftover Princess Theatre song with lyrics by Wodehouse).

For the next decade, musical comedy and operetta flourished side by side; but now even the operetta was of domestic origin. It is true that the great operetta singers of the time, Romberg, Friml, and Herbert were born on the other side, but they lived in America, the libretti were by Americans and all their shows were written for Broadway. For musical comedy it was what Oscar Levant called "the classic period of American popular music." Jerome Kern, George and Ira Gershwin, Vincent Youmans, Irving Berlin, Rodgers and Hart—and later in the twenties, Cole Porter. The American theatre had never known and, sadly enough, will probably never know another decade like it. Radio in its infancy. No T.V. Motion pictures were still silent. And sixty-three theatres on Broadway. One season there were over thirty musicals running simultaneously and in December, 1927, eleven shows opened on the same night.

The musical books were lighthearted, simple-minded, and

innocent. Most were tailored to the talents of stars—as a rule, comic stars. The "love interest" was disposed of in short order in an occasional scene in front of a curtain downstage while the set was being changed. Its functional raison d'être was to give the composer and lyricist an opportunity for a ballad.

When the stock market crashed in November 1929 it took operetta with it. The disillusion of the great depression could no more stand the rose-colored spectacles of operetta than it could those of Herbert Hoover. As the institutions of the republic came under reexamination and attack, the legitimate theatre became a theatre of protest, and musicals became brash and satiric. "A satire," said George Kaufman, "is a play that closes Saturday." Not in the thirties. In 1933 a musical won the Pulitzer Prize for the first time, and it was a satire on the American political system called *Of Thee I Sing,* written by the Gershwins, Morrie Ryskind, and Kaufman himself. During that agonizing decade there was not a phase or figure of American life not considered fair game by a lyricist who knew how to use words for darts; from the tinsel-hearted clowns of the Cartier set to the man in the White House himself. The books during the thirties, with the occasional exception, such as *Pal Joey,* the triumph of the unsentimental musical, remained coat racks on which to hang some good jokes and good songs. But movies talked, radio scooped up the stars, vaudeville died, the haves fought gamely on against the future, and too many have-nots still had not—and the number of legitimate theatres throughout the country and on Broadway grew less and less.

During the thirties two European giants came to this country and both of them had a considerable influence on the direction musicals were to go. The first was Kurt Weill who came by invitation of Hitler. Celebrated in Germany, where his music had been the essence of the dead German romanticism of the twenties, he had also lured serious dramatists and poets like Georg Kaiser and

Bertolt Brecht into the musical theatre to collaborate with him. When he came to America he did the same. Instead of looking for a partner among the steady practitioners, he turned to the dramatists like Paul Green, with whom he wrote *Johnny Johnson,* an anti-war musical, and Maxwell Anderson, with whom he wrote *Knickerbocker Holiday.* That most beautiful of songs, "September Song," came from *Knickerbocker Holiday.* In the early forties he collaborated with Moss Hart and Ira Gershwin on *Lady in the Dark,* the first play, let alone musical, to attempt to dramatize the psychoanalytical process.

The other giant was George Balanchine. Balachine, a refugee from Russia in the early twenties, had joined Diaghilev's ballet company in 1924 and during the next five years established himself as Diaghilev's greatest choreographer since Nijinsky, whom he had fired for deserting him for a woman. In 1933 Balanchine had a small ballet troupe in London, where he met Lincoln Kirstein who encouraged him to come to America. The result was the School of American Ballet and eventually the New York City Ballet, one of the outstanding ballet companies in the world. Shortly after arriving, Balanchine was persuaded by Rodgers and Hart to choreograph *On Your Toes.* And ballet came to the theatre. Previously, choreography had been "production numbers," a "divertissement" composed of effects, legs, and taps, and you cannot tell a story with a time-step. With the full range of ballet movement, anything is dramatically possible.

As the depression had killed the sentimental musical and squirted adrenalin into the veins of satire, World War II killed satire and revived the sentimental musical. The mood of the country switched like a traffic light to escapism, nostalgia, and fantasy. *Oklahoma* was all those things, told in a new, literate, musical way with affection, charm, and infinite skill, and with song, word, and movement blending together to reveal character, establish atmosphere, and advance the story. Agnes De Mille's ballet at the end of the first act, in which the central characters are deftly replaced by dancers and the story continues balletically, is lyric theatre at its most original and most brilliant.

De Mille's artistry was all over Broadway for the next few years, either by the real article herself or by her imitators and followers. But her special kind of lyricism required a special kind of lyricism in book and treatment, and by the end of the forties musical books started hardening up and heading down a more realistic road— and the era of the "big ballet" came to an end. In *South Pacific, The King and I, My Fair Lady,* and *Camelot,* choreography varied from nonexistence to the isolated ballet and local color. Only with Jerome Robbins did it retain its dramatic and theatrical lustre, as in *West Side Story* and *Fiddler on the Roof.*

By 1954 it no longer seemed essential that a musical have a sub-plot, nor that there be an ever-present ensemble filling the air with high C's and flying limbs. In other words, some of the obstacles that had stood in the way of converting *Pygmalion* into a musical had simply been removed by a changing style. What causes the change? It is not the desires of the audience. It is the restlessness of authors for new forms of expression, which audiences then discover to be exactly what they were unconsciously longing for.

The accent on the emotional reality of character and story that had begun with the collaborators of Kurt Weill grew stronger and stronger. The content and style required to accommodate ballet all but disappeared, and the singing chorus as an integral personality that characterized the locale—such as the Western "folk" in *Oklahoma* and the Scottish "folk" in *Brigadoon,* who have always remained "folk"—seemed less and less essential.

As Fritz and I talked and talked, we gradually began to realize that the way to convert *Pygmalion* to a musical did not require the addition of any new characters to give the score the variety usually demanded. There was enough variety in the moods of the characters Shaw had created and we could do *Pygmalion* simply by doing *Pygmalion* following the screenplay more than the play and adding the action that took place between the acts of the play.

Example: *Pygmalion* is in five acts. In the first act Higgins meets Eliza in her native habitat on Covent Garden, then meets Pickering who is on his way home from the opera, explains to him how, by phonetics, he can turn this "squashed cabbage leaf" into a Duchess at an embassy hall, invites Pickering to stay with him at his house on Wimpole Street, and off they go. End of Act One. Act Two. It is the following day and Higgins is demonstrating to Pickering his phonetic equipment when Eliza appears, asking for speech lessons. "Now," said Fritz and I to each other, "what was Eliza doing between Higgins' departure from Covent Garden and her arrival at Higgins' house the following morning?" She probably went home to her parents. But she had no parents—that is, at home. Later in the play we are told that she lives alone, has no mother, and that her father is a dustman living with another woman. So that is precisely what we wrote. Eliza goes home, meets her father and two of his cronies. Brief scene between them. Song by father to establish his character, "With a Little Bit o' Luck," and on into the next scene when Eliza comes to Wimpole Street.

Concerning the musicalization of Higgins, any character in any play is a condensation. From the mass of mosiac pieces that form the pattern of each human being, the author selects the few predominant ones that he wishes the audience to know and that make it possible to tell the story. No character in the theatre is actually "true to life." In fact I do not believe there is such a thing as "realism" in the theatre at all. If there were, there would never be a third act.

What Shaw wanted us to know about Higgins was that he was passionate about the English language, believed it to be the principal barrier separating class from class, and that he was a misogynist. Because they are the outstanding aspects of his character, it seemed to us they should be dramatized in music and lyrics.

I say all this now rather glibly, but none of it occurred in one blinding moment of divine revelation. We discovered it by trial and error, often by writing songs and later discarding them, until we finally arrived at those moments where music and lyrics could reveal what was implied and not repeat what was already in the text, and could catch the drama at the hilltops where it could ascend no further without the wings of music and lyrics, at the same time remaining faithful to the spirit of the Irish Pope.

About two weeks later Herman Levin, who had left me struggling with *L'il Abner,* returned from Europe and called me in the country to see how I was getting on. "Very well," I said. "Have you found a way to do it?" he asked. "I think so," I replied. "How does Lane like it?" he asked. "I haven't the slightest idea," I said. "Why not?" he inquired. "Because he's not doing it, Fritz is," I replied. "Fritz!" he exclaimed. I went right on. "But the problem now is to get the rights." Levin was bewildered. "Get the rights? We have them." "No we don't," said I. "As a matter of fact we're not even sure whether the estate owns them or if they reverted back." "Estate!" exclaimed Herman. "Who died?" It suddenly dawned on me that there was a minor bit of information I had failed to mention. "Oh, Herman," I said, "I forgot to tell you. You're not producing *L'il Abner.* You're producing *Pygmalion.*"

Bernard Baruch, the American financier, used to say that the way to get rich was with your ass: buy property and sit on it. Herman did not even have to do that. He left me sitting on *my* ass while he cruised the Mediterranean.

During those autumn weeks while Fritz and I were writing, several other activities necessary to the production of the play also went into motion. Periodically we would meet with Herman to discuss the sets, the costumes, the lights, and the cast. But far out-ranking all these artistic considerations, there also began a long, complicated game of international intrigue, high finance, and legal shenanigans that so often adds wrinkles to the brow of artistic expression. The game is called: acquiring the rights.

The man who took on this formidable task was Irving Cohen, my lawyer and trusted friend for many years and one of the most experienced, respected, and honest members of that small group of the legal profession who specialize in the affairs of the the-atre. The legal representative of Rodgers and Hammerstein, Moss Hart, George Kaufman, Victor Borge, Alistair Cooke, Feuer and Martin, and an endless list of toilers in the theatrical vineyard, Irving refuses to this day to accept a fact of legal life which is automatically assumed by every other lawyer I have ever met, i.e., that there is a wide difference between what is right and what is legal. In a profession that has distinguished itself by having sixty-three of its members indicted in the Watergate scandal, where an ever increasing number of ambitious young men go to law school and study law in order to learn how to evade it, whose Bar Association constantly rallies to the defense of any scurrilous member under public attack and only raises its voice in censure when one of them has finally been caught red-handed and sent to jail, and where legal victory is seldom encumbered by truth or morality, Irving Cohen with every passing year becomes one of its loneliest members. America inherited from Mother England the concept that a civilized nation means a nation of laws. Unfortunately, as Judge Learned Hand once observed: "You cannot legislate the human heart"; and the word ethics in the legal profession is fast becoming as extinct as the bald eagle. So Irving, with an assist from Herman, an ex-lawyer himself, began to unwind the impossible tangle.

He found out, in short order, that the musical rights to

Pygmalion were owned by the Pascal estate and that the Pascal estate was in a state. It was under attack from two sides. Although it may seem redundant to mention it, the adversaries were both women. One was his wife with whom he was *not* living when he died; the other was a Chinese lady with whom he *was* living when he died. Further, whoever eventually acquired the rights from Pascal's estate would then be obliged to seek approval from those in charge of the estate of Bernard Shaw in London. Still further, Fritz and I were not the only ones in quest of those rights; there were several other competitors, including MGM—a worthy and well-heeled foe.

The Chase Bank (now the Chase Manhattan Bank—tomorrow the world) whose trust department, like that of most banks, is a model of catatonic timidity, had been named the executor of the Pascal will. The vice president of the bank in charge of the trust department was a gentleman named Mr. Bridgewood. Mr. Bridgewood was not an unfamiliar name to me. The previous July my father had died and had named the selfsame Mr. Bridgewood as the sole executor of his estate. This, of course, did not mean I had a friend at Chase, but at least there was someone to whom I could go for information.

A short time later, I received a phone call from a Mr. Moskowitz who identified himself as an executive of MGM in New York City. He asked if I could come in to see him. Thinking that he might want to join forces with us, perhaps even finance the play as motion picture companies often did in those days, I went. Mr. Moskowitz was not a man to waste time on social graces. Within three minutes he informed me that MGM intended to acquire the rights to *Pygmalion* for themselves, that the coffers of the Chase Bank were filled with MGM money, and that the bank would not dare risk incurring the wrath of MGM by awarding those precious rights to anyone else. I asked Mr. Moskowitz why he felt it necessary to tell me that. He did not answer. He simply said, "goodbye."

I reported this to Fritz, Herman, and Irving and then called Mr. Bridgewood. I told him of my discussion with Mr. Moskowitz and asked him how the bank would determine who, among all the competitors, would best serve the interests of the Pascal estate. His answer, as I recall, was that the bank would decide who, among all the competitors, would best serve the interests of the Pascal estate. How it would do so remained, for the time being, moot.

Anyone with a grain of common sense and an ounce of caution would have sat back to await the outcome before continuing further; but common sense is a transgression not tolerated in the theatre and caution is for women who wish to remain childless.

Fritz, being far more practical, said: "My boy, there's only one thing to do. We will write the show without the rights, and when the time comes for them to decide who is to get them, we will be so far ahead of everyone else they will be forced to give them to us."

Concerning the sets, costumes, lights, and casting, our simplest decision was in the choice of who would design the scenery. It had to be Oliver Smith. Oliver was not only Herman's producing partner in *Gentlemen Prefer Blondes* as well as the designer, but he, Fritz, and I had "grown up" together, and he had done both *Brigadoon* and *Paint Your Wagon*.

Oliver is one of the human race's most irresistible and drollest creations. He has the proportions of a tall, modern standing lamp and we always greet each other with warm embraces. Fritz, who is five feet and five inches tall always hopped onto the nearest table to reach hugging height. I am not much taller, but I settle for two-thirds of him.

Oliver is one of the few set designers who not only is as imaginative as he is practical, meaning that he has all the technical and mechanical knowledge necessary to make a multi-set show function, but he is one of the few designers who is a painter and can achieve mood, perspective, and beauty with a brush. He also has a talent for disappearing that borders on the metaphysical. Long before the first rocket went into orbit, Oliver Smith had discovered how to leave the planet and return at will.

When the sets are first mounted onto the stage at the out-of-town tryout, the technical problems, especially with a musical, are monumental. In every show we ever did together there was always a moment when cries of "Where in God's name is Oliver?" would rent the air, and everyone would take loud, solemn, angry vows never to work with him again. Suddenly a couple of stage hands would move a tree or a door or a garden wall and there would be Oliver, calmly chatting with the stage manager.

We unanimously agreed that the ideal man to do the costumes was Cecil Beaton, whose very look is such that it is difficult to know whether he designed the Edwardian era or the Edwardian era designed him. The question was whether or not he would agree to do only the costumes. As a rule he liked to design the entire show. But that would have to be settled if and when.

Thinking about actors at this early creative stage and the possibility of approaching them was a luxury I had never enjoyed before, because it was the first time I had ever adapted a play instead of creating an original work of my own. The difference between the two is that in an original musical one may have ideas for casting at the very beginning, but one must wait until something is written in order to arouse anyone's interest. In this case I was not only adapting the work of another author, but an author whose plays were as great as he himself said they were. And as famous.

Although *Pygmalion* had been written for Mrs. Patrick Campbell, and Eliza Doolittle had always been considered a star vehicle for a great actress, to me Higgins was far more interesting, far more complex, for whom empathy came easily to me. There was no doubt in my mind that Higgins was Shaw, and Shaw, as far as women were concerned, was a man of overwhelming shyness. His love affairs existed on paper only and his ardor, though magnificently articulate, romantic, exalted, and bewitching, was all by post. What always moved me so deeply about Higgins was that he, a master in the language of the poets, was incapable of putting together a few words to relieve his own loneliness; a loneliness which he (Shaw and/or Higgins) so gallantly and wittily concealed. So the first person we began to look for was not an Eliza Doolittle, but a Henry Higgins. And the first person I thought of was Rex Harrison.

I had met Rex and his wife, then Lilli Palmer (she is still Lilli Palmer but no longer his wife) a few years earlier when he was appearing on Broadway in Maxwell Anderson's *Anne of a Thousand Days*. Rex and Lilli frequently came out to Max's house after the performance on Saturday night and stayed till Monday. On Sunday nights we often had a penny poker game and one morning after one of them, Kurt Weill spoke to me about doing a new English version of *The Threepenny Opera* for Rex. "Does he sing?" I asked. Kurt replied, "Enough." I have no idea to this day how he knew that, but it stuck in my mind and I reported it to Herman and Fritz.

Rex was in London at the time appearing in the West End with Lilli in *Bell, Book and Candle*. I called him, told him what we had in mind and asked if we could come over and talk to him about it. I could tell by his answer that he thought we had all gone around the bend. But his curiosity was piqued just enough not to say no. Needless to say I did not mention that we did not have the rights, but we figured by the end of December we either would have acquired them or lost them. So I said that we would be over the early part of January.

During November the story of our project crept into the

newspapers. Two or three days later I received a phone call from Mary Martin's husband, Richard Halliday. Mary at that particular moment was appearing in *Peter Pan* on Broadway. Fritz and I had known them both for many years and I was as delighted to hear from him as I was surprised by the reason. He said that he and Mary had read that we were doing *Pygmalion* and that they would love to hear what we had written.

Mary Martin as Eliza Doolittle? Mary had no greater admirers than Fritz and I, but did not seem, shall we say, a "natural." But, on the other hand, one never knows the limits of a great star's talent, and I remembered Larry Hart saying to me one day something to the effect that if a star seems interested, do not say no for at least twenty-four hours. So Fritz and I decided that although there might be nothing to gain, there was certainly nothing to lose by showing it to her.

By this time we had decided to move the famous tea party to Ascot and had written "The Ascot Gavotte." We had felt it essential that Eliza's fury at Higgins' "inhuman" treatment of her be captured in music and lyrics, so after many stops and starts we had settled on "Just You Wait 'enry 'iggins" and completed that, too. Our first attempt to dramatize Higgins' misogyny resulted in a song called "Please Don't Marry Me." We were certain that Higgins would have to reassure Eliza before going to the ball and so we had written a song called "Lady Liza." And we were equally certain that it would be necessary for Eliza's misgivings before the ball to be translated into music, and had written "Say a Prayer for Me Tonight." These were the five songs we played for Richard one afternoon. He was *most* enthusiastic. I underline "most" because Richard was Southern and had a habit of accenting words. He asked us if we could repeat our performance for Mary one night after the show. We agreed.

Neither Fritz nor I was living in New York City at the time, so we arranged to meet at my mother's apartment a few nights later. That morning Richard called to ask if Mainbocher, the famous couturier, could come along, too. Mainbocher's actual name was Main Bocher and he came from the mid-West. He had gone to Paris to study singing, lost his voice, and when he turned to designing, pushed his two names together to Frenchify them. I knew him reasonably well, liked him enormously, and had great respect for his theatrical judgment. So, shortly before midnight, Mary, Richard, and Main arrived at my mother's. We played the five songs. They listened in silence and departed almost immediately after the last song. Only Main made any comment—saying he liked them very much.

A week went by and we never heard from either Mary or Richard. Finally my curiosity got the better of me and I called Richard and inquired what Mary had thought. His tone was very serious. He asked me if we could have lunch together two days hence. We met at the Hampshire House and after the usual amenities, and having disposed of the menu, he turned to me gravely and said: "Alan, you don't know what a *sad* night that was for Mary and me." I was lost. "Why?" I asked. "Mary," he continued, "walked the floor half the night saying over and over again, *"How* could it have happened? How *could* it have happened? Richard, those dear boys have *lost their talent."* (My memory may be a little hazy about some of his words, but "those dear boys have lost their talent" are forever engraved on the walls of my duodenal lining.) I was so stunned I could not think of anything to say, but it was not necessary because Richard continued. "Alan," he said, " 'Just You Wait' is simply *stolen* from 'I Hate Men' in *Kiss Me Kate* and the 'Ascot Gavotte' is *simply* not funny. It's *just* not *funny* at all." He had nothing to say about the other three, or if he did I cannot remember because at that point I was numb. They were, after all, the first people to have heard anything and the reaction was so violent that I was shaken to the core. I changed the subject as quickly as I could, ate my lunch in three mouthfuls, and left. The last words that I remember Richard saying, as he shook my hand, were: "I'm *so* sorry. *Really, Alan. We're so sorry.*"

I went back to the country and reported it all to Fritz, who thought about it for a moment and said: "Well, I guess they didn't like it." Little did I realize the future repercussions of that lunch.

While Mary Martin was flying through the air on concealed wires as Peter Pan, another musical, an English importation called *The Boy Friend,* whose feet also barely touched the ground—but for quite different reasons—was playing a few blocks down the street. It was a candy box of all the musical comedy clichés of the twenties as seen through the eyes of someone who was not there, a prerequisite of camp. Since then there have been related versions of the thirties, the forties, and the fifties, and I have no doubt that at the appropriate time the sixties and seventies will follow. Nostalgia has always been one of the theatre's most popular deceptions.

The ingénue lead on Broadway was an eighteen-year-old girl named Julie Andrews and she had received a rapturous press. From the moment she set foot on the stage, one could see she fairly radiated with some indefinable substance that is the difference between talent and star. Whatever that substance is you know it is there because you find yourself caring about him or her spontaneously and illogically, far beyond the dialogue, the role, or the play. The substance is not always the same. Gertrude Lawrence, for instance, was electric: Laurette Taylor was all humanity; Julie was all that is endearing.

There is no doubt that being talented as well always helps, but I can even remember one or two great stars whose abilities were limited and yet had so much of that other "whatever-it-is" that the missing talent went by unnoticed.

Julie, fortunately, had a dazzling array of gifts: a charming soprano voice, so flexible she could sing light opera and popular with equal ease; probably the most immaculate diction of any soprano in memory; she danced; she moved with grace; whatever she had to say in *The Boy Friend* she did with conviction and style; and physically she was as pretty as any eye might decide her to be.

Fritz, Herman, and I went to see her in the show and shared the general enthusiasm. What was most amazing to me was that even in that fluffy bit of theatrical patisserie, when "boy lost girl" at the end of the first act, I found myself embarrassingly unhappy about it. Could she play Eliza Doolittle?

Although Shaw wrote *Pygmalion* for Mrs. Patrick Campbell who was forty-nine years old when she did the part, Shaw states in his stage directions that Eliza is eighteen. He may have written that in to flatter Mrs. Campbell, but, nevertheless, there it is. We began to think how refreshing it might be if, for the first time since the play was written, a girl of precisely that age played the role. We did not have a director (because we did not have the rights), but we auditioned Julie and she read one or two of the scenes for us. A few days later she and I went into a studio and worked alone together for the better part of a day. She had a composure and ease beyond her years and I was curious to see if, perhaps, there might be some indication of how much feeling lay buried beneath her Walton-on-Thames coating of middle-class niceness. One day is hardly sufficient for that kind of exploration, but we did a few scenes from different plays together and I vividly remember an occasional, unexpected flash of fire and, at one point, a sudden downpour of tears. I reported to Fritz and Herman that quite possibly there was a lot more to Julie Andrews than met the eye and ear. We told her of our interest and that we hoped she would make no commitments until we had—please God—acquired the rights. "Lovely," she said, as she usually did. And we parted.

By the end of November the Chase Bank began to stir. Having

come to the conclusion that it knew even less about the theatre than it did about forecasting economic trends, and that it was incapable of making an artistic decision of such consequence, it decided to ask the court to allow it (the bank) to appoint the most celebrated literary agent of the time, Harold Freedman, to make that all important decision. When Fritz and I heard the news we decided it could not hurt if we asked Harold Freedman to be our agent. Feeling his responsibility keenly, he said that he would have to think it over carefully—and before we left the room he agreed.

A week or so later, Mr. Freedman notified the court that he had decided in his infinite wisdom that we be awarded the rights. Having been told of his choice in advance, Irving Cohen insisted that Mr. Freedman also inform the court that he was our agent. To the kind of court we have in New York City this seemed eminently satisfactory, because it proved that Mr. Freedman was indeed a man of great intelligence whose judgment could be trusted.

The first victory was ours.

The next battlefield would be London. Our little brigade consisted of Fritz, Herman, Irving Cohen, Nancy (still my wife), and me, and the cost of moving us overseas for what could very well be several weeks involved a formidable sum of money, more than our worthy producer possessed at that moment. Although I knew my father had been generous to my brothers and me in his will, there would be no distribution of the estate for many months. However, sometime in my teens my father had purchased an interest in a gold mine for us, and each of us was to receive the stock when we became twenty-one years old. Each of us was now well past twenty-one, but none of us had ever had the nerve to ask my father for the stock. With his death it was handed to us. I immediately decided to sell my share to bankroll the expedition to London. Had it been necessary, I would have mortgaged my house and gambled every cent I possessed.

Under the varnish of professional behavior and lighthearted camaraderie that characterized the relationship between Fritz, Herman, and me, I still burned with the desperate feeling that this project had to be it, and, more than that, could be.

Fritz had become enthusiastic enough to postpone the play on which he had been working with Harold Rome. We were working well together and enjoying every moment of the struggle. Edna Ferber once remarked that the excitement of writing is having written. True. But in the creation of a musical, the excitement of having written can come after every song. When Fritz and I would finish a number, we would dash around the neighborhood, looking for "customers" as Fritz would say, meaning neighbors for whom to play it. Naturally, our captive audience was complimentary, but somehow we always could tell if the compliments were because of the song or because of the friendship. Very often it influenced us and made us aware of a weakness.

Arthur Freed once told me that when he was producing a film by Irving Berlin, Berlin would come to the studio and play a new song for the production group (more about that later); the moment he finished he would look around the room and if he did not see the exact reaction he wanted in the eyes of his listeners, no matter how they may have raved, the song was never heard again.

For me, over the years I have discovered that when I am writing, occasionally, perhaps not more than a few times a year, I write a line or a couplet that for all I know might be discarded the next day, but at that moment gives me a flashing sense of exhileration so deep and so consuming that I know it is as close to the heart of living as I shall probably ever reach. Once or twice it had happened again that autumn.

I sold my stock for $150,000. My brothers sold theirs later for 25 percent more. At the time I never dreamed that a loss could be so profitable.

And so it was that shortly after the first of the year, we took off to visit the original scenery.

When we arrived in England that cold January night, it was the first time I had set foot in the Old World since 1937. I had not gone to London either for the rehearsals and opening of *Brigadoon* in 1949 or for *Paint Your Wagon*, three years later. Fritz had, but not I. Even though both shows had been hits and had run over two years in the West End (the London Broadway), I had never regretted not being there.

During my prep school years and through my first year at college, the day after school closed at the beginning of June my younger brother Bobby and I were packed off to Europe with my mother, where we stayed until the day before school began at the end of September. After a few weeks of Thomas Cooke-ing it through England, France, Austria, Hungary, or Italy, my mother eventually settled us down for the summer at the Lido in Venice. I cannot pretend they were not marvellous summers, but as each September came around I found myself happier and happier to be going home. When I got off the boat in 1937 and returned to college to begin my second year, I never wanted to travel again. After the war, when so many Americans started making their personal contributions to the economic recovery of Europe, I discovered that no wandering minstrel still was I, and I remained stubbornly entrenched in the land of the free and the broken home of the brave.

But as we drove from Heathrow airport and London began to unfold around me, my pulse began to quicken. When we left, a few weeks later, I never quite came home again.

The following day we telephoned Rex and made an appointment to have supper with him after the show. When we all trooped

backstage to see him, there was an unmistakable strain and froi-
deur in the air. After visiting Rex I stopped in to see Lilli, who
greeted me with distinct reserve. I later found out that despite the
fact they were co-starring together and playing love scenes in the
most convincing fashion, offstage it was "goodbye" until the next
performance. They were separated and Rex was in love with Kay
Kendall, whom he joined every night after he and Lilli had taken
their curtain calls. This rather prickly situation was covered in a
cloak of secrecy so large it could be seen for ten miles.

Pause.

Rex. Because so much of the story of *My Fair Lady* involves
Rex Harrison, both on stage and off, and because it is his fate in life
to be a human thermostat who changes the temperature of every
room he enters, turning summer to winter or ice to steam in a matter of seconds, I would like to introduce immediately the music
that underscores any words I write about him. The theme is a warm
one. It may come as a surprise to some and a dire disappointment
to others, but I am devoted to him. He is one of the few enduring
friends I have made in the theatre. He has been unfailingly loyal,
sympathetic, and generous—on one occasion flying from Italy to
New York in mid-winter to help me out for one night—and at crucial times, and in special ways he has been good for me. This does
not mean, however, that I am unaware of the fact he has, shall we
say, a unique approach to human relations. During *My Fair Lady*
I collected a trunkful of samples.

Concerning the trail of female fury that has followed him from
parlor to print, I for one could not be less impressed. It is impossible to be a ladies man without the ladies and none of them married
him at gunpoint. Each did it voluntarily, presumably with her eyes
open. Nor can I believe they were strangers who met him for the
first time at the altar.

The female sex has no bigger fan than I. I am firmly convinced they could run this world far better than men. They are infinitely more practical and more realistic. They are not victimized by that idiotic, destructive disease called male vanity and I cannot remember one instance of a woman in business going bankrupt because of over-expansion. And God knows they are prettier. But, and a large but it is, to marry a man who may have moods that cannot be tracked by a radar system, and then be astonished to discover that he has moods that cannot be tracked by a radar system, is a phenomenon worthy of serious scientific attention.

The commitment of marriage can frequently arouse some rather peculiar behavior in men and women alike, but the bizarre notion that one can change the character of one's mate seems to occur more often to women than to men. In fact, there are many French women who believe that a wife only owns that part of a man she has changed. So much for French logic!

The male anthem that a woman does not know what she wants usually means: "Why can't a woman be more like a man?" All too often, however, what she does want is the man she hopes she will make out of the man she has.

Rex is a man of charm and the unexpected. The most idle remark can suddenly produce a tempest of vituperation that flashes and thunders and passes like a summer storm. I remember one night in Philadelphia, before *My Fair Lady* came to New York, when he, Nancy (still my wife) and I were having a pleasant supper after the theatre. Rex was in the very best of spirits. Some topic of no consequence at all came up in the conversation to which I volunteered a totally casual opinion. Nancy, not at all argumentatively, said: "No. I don't think so." That is all. "No. I don't think so." "You bitch!" roared Rex. "How dare you disagree with him? Who the hell do you think you are? If he says that's the way it is, then that's the way it is and you've got no business . . ." etcetera, etcetera. The explosion was so unmotivated and it vanished so quickly that there was no time for Nancy even to be hurt. She just stared at him in bewilderment, I quickly changed the subject and our pleasant little after-theatre supper continued.

On another occasion, much more recently, Rex was visiting my wife, then Sandra Payne (she is still Sandra Payne, but no longer my wife) and me in the country, and sitting around the fire one evening he was discussing, most sympathetically, how difficult it was for his wife, then Elizabeth (still Elizabeth, but) to put up with his past which, time after time, kept cropping up either in the press, social conversation, or in the shape of children. I said, also sympathetically, that I could understand that. Sandy said, also sympathetically, that she could, too. That is all. She could, too. "God damn you women," screamed Rex. "What about Alan and me? It's bloody difficult for us, too, but none of you ever thinks of that." Look of bewilderment. Change of topic. Scene around the fire continues pleasantly.

In the final analysis, no one knows what goes on in the bedrooms of life. But there is no question that Rex's domestic history has caused considerable anatomic fallout and most of it has fallen on him, creating employment for would-be journalists and reading exercises for those who, as a rule, buy newspapers for the pictures.

The hurdles we had to overcome in persuading him to play the part were high and many. Fritz and I still had the five songs, Richard and Mary notwithstanding. Two of them, as I mentioned earlier, were for Higgins. Rex hated them both. We knew it because he immediately said, "I hate them." Strangely enough, merely seeing him again and feeling his personality, Fritz and I knew before we even played them what his reaction would be, and we knew he was right. The songs were slick and instead of being acting pieces set to music, they were skin deep and clever word games. It took considerable time to reassure him that first attempts are frequently stopovers on the way to the eventual destination.

Secondly, we had to convince him that Leslie Howard was not the definitive Higgins of our time. I personally believed that brilliant as he was in the film, Howard was not the complete Higgins. We all ran the film together and I said to Rex that my entire argument could be based on the reading of one line. The line occurs in the scene after the ball when Higgins is "humbly" taking full credit for Eliza's triumph. When they are alone together, there is a moment when Eliza cries out: "What is to become of me?" Higgins looks at her and says: "Oh! That's what is worrying you, is it?" To me, when Leslie Howard delivered the line one could tell he knew full well what she was talking about. You could almost see in his eyes that he was aware of her pain and of strange stirrings within himself. I said to Rex that I thought it was wrong. I did not believe Higgins had the slightest idea what was troubling her, and when he said, "Oh! That's what is worrying you, is it?" he was genuinely amazed by the discovery. Using that as the watershed, after running the film we talked through the play together and Rex finally agreed that perhaps Leslie Howard was a touch too romantic and, consciously or unconsciously, told us ahead of time something Higgins should not have found out about himself until later in the play.

Third hurdle, the prickly situation. Kay was doing a film. If *Bell, Book and Candle* closed and we had finished the work and were ready for rehearsals and Kay was still doing her film, how could he leave her? Rex felt comfortable enough with me to say to me one night, with the kind of touching confusion that so often seasons his comedy with tenderness: "You see, it isn't how much I will miss her that bothers me. But what will I do for fun?" I had no answer to that. There is none.

Fourth hurdle. Could he do a musical at all? We were staying at Claridge's and Fritz had a piano in his room. One day Fritz said: "Come up and let's see how you sing." He came upstairs and sang one verse of "Molly Malone." Fritz stopped him before he began the second verse and said: "Fine. That's all you need." His voice had a tenor timbre, which meant it would carry over an orchestra and, we later discovered, his sense of rhythm was faultless. He is instinctively musical.

All stars are hesitant to commit themselves. Some take longer than others and a few practise the sadistic art of fence walking until the authors and producer have telephoned Memminger's for reservations. Rex was slow, but it was understandable. For a man of his theatrical stature, at that point in his career to leap on to the musical stage was not an easy decision to make. And so we waited.

Waiting, for me at least, was not difficult. My oldest and dearest friend, Ben Welles, with whom I had collaborated on one of the Hasty Pudding shows at Harvard, was then working for the *New York Times* in London and he and his wife, Cynthia, had a charming house in Wilton Place. Every moment I was not engaged on official business was merrily spent with them. I also ran into another old friend from Hollywood, Lewis Milestone (Millie, as he was called) the director of the immortal film *All Quiet on the Western Front*. I told him what Fritz and I were doing in London and he asked if I had ever been to Covent Garden when the market opened. "Never," said I. "Well," said Millie, "it seems to me if you are going to write about a flower girl from Covent Garden, you ought to go there." "What time of the day?" I asked. Millie replied, "When the day's activities usually begin, of course. At four in the morning." Ergo, one night I brought Fritz and Millie to Ben's house where we kept everyone up until it was time to depart for Covent Garden.

It was cold that early morning and I had forgotten from my childhood schooldays how cold English cold can be. The celebrated English humidity responsible for the celebrated English complexion may have added a dash of English pink to our cheeks, but from the neck down I was a large dash of blue. Millie, for some reason, was impervious to the weather. "Keep walking," he said "and you will be all right." We walked around Covent Garden for three hours. It was the first time I heard the Cockney rhyme language in action. It is a fascinating invention and for the uninitiated, worthy of a few lines of explanation.

Simply put, instead of a word they use its rhyme. "Wife" becomes "trouble and strife"; "man" becomes "pot and pan"; "stairs" are "apples and pears." So a typical sentence might be, "A pot and pan walked down the apples and pears with his trouble and strife." If that were not complicated enough, they then proceed to lop off the rhyming word. A "queer" is a "ginger beer," which becomes a "ginger." I had always wondered at the etymology of the expression "giving someone the raspberry," and I found the answer to it at Covent Garden that morning. The full rhyme is "raspberry tart." It takes little imagination to figure out what rhymes with "tart" and sounds like a "raspberry." They also insert words into the middle of words, as in "absobloodylutely." I made use of it in the lyric of "Wouldn't It Be Loverly?" but changed it to "absobloomin'lutely."

As we wandered around the market we saw a group of costermongers warming themselves around a smudgepot fire. It seemed to dramatize the climate perfectly and we used it in the play. At seven o'clock we walked over to the Savoy Hotel for breakfast, but it was not until late that afternoon that I finally thawed out.

Two or three days later Fritz and I began to work on Eliza's first song, and after our experience in Covent Garden I realized that it had to be about the longing for creature comforts. I gave Fritz the title "Wouldn't It Be Loverly?" and he wrote the melody in one afternoon. What I thought was most impressive about the music was its cheerfulness, so characteristic of the Cockney spirit.

While we were in London, we also met with Cecil Beaton. He

said that only with Oliver Smith, for whom he had the greatest respect and affection, would he consider doing only the costumes. Therefore he would do the costumes.

In New York, when we first discussed the part of Doolittle, both Herman and I had the same first thought: Stanley Holloway. I remembered him well from my schooldays in England and we both had seen some of his recent motion pictures. Herman called him and we all had lunch together at Claridge's. He loved the idea of playing Doolittle. We asked him if his singing voice was still intact after all the years he had been away from the musical stage. Without a word he put down his knife and fork, threw back his head and unleashed a strong baritone note that resounded through the dining room, drowned out the string quartet and sent a few dozen people off to the osteopath to have their necks untwisted.

While we were busy with Rex, Stanley, and Cecil, Irving Cohen was meeting with Miss Barber of the British Authors' Society who was responsible for the disposition of the rights to Bernard Shaw's plays. How those rights were to be assigned had been very precisely specified in the old boy's will, and his will was as original and provocative as all his other works.

When his wife had died many years earlier, she had bequeathed a sum to be used to teach the Irish manners. At the time when Shaw was asked about it, he said that he thought it an admirable idea, so admirable, in fact, that he himself intended to do the same for the English. However he did not. Instead he left all the proceeds from his writings to the creation of a foundation to increase the English alphabet to forty-nine letters!

The theory that if the English language could be written phonetically it would standardize pronounciation and thereby remove class distinction was not an invention of Shaw's, but he was its leading proselytizer. I cannot believe he truly expected anyone to sit down and recreate the English alphabet, and even if anyone were fanatic enough to do so, that the English, of all people, would adopt it, because there is also a provision in his will that if, after a reasonable period of time and effort, it proved unfeasible the monies were then to be divided equally between the National Gallery in Dublin and the National Gallery in London. But who was to say what constituted a reasonable time?

That question became very pertinent to us because it is also stated in the will that no one was to be given the rights to any of his plays for a period longer than five years, and the only way that clause could be altered would be if the "reasonable time" clause came up for review and someone—presumably the British Government—decided to take action. And what would make the British Government decide to take action? Many years had elapsed since Shaw's death and nobody had seemed at all interested in establishing the foundation, and the British government had done nothing. Ah! But if the musicalization of *Pygmalion* should be, by some chance, a great success and the royalties began pouring in, it was "bloody likely" that the government would decide the English language could do very well without twenty-three additional letters and move rather swiftly to grab the loot. In other words, according to the time-honored Gospel of St. Lucre, they would see to it that the will was broken and make any arrangements that would continue the golden flow.

However, it is an unfortunate fact of theatrical life that not every play is a smash hit. One can not only fail, but one can also have a modest success which finally returns its investment over a long period from many sources other than the Broadway run. *Paint Your Wagon,* for example, which was the last play Fritz and I had written, did not go into the black for almost sixteen years. Not only that, but the five-year clause would automatically preclude the sale of the play to motion pictures. Normally the authors have rights in perpetuity and the producer and backers participate for a minimum of eighteen years. To try and finance a play without the possibility of a motion picture sale and with all bets off after five years would make fund raising difficult, to say the least. That is, unless there were a backer to whom the rights would have a limited value even if the play were a failure: i.e., a television company. If a television company financed the play and the play failed, it would still have the right to do a television performance of Shaw's *Pygmalion* or the musical version itself.

At that time there were only two networks in a position to undertake such a venture, NBC and CBS, and neither of them had been active in the theatre to date.

To proceed any further against such overwhelming odds was as illogical as writing the play before acquiring the Pascal rights in the first place. So naturally we decided to proceed at full gallop, hoping that if fools rushed in, perhaps Broadway angels would follow!

On the Sunday of our fifth week, Rex called and suggested that he, Fritz, and I take a walk in Hyde Park. Rex is over six feet tall and Fritz and I, as I have mentioned, are over five feet tall. Rex also takes long strides which he executes briskly, his head high and pointing in the direction in which he wishes to go. The walk through Hyde Park consisted of Rex walking and Fritz and I jogging along next to him. We "walked" for almost three hours, Rex chatting away, Fritz and I panting away. Then all at once he stopped. He turned to us and said, almost out of nowhere: "All right. I'll do it." Fritz and I were almost too exhausted to register any joy, but it did not matter because I do not think he would have noticed it.

We exited out of Hyde Park and Fritz said he thought he would go back to the hotel and take a little nap before dinner. He woke up two days later. I, however, was going on a bit further and so Rex and I continued on together. When we parted he turned to me, looked at me for a long moment, and then said: "I don't know why, but I have faith in you."

No one before in my life had ever said those exact words to me, and Rex will never know the difficulty I had in controlling what might have been a rather un-British emotional display. Throughout the years that moment has returned to me often, always with the same flush of everlasting gratitude.

It was estimated that *Bell, Book and Candle* would undoubtedly close by late spring, and so we notified Stanley and Cecil that rehearsals would begin in New York in the early autumn. We suggested to Rex that he take some vocal lessons, not to learn how to sing, but to strengthen the machinery, and he promised to do so. We, in turn, promised him that we would fly over to see him to show him his songs as we wrote them, to make certain he felt comfortable with them.

In mid-February we left London with the Shaw rights in one hand, commitments from Rex Harrison, Stanley Holloway, and Cecil Beaton in the other, two less songs than we had arrived with and a year's work ahead of us.

Returning to New York, Fritz and I retired to Rockland County to begin the long haul. Although there was adequate space in my own house for Fritz to move in, for a very good reason he refused, and rented a house at the top of the hill from Burgess Meredith.

That particular section of the Hudson River valley is known as the Dutch country and many of the houses are reputedly haunted. Mine was built in 1732 by the father of Mad Anthony Wayne, the famous general of the American Revolution. When I purchased it I was forewarned that the ghost of Mad Anthony patrolled the premises. In the seven years I had lived there I had never bumped into him. But Fritz had. In fact he had had two "meetings" and the second had so unnerved him that he refused to spend another night in the house.

The first meeting had occurred the previous October. In the guestroom there were two double beds. One night Fritz was asleep in one bed and Virginia, the woman with whom he was living, was in the other. He was awakened suddenly by the sound of heavy footsteps coming up the hall that seemed to pass right through the locked door and into the room. The room turned ice cold. He thought for a moment he was dreaming, until he heard Virginia cry out from under the covers in the next bed: "Go away! Leave us alone! What did we ever do to you?" The footsteps and cold air then seemed to pass through the wall and out into the night. Fritz turned on the light. The door was still locked, but there was no question they had both heard and felt the same presence.

On the New Year's Eve before we left for England, they were again fast asleep and again heard the footsteps coming up the hall and walk through the door. But this time the footsteps continued on into the bathroom where, a few seconds later, they both heard the lavatory flush. Then the steps continued through the wall and disappeared into the forest. When I awoke the next morning and went to their room, Fritz and Virginia had gone. They had gotten up immediately, dressed and driven back to New York. Fritz had left me a note which said: "Dear boy, a ghost who wakes me up in the night is one thing, but a ghost who goes to the bathroom and takes a crap is more than I can stand. I will call you tomorrow. Fritz." And that is why he lived at the top of the hill.

Before settling in and down we addressed ourselves to the problem of the financing of the play. Robert Sarnoff was the president of NBC and I had known him since "swingtime" in Central Park. I called him. Bobby said he would think about it and "get back to me." In all branches of the performing media, no one ever calls one later, you are "gotten back to."

William Paley was the president of CBS and there our hopes lay with Goddard Lieberson, then the vice president of Columbia Records, a division of CBS, and a friend of Fritz's and mine since the beginning of our collaboration. Goddard evinced much more interest than Bobby and said he would discuss it at the first opportunity with Bill Paley.

Herman, meanwhile, immediately got in touch with Julie who had, despite numerous offers, indeed kept herself available and concluded an agreement with her agent for her to play Eliza Doolittle.

The most important cog in any theatrical enterprise is, of course, the director, and although we had discussed many names with Rex we still had not agreed upon whom to approach. Herman had suggested Moss Hart, but upon investigation we discovered that he was writing a musical himself with none other than Harold Rome. We decided to wait a while until Fritz and I had written a few more numbers before presenting it to anyone.

Every permanent collaboration develops its own idiosyncratic ways of working and Fritz and I had ours. After we had arrived at a general outline of a play—in this case there was a play and so it was a matter of treatment—we would then begin discussing the musicalization. As I mentioned earlier, although one writes to please oneself, there are "rules" and an audience is preconditioned by those rules. I happen to believe that if a group of spectators came to the theatre expecting to see a musical and instead saw *Hamlet* for the very first time, after five minutes they would grow restless waiting for the music. This may be an exaggeration but it proves a point. There are also conventions in the musical theatre: conventions involving the balance of the score, the proper distribution of solos, ensemble singing, and choreography. What is exciting is to be aware of these conventions and use them for fresh expression. It is not enough that there be a fast song after a slow song. Legitimate, dramatic ways must be found so that the character or characters arrive at the emotional moment that demands the right kind of music to balance the score.

Fritz and I were determined to retain as much of Shaw's dialogue as possible, which would automatically mean there would be more dialogue than in any other musical to date. The only way to accomplish this, we felt, was to fill the score with tempo and to search every emotion until we found that aspect of it that demanded it. A case in point is "Show Me." Eliza leaves Higgins' house shattered and alone, not knowing where she belongs or where to turn. It is preceded by a long dialogue scene. Her mood is fundamentally a sad one and sad songs make slow songs. But an emotion is a mountain with many sides and we chose the road marked hurt and fury. Hurt and fury translate themselves into passion and passion into tempo. Fritz decided on almost a Spanish tempo and write it in an agitated 5/4.

Having decided on the approach we would then become specific. We would discuss a musical moment until we knew exactly what we were trying to accomplish, and then Fritz would wait until I had found a title. He would then begin composing to the title.

Some composers think for a long time before they begin writing. Some write it at a desk, as did Kurt Weill. Fritz would sit at the piano and improvise and improvise. While he was doing so, I was always in the room. After a while he would almost go into a trance and not even quite realize what he was playing until I would suddenly say: "Wait! That's it." Usually he would then reply: "What?", and I would hum a few bars of what he had just played. "Oh?" Fritz would say. "You like that?" "Yes," I would reply. He would play it again and either say, "Not bad," and continue; or "What's the matter with you? That's terrible!", and go back into his trance.

During this exercise I did nothing but sit and listen. Occasionally, perhaps, jotting down an idea for the lyric. Sometimes he would find the melody in a matter of hours. Sometimes two or three days. Once he had composed it he would leave it with me, always remaining within reach in case I wished to try a line on him, or find out if a small change could be made in the melody to accommodate a lyrical idea. I was always manic with excitement when he finished a piece of music. Fritz, on the other hand, was usually riddled with uncertainty. His uncertainty, however, was something he shared with me only.

The outside world saw many Fritz Loewes, but I knew only one. Sometimes he would publicly announce with inverted bravado: "I don't like my music at all!" On other occasions he would compare himself to almost anyone from Beethoven and Brahms to Ravel. Those who knew him well knew he was never serious, but I believe I was the only one aware of the deep emotional reason for the masquerade.

He never regarded a song as finished until the lyric was written and always refused to play anyone a naked melody. He was always conscious of range and if I had trouble singing a melody—not that I am a singer, God knows he would continue working on it until I could.

The first song that we tackled was "Wouldn't It Be Loverly?"

He made a few changes in the middle and then left me to my labors. With the memory of Covent Garden fresh in my mind— and in my bones—and riding a crest of excitement because of our successes to date, I could hardly wait to put pen to paper. I told Fritz that I was convinced it would be finished in a few days.

I never begin a new song at any time of the day other than early morning. If Fritz finished a melody, let us say, by noon, I still would wait until six-thirty the following morning before I locked myself up and plugged in the coffee pot. And so at six-thirty one morning I began "Wouldn't It Be Loverly?" For some reason the page seemed far away and I could not organize my thoughts or empathize the emotions that I wanted to write. By six that evening not one word was on the page. I thought perhaps it was because the lyrical muscles needed limbering up. It had happened to me many, many times before. The next morning I returned to my chair. By six that evening I still stared at a blank page. It continued for a week. During the second week panic, slowly and insidiously, began to join me and by the third week it had become my constant companion. I had known lyrical paralysis before. It usually came in two varieties. The first was when I thought I knew what I was going to say and then discovered I did not know what I was going to say and began searching for another way of saying what I thought I was going to say; the second was when I knew precisely what I wished to say and was unable to find the words to say it. In this instance I still knew what I wished to say, but I had lost all faith in it and was trying to find words to say what I had lost faith in that would be so miraculous I would once again have faith in it! But I knew that no such words existed. I was not, in fact, lyrically paralyzed. Obviously it was something much deeper. By the fourth week I had lost eight pounds and had become a basket-case. In desperation, I went to see Dr. Bela Mittelmann, a psychiatrist whom I had gone to for a spell eight years earlier. Besides being one of the nation's most respected analysts, he was also the only psychiatrist I had ever encountered who had a sense of humor and did not have modern furniture in the waitingroom.

Collapsing onto the couch I poured out my tale of woe. In the course of the hour I remember him saying to me, "You know, you write as if your life depends on every line." "It does," I replied. Passing that by, he continued to explore my recent past. Suddenly, from nowhere, I found myself spilling out the incident with Mary Martin and Richard Halliday. In the most sympathetic way imaginable, he began to chuckle. In an instant I saw clearly that that brutal lunch in the Hampshire House had shaken me more profoundly than I had realized. When the hour was over, I asked him if I might come and see him again that week. "Of course," he said, "but first, why don't you call me in a day or so." When I had walked into his office my head had felt twice its size and my body about two feet tall. When I left I felt my normal proportions returning.

At six-thirty the next morning I returned to my solitary haunt and began work again. By mid-afternoon half the lyric was written. The following day I finished it.

Richard and Mary were at their home in Brazil when *My Fair Lady* opened and we received a warm cable of good wishes from them. I have seen Mary a few times since and certainly bear her no malice: she was entitled to her opinion. But why that insensitive lunch? I will never know. Richard died a few years later before I had a chance to ask him. Or would I ever have asked him? I doubt it. But ever after when either Fritz or I was stuck, one of us would say to the other: "You *poor dear* boy. You have *lost your talent.*"

After a successful tour around the neighborhood with "Wouldn't It Be Loverly?" we turned our attention to the musicalization of Henry Higgins. In a very short time Higgins and Harrison became interchangeable in my mind, and instead of Rex's vocal limitations becoming an inhibition, his personality and style seemed to clear away fresh creative paths. I realized that the secret in writing for him was to make certain at all times that the lyrical and musical line coincided exactly with the way one would speak the line. For example, "Let a woman in your life and your sabbatical is through" was composed in such a manner that it could either be spoken or sung without altering the music. It had nothing to do with range; only that. Fritz and I also slowly began to realize that his songs, most of which could be classified as comedy songs, had to be built on a strong foundation of emotion. The first one we attempted was "Why Can't the English?" After one or two false starts, we found out that it could not be a mere statement of an intellectual position: what it required was anger and frustration. Music is an emotional language and this was something it could express. We followed it with "I'm an Ordinary Man" which replaced the totally inadequate "Please Don't Marry Me." The two songs took about six weeks in all to complete.

While we were thus engaged I was interrupted one day around noon by a breathless phone call from Goddard Lieberson. He said he was on his way to "21" to have lunch with Bill Paley. He had not forgotten our conversation, but he could not remember exactly which of Shaw's plays we were doing, who was going to be in it, and any and all other details. I filled him in in staccato telegraphic sentences "I'll get back to you," said Goddard and plonked down the receiver. A few hours later he called back to report that Mr. Paley, who was, incidentally, a good friend of Rex's, was immensely interested and could Herman Levin come to see him.

I communicated this to Herman. He assured me he would have no difficulty in fitting Mr. Paley into his busy schedule and the next day they met. At the conclusion of their meeting there was an understanding ready to be put to paper that CBS would finance the entire production, which was budgeted at $400,000, and that Columbia Records would make the cast album.

Now we had the rights, the principal members of the cast, the scenic designer, the costume designer, the financing, but no title— and no director.

When we finished "I'm an Ordinary Man" we met with Herman in the office to discuss the director. Despite Moss Hart's involvement in his own play, Herman felt we had nothing to lose by calling him and asking him if he would be interested in hearing what we had written so far. He called him, and to our surprise and delight Moss said he would love to hear it.

A few days later he came to Herman's office and Fritz and I displayed our wares. Moss's reaction was immediate and enthusiastic. He agreed to postpone his own project and direct ours. We all breathed a sigh of relief that could have sent a battleship halfway across the Atlantic.

Pause.

Moss Hart. Moss Hart, as I was to find out, had no understudies. He is and forever will be irreplaceable to more people in more ways than any man I have ever known. When he died in 1961 it was more than simply the death of one man. It seemed as if the gods had broken in and robbed us of some of our most precious humanity. For me hardly a day goes by that I do not find myself beginning a sentence with: "As Moss used to say . . ." And time after time when I have blundered, the first thought that comes to me is: "Damn it. Moss told me not to do this or . . ."

"I have had many successes in my life," he said to me one day, "and many failures. Each time I had a success it was for a different reason. Each time I failed it was for the same reason. I said yes when I meant no." Much too often have I remembered that much too late.

Following his first success with George Kaufman, *Once in a Lifetime*, about which he wrote so movingly in his memorable book *Act One*, for the next dozen years there was not a season on Broadway that was not brightened by the gifts of his pen. He wrote six plays with Kaufman, including *You Can't Take It with You*, which won the Pulitzer Prize in 1937. He wrote books for musicals with scores by Rodgers and Hart, Cole Porter, Irving Berlin and Kurt Weill and Ira Gershwin. When he turned to directing, he did so with the sure hand of a master of his art and an eye that clearly perceived the goal at the far end of the road. Probably the most important part of a director's role is in the preparation of a play, in the casting, the planning, and the work with the author. He was a superb constructionist and could put his finger on the most subtle dramatic weakness. He appreciated the actor's craft and always sought the best. He understood the producer's problems and the economic limitations, and was as practical as he was creative. He was in every sense of the word a man of the theatre, a gentleman of the theatre, and the last of his breed.

Undoubtedly his most inspired bit of casting was in his private life when he married Kitty Carlisle. A friend of his, the playwright and screenwriter Norman Krasna, was in love with Kitty and brought her to Moss's house in Bucks County one weekend for his approval. If that seems surprising, it gives one some idea of the importance of Moss's opinion to all his friends.

Kitty had been educated in Europe to be, as she frequently says, either a soprano or the wife of a Count. She became a soprano and after her debut on Broadway—mentioned earlier—she went on to Hollywood where she starred opposite Bing Crosby for Paramount, and later introduced the famous song "Alone" in the Marx Brothers' film *A Night at the Opera*. She then returned to New York, the theatre—and ultimately to Moss.

After the weekend, Norman called Moss for the "reviews." Moss said he thought she was a lovely girl but he could not see them as a couple. It was an unbiased opinion because at the time he had no idea that one day he would see himself as Norman's replacement. But a few years later they met again, and in 1946 they were married. Moss was in his early forties and until then had been a confirmed bachelor—pursued, but a fast runner. But with Kitty he hung up his track shoes.

They were not only an ideal couple, they were the ideal couple. One of Moss's most endearing traits was his innocent surprise at being Moss Hart. It was said of Scott Fitzgerald that he was not only at every ball, but he was also outside with his face pressed against the window. It could also have been said of Moss and it could also be said of Kitty. The only "misfortune" that befell their marriage was that Moss immediately lost his butler, but that happens to every bachelor (who has a butler). They lived in the grand manner and no one ever loved the grand manner more. Moss always said that money was to be spent foolishly. But he did not mean foolishly, he meant "enjoy it, kid." They lived in a beautiful apartment on upper Park Avenue. Moss loved to decorate and Kitty, wise lady that she is, let him do it. They entertained regularly and were sought after everywhere. In time they had two children, a boy, Christopher, and a girl, Cathy.

In the forties, following *Lady in the Dark,* dark clouds began to speckle his path. Determined to write alone his first effort, *The World of Christopher Blake,* did not, as we say in the trade, come off. Shortly after he wrote *Winged Victory* for the Air Corps which was greeted with trumpets and huzzahs. But after that the words came more slowly and more painfully and his output diminished. From time to time he would wander West to gather a few gold nuggets from the Hollywood soil, and in 1946 he wrote the screenplay for *Gentleman's Agreement* which won the Academy Award for the Best Picture of the Year.

But whether he walked in sunlight or shadow, his aura never dimmed. He was always the great Moss Hart—and the adjective, for once, is accurate.

He was at times witty, at times salty, at times explosively funny. We used to phone each other every day, the phone calls always beginning in the middle of the conversation. The first topic, however, invariably was how he had slept the night before. All his adult life he was racked with insomnia. When we were not near enough to phone, we used to write. The letters were profane and outrageous but very funny—at least to us.

After *My Fair Lady* opened in New York, he and Kitty decided to take a boat trip to Europe. I received a letter from him written on board which ended abruptly, as follows: "I have to stop now. There's a lifeboat drill and I have to try on Kitty's clothes."

On another occasion, in mid-winter, he and Kitty went south

to Montego Bay in Jamaica for two weeks of sunshine. After he had been there a few days I received the following letter from him:

> Dear Chap,
>
> I am a true friend—the vrai! I could tell you it has been marvelous—but it would not be the vrai. Wretched is the word for Mossie! We arrived in a downpour and it has been torrential ever since.
>
> Only one thing has dissipated the gloom for me—in yesterday's local newspaper there occurred a glorious—a collector's item—typo error. They were reporting a wedding and went into great detail on the bride's costume. Then—the last paragraph read—"and the groom, not to be outdone, wore a large red carnation in his bottomhole."
>
> If the rain keeps on I may stick one in mine.
>
> Your dolorous friend

He could say things that uttered by anyone else would have been answered with a broken jaw.

One day we were walking down Fifth Avenue when a man suddenly came over, stood directly in our path, and said: "Well, if it isn't the great Moss Hart! I'll bet you're too big and famous to remember me." Moss looked at him for a moment and then with a warm and winning smile said: "No, you are quite wrong. I remember you very well indeed. We went to school together in the Bronx. You bored me then and you are boring me now." He side-stepped around the man and we walked on. I was stunned with admiration and told him that I found his performance more impressive than his Pulitzer Prize and all his other accolades.

Although an informal man, because of his vast experience in every form of theatrical expression, from revue to musical, to comedy, to drama, his opinions seemed oracular. He was also one of the three directors I have ever known who understood lyric writing—the other two being Joshua Logan and Vincente Minnelli. When Fritz and I played a new song for him and he liked it it was tantamount to universal critical acceptance.

He had a monumental warehouse of stories. From time to time he would repeat one that he had already told us, and yet it still seemed amusing. There was one in particular that we heard more than most because it usually came to his mind after we had played him a new song. In the early thirties he had written a satirical review with Irving Berlin called *As Thousands Cheer*. (He was, incidentally, one of the best sketch writers in the history of musical review.) One day Irving came rushing excitedly into his apartment. He had found the finale for act one. It was called "Easter Parade." Irving is a self-taught pianist and musician, but his musical invention is so original and so musical that trained composers like George Gershwin and Jerome Kern used to shake their heads in envious disbelief. "That son of a gun," Jerome used to say helplessly. "How does he do it?" But there is no doubt Irving is no Gershwin at the keyboard.

He sat down and played "Easter Parade" for Moss. It sounded terrible. Moss was in a dilemma. Finally he said: "Irving, play 'Blue Skies' for me." Irving played "Blue Skies" and that sounded terrible. Moss then said: "Irving, the finale is terrific."

They say a charming woman is a woman who makes a man feel charming. Moss was a writer who made you feel like a writer. He was amusing and made you feel amusing. One of his devices was to pin an exaggerated character label on you. Fritz, he had decided, was the world's worldliest sophisticate. I, on the other hand, was the possessor of an enormous fortune and traveled in international circles far beyond his lowly reach. Unconsciously I began to make outrageous statements that suited the character he had created for me—just to amuse him.

I was living for a while in the Waldorf Towers and my day started with the usual phone call to Moss. "God damn it," I began one day. "What's the trouble?" he asked. "The Duchess of Windsor's air conditioning is dripping on my Rolls Royce," I replied. He roared with laughter, as I knew he would, and somehow because it was Moss, whenever I made him laugh I felt as if I had just received a present.

I was soon to discover that his objective as a director was to produce what the author had written, tastefully, theatrically, and truthfully. He did not intrude—he guided. The most difficult thing to find in the theatre today is a director who will not make a contribution, that is, force the author to make unnecessary change to suit a directorial concept. Being a writer himself, Moss had profound respect for the written word of others.

However rewarding our early meetings were together, and however overwhelmed I was by the acuteness of his perception and understanding of what we were trying to accomplish, I had no idea of the theatrical experience awaiting me when rehearsals began.

With our new director's stamp of approval on "I'm an Ordinary Man" and "Why Can't the English," Fritz and I flew to London to show them to Rex, as we had promised we would. We found him a little anxious, concerned, and beginning to question his decision to be in the play. One of the main reasons for his disquiet, we discovered, was the vocal coach to whom he had been going. He was a voice teacher whom—dare I say it?—Mary Martin suggested to him, and said coach had been preparing him for Puccini. Rex belted out a few pear-shaped tones for us with the large end of the pear coming out first. Fritz jumped up and immediately told him that whomever it was he was seeing, he was not to ever again. Rex was immensely relieved to hear that. With the help of Teddy Holmes at Chappell Music, our publishers, Fritz found an admirable man for him, someone wise enough to understand what was needed.

We played Rex the two songs and he liked them both. We made a tape recording of them so he could listen to them over and over again, and left him the music and lyrics.

Our pleasure and relief at his reaction to the new songs was considerably dampened, however, by the continued strength of *Bell, Book and Candle* at the box office. Far from falling off in the late spring, the houses were getting better and better and there was no end in sight. Furthermore, there was no theatrical tradition for extracting a star from a play. He had a contract and could not give notice, and the producer has no right to summarily close a play. Only the theatre owner has the right to order you out and only when a play has fallen below a specified weekly figure, called the stop clause, for two consecutive weeks. It was clear that the only solution involved some financial arrangement between Herman and the English producer, who happened to be Hugh "Binkie" Beaumont, managing director of H. M. Tennent Limited, and undoubtedly England's most influential and powerful theatrical manager. If such could be accomplished, then, we hoped, he in turn could make some arrangement with the theatre owner to effect a release from the theatre contract. One thing was certain: as long as *Bell, Book and Candle* continued to run, rehearsals could not be scheduled, and without a rehearsal date the entire production could conceivably disintegrate.

Fortunately, Binkie, Rex, and I were blessed with the friendship of Irene Selznick, a dear and remarkable woman, the daughter of Louis B. Mayer and ex-wife of David O. Selznick, and a theatrical producer of considerable stature in her own right. Among the plays she had brought to Broadway were *A Streetcar Named Desire, The Chalk Garden* and, of special interest to us at this moment, *Bell, Book and Candle.*

No arrangement could be made with Binkie without her approval, because, as is always the case, the New York producer shares in the British reproduction just as the British producer of an English play shares in the American reproduction.

The moment we returned to New York I had lunch with Irene. She felt very strongly that our musical—still untitled by the way— should not and could not remain in limbo. It is typical of her that her conviction was not based on friendship, but because she felt it was not good for the theatre. Irene assured me that if Herman were able to make an arrangement with Binkie she would give it her blessing.

The following week Herman took off for London for a meeting at the summit with Binkie. After a few days of argle-bargling they arrived at an agreement which specified a November closing date for *Bell, Book and Candle,* in return for which Binkie and H. M. Tennent would receive a cash settlement and the rights to produce the British production of the musical *Pygmalion.* It is also typical of Irene that she not only was instrumental in persuading Binkie, but refused to share in any of the proceeds.

When Herman returned we were able to announce a rehearsal date of January 3. We could have started earlier, but because so many of the cast were English we felt it only fair to allow them to celebrate Christmas at home.

We now had the rights, the principal players, the scenic designer, the costume designer, and the director—but still no title.

It has been my experience over the years that unless the title is born with the idea, as it was with *Brigadoon* and *Paint Your Wagon,* after a while it becomes a parlor game, and like all parlor games the longer you play it the sillier it is apt to become. To date we had had "Liza" and "Lady Liza," both of which went to their final resting places in the trash basket—because it would have seemed peculiar for the marquee to read: "Rex Harrison in 'Liza'." For a short time we had "My Fair Lady," but discarded it because it sounded like an operetta. While we were in London, Fritz came across "fanfaroon," a rarely used English word meaning someone who blows his own fanfare. He clung to it tenaciously, primarily I believe because it reminded him of *Brigadoon*. The song on which we were now working was called "Come to the Ball," and for a while we even considered that.

The number was for Rex. There was to be a scene following Eliza's catastrophic blunder at Ascot in which she refused to go on. The idea of the song was, having tried every form of persuasion from cajoling to steamrolling, Higgins finally resorts to charm. It was written as a waltz and I was on it for three weeks. Three-quarter time invariably requires an endless amount of interrhyming which can raise havoc with the central nervous system. Eventually it was finished and we went on to "On the Street Where You Live."

The idea for it had come from a personal experience of pre-adolescence, which seemed to me about the emotional level of Freddie. When I was ten years old I had been sent to a dancing class on Sunday afternoons, white gloves and all. The prettiest girl was, of course, the most popular, but I was too shy to make my presence felt. She lived on Fifth Avenue, so every Saturday I would place myself on a bench outside Central Park opposite her house, hoping I would see her come in or out and be able to dash across the street and speak to her without the competition of all the other white-gloved little brats. But she never came by. I found out later I had the wrong address.

With those two songs completed, off we went to play them for

Moss. He and Kitty were living that summer in the unlikeliest spot one would have ever expected to find Moss and Kitty Hart. They had bought a beach house on the Jersey coast in a town called Beachhaven, a model of middle-classic America. "Summer is not summer," Moss used to say, "unless you get sand up your ass," and they had selected Beachhaven not only for the sand, but because there was not a soul there whom they knew.

I was very proud of "Come to the Ball" and was doubly so after hearing Moss and Kitty's reaction. We all felt that undoubtedly this would be Rex's *pièce de résistance* in the first act.

Leaving Beachhaven, it was back to Rockland County and on to the opening of the second act, which was called "You Did It." After we did it, back we went on to the Jersey Turnpike. The reviews in Beachhaven were good, so with two more songs for Rex now ready, we packed our bags and left for London again.

We found Rex in much better spirits. He had had a week off from the play and seemed to be enjoying himself working on "I'm an Ordinary Man." He was not happy, however, with "Why Can't the English?" As he tried to learn it, he said he felt he sounded like an inferior Noel Coward. I could not understand what he meant until it occurred to me that perhaps it was the rhyme scheme. I had first written it:

Why Can't the English teach their children how to speak?
In Norway there are legions
Of literate Norwegians
....

I changed it to:

Why can't the English teach their children how to speak?
This verbal class distinction by now should be antique.

And so on. The change made the lyric far less "lyricky," more act-able and Rex comfortable.

He was most enthusiastic about the two new songs, which I must confess did not come as a surprise to me. Over the summer, the more I worked on his material the more I began to enjoy it, and the more at home I became. Somehow I had the feeling that in find-ing a style for Rex I was also finding a style for myself. Kurt Weill had told me many years earlier that he had met Lotte Lenya while he was writing *The Threepenny Opera,* and he had written the songs for Jenny with her in mind. From that moment on, he told me, he kept hearing her voice in every melody he wrote—this in spite of the fact she only appeared in one other musical of his. To this day, time after time I find myself instinctively writing for Rex and con-stantly reminding myself that I am not writing for Rex. Neverthe-less, he was then and will always be my natural extension.

As Fritz and I continued working on the rest of the score, the activ-ity involved in the physical production of the play accelerated.

To light the show, Moss suggested Abe Feder to which we all, naturally, agreed, even Oliver. As a rule, scenic designers are against Abe because he constantly commits the cardinal sin of lighting the actors first and the scenery second. Lighting a show is a long and maddening process which is seldom completed until just before the show opens in New York. I have since done three more shows with Abe and thanked God for him every time, and I hope I never do another without him. He is undoubtedly the best lighting man alive today.

I will never forget him at President Kennedy's last birthday party. At first the president had said he did not wish any entertain-ment, and so two dinners had been arranged to take place simul-taneously in the large, two ballrooms either side of the foyer of the

Waldorf Astoria, the Sert Room and the Empire Room. It was to be a $1,000-a-plate dinner and the president would go from table to table thanking everyone. Suddenly, two weeks before the affair, I received a call from Washington saying the president had changed his mind and would very much like some entertainment after all. (I was still staging Democratic rallies in New York.)

Obviously one cannot put on a show in two rooms at the same time, so I decided that while the dinners were taking place, we would put up grandstands in the foyer and drop enormous drapes to mask the foyer from the rest of the lobby. The Park Avenue entrance to the Waldorf would simply have to be closed that night.

Abe had been kind enough to help me out at the last two rallies I had done at Madison Square Garden, and so I naturally turned to him again. He arrived, looked up at the ceiling, which is some three stories high and a mass of tiny lightbulbs, puffed on his ubiquitous cigar for a moment and then summoned the manager. Pointing up at the ceiling he said: "See all those lights up there?" Of course the manager saw all those lights up there. "Take them out," said Abe. The manager's skin turned olive green. Abe was nonplussed. "Oh, don't worry about putting them back," said he. "I'll take care of that. You just get them out!"

The night before the party, Abe brought in his crew and from eleven o'clock at night until six in the morning not only were all the lightbulbs removed and replaced with the lights Abe wanted, but four huge scaffoldings were erected in the four corners of the foyer on which Abe placed his spotlights. Exhausted, we all went home. At seven in the morning the Waldorf crew arrived, saw the four scaffoldings, thought someone had left them there by mistake, and took them all away. We arrived during the afternoon to rehearse and found them all gone. I was aghast, but not Abe. He found it very amusing, went to the phone, called his crew who returned within minutes, and by "show time" the scaffoldings were all up again. "I told you not to worry, kid," he said. "Have I ever let you down?"

He has lit entire national parks, the grounds of the White House for various occasions, Kennedy airport, Miami Beach, and every major arena in the country. It is my firm belief that if God had turned over the lighting of the Milky Way to Abe Feder, Abe would not only have done a much more artistic job, but we would have seen who was up there.

To play Pickering, Rex had suggested Robert Coote when we were in London. We brought the news back to Moss, who thought it was a splendid suggestion, and Herman made the necessary arrangements.

By now Cecil had arrived "in the colonies" to begin conferences with Moss. He came with dozens of sketches in his portfolio, all of which we found beyond our expectations. Cecil is the only man I know who can design clothes that are both witty and beautiful at the same time. He is, of course, maniacal in his search for materials.

Binkie had warned me. He had told me a story about Cecil that I will never forget. For many years there was a lady named Lily Taylor who was Binkie's all-around assistant. After the war, H. M. Tennent decided the time had come to treat London to an extravagant production, and the instrument was Noel Coward's play *Quadrille,* starring Alfred Lunt and Lynn Fontanne. Binkie asked Cecil to design the sets and costumes. Cecil sketched or described to Lily Taylor the type of materials he needed for the costumes and she scoured London, bringing him the best she could find. Cecil was horrified and rejected them all. So Binkie sent Lily on an extended shopping spree, which literally took her as far as India in search of rare silks and luxurious fabrics. She returned two months later with a collection that would have dazzled Kubla Khan. Binkie telephoned Cecil and asked him to come to London.

Arriving at H. M. Tennent, he sat down and went through the swatches without a word. When he had finished inspecting them he looked up at Lily and said: "Lily Taylor, you're just not trying."

Fortunately for us he was able to find the materials he needed right here in little ole Manhattan. One day he showed us the fabrics he had selected for the ballroom scene. They were of a delicate pastel in color and extraordinarily beautiful. Moss and Oliver were enchanted. Abe looked at them through the cloud of cigar smoke which follows him everywhere and said: "Very pretty. But would you mind bringing them over to my studio." We all shrugged, agreed, and went. Taking us into his big workroom, he said to us: "I'd like to show you the kind of light that is going to hit those costumes." He turned on a lamp and the colors disappeared. I looked at Cecil, expecting him to be miffed. I underestimated his professionalism: he was delighted to find out. That little journey across town probably saved the production $10,000.

There is no person involved in the production of a musical who is for me more frightening, more mysterious, and, next to the director, more essential than the choreographer. He is frightening and mysterious because one never knows what one is going to get until well into rehearsal. As the composer creates with a piano and the author with words, the choreographer creates with human beings, and one cannot peer over his shoulder as he works—no more would a composer or author tolerate someone observing them. One can know what number is being choreographed, but one cannot know until one sees it. For a good choreographer to accept a commission, he must see at least one moment in the play where he can give vent to his own special flare. But will *his* big moment be what is required? If it is, his contribution is incalculable: if it is not, it is a nightmare. The problem of selecting a choreographer for

Pygmalion was further complicated by the dramatic fact that neither Moss, Fritz, nor I felt the show required a great deal of dancing, and how does one get a first rate choreographer to agree to do a show where there is to be not much choreographing?

The first person we decided to talk to was Gower Champion. He had only choreographed two or three shows on Broadway previously, but a major talent was clearly beginning to unfold. We played him the score. He loved it and expressed great interest in doing it. Unfortunately, when Herman sat down with his representatives, his terms were more than we could afford.

We then turned to Michael Kidd, with whom I had worked many years earlier in a show I had written with Kurt Weill, and who had received high critical praise for *Finian's Rainbow* and *Guys and Dolls.*

I will never forget the night we played for him because it was one of the few times I ever saw Moss become angry. Mike is a rather unemotional fellow, not given to much facial expression. He listened to song after song without comment, until we arrived at the opening of the second act, "You Did It," in which Higgins and Pickering recount to the servants what has transpired at the ball. When we finished it, Mike said, "That's wrong." Moss's face flushed. He turned to him slowly and his words hissed through his teeth. "It's wrong?! Two very talented men have spent a great deal of time and effort creating that number and after one hearing you pass judgment and say it's wrong?" Mike seemed oblivious to Moss's anger and said, "It's describing offstage action." "We are aware of that," replied Moss and turning to Fritz and me said, "Please go on." Fritz and I continued but I knew it was merely for the exercise. Moss would never, under any circumstances, accept Michael Kidd. When we completed our "performance" Mike also made a few comments about the second act, which he did not feel had been properly solved as yet. Moss had nothing to say and obviously could not wait for the meeting to end. After Mike left, Moss looked at Fritz and me and from his lips came an over-articulated, "No."

The next person we spoke to was Hanya Holm, who had recently done a brilliant job choreographing a musical called *The Golden Apple*. Hanya is a sedate little lady with a vast classic background, and she seemed to understand immediately the needs of the play. She almost made me lose my fear of choreographers.

Hanya signed on.

In November, as Cecil and Oliver were drawing near to the completion of their designs, public auditions began for dancers and singers. Vocal auditions were supervised by Franz Allers, who had conducted the orchestra in every show of Fritz's and mine since *The Day Before Spring*. Although I have never made an actual count of the number of candidates who audition for the ensemble of a musical, for both *My Fair Lady* and *Camelot* the number was somewhere in excess of five thousand. For *My Fair Lady* sixteen were to be selected. The number of auditioning dancers was over one thousand and from that number twenty-two were to be selected. Hanya, of course, conducted the dancing auditions.

For the singing ensemble, Franz first eliminated all those who were not vocally adequate. After two weeks of this the number was reduced to approximately two hundred. Then Fritz joined him and that number was halved. Then Moss, Fritz, Franz, Herman, Cecil, Hanya, and I made the final choice. Besides vocal ability and appearance, it was necessary for Hanya to see how each person moved, for Cecil to approve of their ability to wear his clothes, and for Herman to find out if those selected approved of the salary he was offering.

Nothing in the theatre is more painful to me than these final auditions, and I suffer for every performer who has to walk out on a bare stage and sing for a handful of judges sitting halfway

back in the theatre, who most of the time seem to be paying little attention and are constantly conferring. Fritz and Franz added
a bit of exoticism to the affair by discussing every candidate in
German. As far as looks were concerned, if a woman sang beautifully Fritz automatically believed she was beautiful, no matter
what her measurements.

There is also a further self-deception that occurs, to which all
of us fall victim. It is the notion that if a young artist is not up to
the physical requirements, he or she will lend "character" to the
ensemble. Unfortunately, "that interesting face" in the ensemble
is only interesting to the half-dozen people watching the audition.
The audience, I have discovered, looks at the ensemble and immediately decides whether they are attractive or not attractive.

It is simpler with the dancers because they are all graceful and
there are no fat ballet dancers. So after Hanya had approved of
their technique, the ultimate choice was made on the basis of type
and their ability to seem at home in Cecil's clothes.

Along with the auditions for dancers and singers, there were
also auditions for the smaller parts and for understudies. As I write
the book of a musical, I always try to write in the kind of smaller
parts in which understudies might be cast.

The one principal character who had not been cast was
Higgins' mother. Cecil, because of his clothes, and Moss, because
of ability and type, both set their caps for Cathleen Nesbitt. "It's
too small a role for Cathleen Nesbitt," I said to Moss. "I know it
is," said he, "but I'm going to try." He personally called her and
invited her to come to the office to discuss it. The manner in which
he did left me weak with awe. He said to her: "Cathleen, the role
of Mrs. Higgins was never a great role and it is even smaller in the
musical version. Furthermore, I want you to know it will not get
any bigger and might even become smaller on the road. But we
want you very much. Cecil has designed some ravishing clothes,

you will look beautiful and you will receive your usual salary." He leaned forward. "Also, Cathleen, I beg you to consider this. For years now you have been appearing in very large roles in very bad plays, to which all your friends have come out of loyalty and suffered through the evening. I believe they will have a very good time at this play and I think you owe it to them to give them a nice evening in the theatre." Cathleen was completely bewitched—as who wouldn't be?—and the following day called Herman to say she would accept the part. What a man!

Betwixt, between and simultaneously, Fritz and I continued working on the score. We had had only one unexpected visitation from the muses and that was "The Rain in Spain." Walking to the office from auditions one day, we began to discuss how to end the sequence of Eliza's lessons. I said to Fritz, "Why don't we just do a number in which all that she has done wrong she now does correctly?" Fritz nodded approvingly. "Like what?" he asked. "Well," I replied, "her main difficulty is with the letter *A* so why don't we call it "The Rain in Spain"?" Fritz thought for a moment and said, "Good. I'll write a tango." We went up to the office. He sat down at the piano and somehow, from somewhere, he played the main theme of "The Rain in Spain." I took out a pad and pencil and wrote the next two lines. He set them immediately. Then the next two. Then the conclusion. I do not believe the entire effort took more than ten minutes. In fact, it had happened so spontaneously and easily that we were suspicious of it. Moss dispelled our suspicions.

At the end of the summer, Nancy and I decided to abandon Mad Anthony and bought an apartment in New York City. Fritz again took up residence in the Algonquin and the final three months of work were completed to the counter-melody of horns and sirens.

Because of Stanley Holloway's background in music hall, we

decided that his two numbers should seem like something out of old English variety. It also seemed the perfect style in which to characterize Doolittle. We had written one of them, "With a Little Bit o' Luck," but still had one to go.

One musical moment with which we were having continuing difficulty was a key song for Eliza. We had been attempting to give her a great lyrical burst of triumph after she had finally conquered "The Rain in Spain," which would, at the same time, reveal her unconscious feelings for Higgins. But every song we had written, despite all efforts to the contrary, had somehow emerged with her true feelings on her sleeve. Over the past few months we had written six numbers and had discarded them all. By mid-November, after sixteen months of work, we were still three important songs short of completing the score.

If this was our worry, Moss had another. Also by mid-November I had not completed the book. The play was there, had always been there, and I knew in my head what changes and additions I intended to make. But Moss found that peculiarly insufficient. One morning he called me and said: "If you have any plans for this weekend, cancel them. We're going away together." I was astonished. "Going away? Where?" "We're going to Atlantic City," said he, "and we're not leaving until you have finished the book and we have had time to discuss every scene together."

I was less surprised by the order of business than the location. Atlantic City, for those of recent or foreign vintage, is a once famous resort along the Jersey coast with a five-mile boardwalk, contiguous to which are a string of palatial hotels, now the shabby relics of a bygone era. In its day it was also a spot where unmarried couples frequently went and never saw the boardwalk. (I describe it as it was then. In the near future Atlantic City may well become the Las Vegas of the East. Gambling has been legalized and reconstruction has begun.) At the time Moss suggested we go there, however, its only visitors were either caught on hooks or dug out of the sand. I assured him that I had only about three days' work left, to which Moss replied, "Good. You will do them in Atlantic City." And so we went to Atlantic City.

The hotel in which we stayed had about four other guests, and so for a very small stipend Moss reserved the entire penthouse. Even when slumming he wanted the best.

As I mentioned before, when I am working I am an early riser and by seven-thirty the next morning I was pecking away at the typewriter. Moss usually arose around eleven. I did not disturb him, however, until I heard the phone ringing and knew he had picked it up. When I walked into his room, I heard him saying to someone on the phone: "I'm in Atlantic City." Pause. "No. Nothing serious. Just another pretty face." After he had had breakfast I showed him what I had written. He was pleased, and we then began a four day schedule that consisted of me working in the morning until noon, Moss reading it over and making suggestions until mid-afternoon, then long, long walks on the boardwalk during which time we discussed every phase of the production from the first moment to the last. I remember them as four of the most delightful days I have ever spent. Moss never failed you. There was never a moment of surprising revelation, as so often happens with others, when you suddenly say to yourself: "Oh ho! I'd better rethink this fellow." I think the greatest compliment I ever received was when he said to me that he hoped we would do another play together after this one.

At the end of the four days the book was finished, and we returned to New York rested and well prepared for the battle to come.

By the first week in December, Fritz and I had found "Get Me to the Church on Time" and had begun work on what was eventually to become "I've Grown Accustomed to Her Face." From time to time, however, I began to notice Fritz holding his stomach and an occasional wince of pain flitting across his face. When I asked him what it was, he seemed disinterested in replying. We finished "Accustomed" a few days before Christmas and, as it turned out, just in time. While the rest of our future company was enjoying their Christmas in London, Rex arrived three days before the holidays to begin work in advance with Fritz, Moss, and me.

It was another example of something that I have found to be true throughout my professional life. Every genuinely great star with whom I have ever worked is a star only because of talent and that indefinable substance, but because he works harder than anyone else, cares more than anyone else and his sense of perfection, which is deeper than anyone else's, demands more of him.

I remember when I was doing a film with Fred Astaire, it was nothing for him to work three or four days on two bars of music. One evening in the dark grey hours of dusk, I was walking across the deserted MGM lot when a small, weary figure with a towel around his neck suddenly appeared out of one of the giant cube sound stages. It was Fred. He came over to me, threw a heavy arm around my shoulder and said: "Oh Alan, why doesn't someone tell me I cannot dance?" The tormented illogic of his question made any answer insipid, and all I could do was walk with him in silence. Why doesn't someone tell Fred Astaire he cannot dance? Because no one would ever ask that question but Fred Astaire. Which is why he is Fred Astaire.

During that last week, perhaps because of the added adrenalin created by the deadline, I finally got the title for "I Could Have Danced All Night," and Fritz set it in a day. When he left me to work with the lyric, he was decidedly not well. I finished the lyric in twenty-four hours, but not to my satisfaction. I was exuberant about the melody, but I thought my lyric was earthbound. There was one line in it in particular that made me blush when I sang it to Fritz. The line was: "And all at once my heart took flight." I have a special loathing for lyrics in which the heart is metamorphosized and skips or leaps or jumps or "takes flight." I promised Fritz I would change it as soon as I could. As it turned out, I was never able to. In time it became far and away the most popular song Fritz and I have ever written. But to this day the lyric gives me cardiac arrest.

Far more serious than the lyric, however, was Fritz's condition. He literally walked bent over double. I immediately took him to my doctor, who in turn rushed him to the hospital and removed his appendix. Fritz was furious. For some reason, neither the doctor nor I was able to convince him that the operation was necessary and to this day he accuses me of putting him in the hospital under false pretences.

On January 3, after miles of traveling and miles of typewritten pages and musical manuscript, rehearsals officially began. When I say officially I mean for the entire company. The dancing ensemble always begins rehearsal a week earlier. There were chairs on stage for the company. Around the edges of the stage Moss had arranged an exhibition of sketches of the scenery and the costumes, and the press was allowed in to do their first day interviews. After an hour or so, all but those involved in the production were asked to leave and the company took their places—the principals in the first row, secondary characters in the second row, and the ensemble behind. Facing the company was a series of long desks. Moss occupied stage centre and either side of him were Cecil, Herman, Abe, Oliver, Biff Liff our stage manager, the assistant stage managers, Franz, Hanya, etcetera, and at the very end near the piano, Fritz and me. Fritz had recovered sufficiently to hobble in for the first reading and play the score.

The cast read the script aloud, with Moss reading the stage directions. Whenever they came to a song, Fritz and I performed it. After the first act the enthusiasm was high. The enthusiasm continued throughout the second act, except Rex's. His face grew longer and longer and his voice softer and softer. I knew exactly why. Somehow Higgins had gotten lost in the second act and because his is the central story, I felt his concern was justified. When the reading was finished, I turned to Fritz and Moss and said that I thought Higgins needed another song in the second act. Fritz was not certain. Moss was. But what? Fritz and I made an appointment for early the next morning to begin staring at each other.

On the way to the Pierre Hotel that evening to have dinner with Rex, I remembered a day a week earlier when he and I had been strolling down Fifth Avenue reviewing our past marital and emotional difficulties and his present one. (It is a melancholy fact that between us we have supported more women than Playtex.) Suddenly he had stopped and said in a loud voice that attracted a good bit of attention: "Alan! Wouldn't it be marvellous if we were homosexuals?!" I said that I did not think that was the solution and we walked on. But it stuck in my mind and by the time I reached the Pierre I had the idea for "Why Can't a Woman Be More Like a Man?" It seemed a perfect second act vehicle through which Higgins could release his rage against Eliza for leaving him.

When I met Rex I told him the idea and he roared with laughter. The next morning Fritz and I went to work.

Rehearsing a musical is a little like running a school. The play is rehearsed under one roof, the singers under another—usually several blocks away; and the dancers under another, again in another part of town. Under the rules of Actors Equity one was allowed to rehearse eight and a half hours a day, with seven hours of actual rehearsing and one and a half hours for meals. Most directors like to begin in the morning at ten o'clock and rehearsing until one or one-thirty, returning at three and continuing until seven. Moss did not. He felt that by the end of the day the cast was usually so tired that little was accomplished in the last two hours. Instead he began rehearsals at two o'clock. The company then broke at five-thirty, returned at seven and worked until eleven. He also so arranged the schedule so that the singers and dancers rehearsed on the day schedule, and he then had the services of Hanya and Franz in the evening when he began staging the musical numbers with the principals.

Because it was Rex's first plunge into the murky waters of a musical and Moss appreciated the necessity of giving him confidence, during the first week the evening rehearsals were devoted entirely to Rex and the staging of his numbers. It was also ideal for Fritz and me. We were able to work during the day on the new song and then be present in the evening.

At the end of the eighth day "Why Can't a Woman?", which I had now christened "A Hymn to Him," was finished and we played it for Moss. He loved it. The next day we showed it to Rex. Rex listened to it without a smile, then looked at me and said: "Quite right! You're absolutely right," and took it home to learn it.

A play in rehearsal is like a country in a world in which only one country exists. The only topic of conversation of interest to anyone is the play and any subject related to the play. The reality of daily life disappears, relationships are tossed into the pressure cooker, strangers become as vulnerable to each other as lovers, and emotions that normally dwell in subterranean caverns rise to the first layer of skin. When Fritz and I returned to the theatre after having completed the song, the weather in the foreign land of *My Fair Lady* was, as to be expected, a mixture of sun, shower, and the unpredictable. Rex, Julie, Stanley, Coote, and all the other performers were getting along beautifully. Naturally, the dancing under Hanya's direction was progressing with the least amount of troubled air. I say naturally because of all the arts in the theatre, the ballet is the most disciplined. I was surprised and amused to discover that at four o'clock every day the cast stopped for tea, as they did in England. On the second day of rehearsal, apparently, Stanley Holloway had insisted he could not continue without his "cuppa" and Moss decided there was no chance of breaking a national habit, several centuries old. Julie had become the little mother and brewed tea for all her countrymen while rehearsals halted for half an hour.

Rex had adopted the attitude of Shaw's defender against the barbaric Americans and kept a Penguin edition of *Pygmalion* nearby at all times. At least four times a day, if a speech did not seem right to him, he would cry out: "Where's my Penguin?" and refer to it to see what damage I had done. After observing this for a week or so, I went to a taxidermist and purchased a stuffed penguin. The next time Rex cried out, "Where's my Penguin?" the stuffed bird was rolled out on to the stage and he, and everyone, howled with laughter. From that moment on, he never mentioned the Penguin again and kept the stuffed edition in his dressing room as a mascot throughout the run of the production.

I did, however, make one grave error. There is a speech just before "The Rain in Spain" where Higgins says: "Oh Eliza, I know you are tired. I know your nerves are as raw as meat in the butcher's window, but think what you are trying to accomplish? The majesty and grandeur of the English language . . ." etc. When Rex got to that scene he said to me: "That's a damn fine speech. Where in Shaw did you find it?" Like a fool I told the truth and said: "I wrote it." From then on he lost respect for it and seldom got it right. But it taught me a lesson. Ever after, if he came to a line I had written and inquired: "Is that yours?", I would always reply that I had found it in one of Shaw's letters or in a preface or an essay. That seemed to satisfy him and we had no more difficulties. I must have been so persuasive that in an interview with the *London Times* two weeks before the English opening, he said that in the entire play there were only six lines not written by Bernard Shaw.

Julie was mastering the songs in short order, but was having considerable difficulty getting into the role. Interestingly enough, one of her technical stumbling blocks was learning how to speak Cockney. To assist her we found an American phoneticist who did in reverse offstage what Higgins was doing on stage. But after the second week Moss decided drastic assistance was needed. He closed down rehearsals for two days and spent them alone with Julie. We were all "barred" from the theatre and over the weekend he worked his own particular magic. On Monday morning when rehearsals began again with the full company, Julie was well on her way to becoming Eliza Doolittle.

In rehearsal, Moss's authority was total, not because he demanded it but because it was so apparent to everyone he knew what he was doing. If an actor suggested a better move, Moss was the first one to recognize it and be grateful. He was the only director I ever knew who could walk up on the stage and say to the actors: "I haven't a clue what to do with this scene. Does anyone have an idea?"—and not lose his authority.

Our working relationship was something I will never find again. We would be watching a scene in progress and he would lean over to me and say: "Are you aware, dear boy, that that is one of the most stinkingest exit lines ever written in the history of the theatre?" Or sometimes he would show me a scene and I would question something. He would immediately stop the action and say to the cast: "The author is unhappy. Let's try it this way."

Between the extra time spent with Julie and the solo evenings with Rex, Stanley Holloway began to feel we had all given up on him. He got in touch with his agent and one morning Herman came to the theatre to bring us the astounding news that

Stanley wanted out. Moss immediately took Stanley off into a corner and said to him: "Now look, Stanley. I am rehearsing a girl who has never played a major role in her life, and an actor who has never sung on the stage in his life. You have done both. If you feel neglected it is a compliment." The moment he said it, Stanley began to roar with laughter, cancelled his notice and there was no more talk of Stanley wanting out.

Towards the end of the second week of rehearsal, Herman came to the theatre at "teatime" with two large pieces of wrapped cardboard under his arm. He called Fritz, Moss, and me together and revealed the secret under the brown paper. It was the layout for the first advertisement for the New Haven newspapers announcing the opening. Our itinerary was to be one week in New Haven, four weeks in Philadelphia, and then New York. The advertisement said: "Herman Levin presents Rex Harrison and Julie Andrews in '?'." "Now listen," he said, "we've *got* to have a title. People have to know the name of what they have seen so they can tell their friends to go and see it!" His logic was irrefutable. "Call it anything," he went on. "You can always change it on the road. After all, when *Oklahoma* opened it was called *Away We Go*." "Why don't we just take the title that we all dislike the least," I suggested. There was a collective, apathetic nod. After a brief summary of all the candidates, we decided the title we found the least indigestible was *My Fair Lady,* and with a helpless shrug we agreed to it. A few months later we all thought it was brilliant—except Fritz, who still liked "fanfaroon."

When a play is in rehearsal, as a rule the two goals of the director are: first, "to get it on its feet" and second, "to get the scripts out of their hands." "To get it on its feet" means to stage the movements of every scene. As each position is given, the actor writes it in his script. "Getting the script out of their hands" is the moment when the actors have learned their dialogue and movements and can put the scripts away. Some directors spend several days discussing the play line by line around a table before "standing it up." Moss was not one of those. He subscribed to the theory once stated to me by Elia Kazan, "an actor doesn't belong on his ass." By the end of the second week, Moss's two goals had been achieved. During this time the principals had also learned their songs well enough to establish the right key, thus allowing the orchestrator to begin orchestrating.

In the theatre there is a wide difference between orchestrations and arrangements. Some composers write the bare song, and all the incidental music surrounding it is left to the orchestrator, who then "arranges" the music. A real composer, such as Fritz, writes every note himself, even indicating in the piano part the instrumentation he desires, and the orchestrator then "orchestrates" it. This is also true of the dance music. A dance arranger will sit with the choreographer and using the composer's themes, arrange the music according to the choreographer's needs. The "arrangement" is then orchestrated. Fritz, however, regarded that arrangement as a sketch, and using it as a guide, composed the dance music from beginning to end. This would then be "orchestrated."

The third week of any rehearsal is traditionally the down week. Through repetition, what once was amusing is now stale and what once was dramatic is now heavy. However, the mood changes and excitement is rekindled when the far flung elements begin to be assembled under one roof and blended into one play. This usually happens at the end of the third week. The cast finds itself performing for a mini-audience of singers and dancers who are always enthusiastic, and the dancers find themselves being applauded by the actors and singers. For some tantalizing reason that in all my years in the theatre I have never been able to understand, whatever lines the ensemble laughs at, invariably no one else does, and they end their days in the dustbin of some out-of-town hotel. Having discovered this early on in my life, I always put a little check against those lines and prepare their alternates well in advance.

During the last ten days of rehearsal, there are constant interruptions as various members of the company are whisked out of the theatre for costume fittings. Even though the director is aware that it is essential and struggles to arrange those fittings at more convenient times, there are no more convenient times. Somehow it never provoked Moss, however, and he was always able to switch gears and move on to another scene where he had a full complement of actors with whom to work.

During the last week, a major storm was gathering on the horizon. The name of the tempest was "Without You," which Julie sang near the end of the play. From the first day of rehearsal, Rex made it vociferously clear he had no intention of standing on the stage doing nothing while this young woman sang to him. "I am not," he said delicately, "going to stand up there and make a cunt of myself."

"What are we going to do?" said Fritz and I to Moss. "I will tell you precisely what we are going to do," he said. "Nothing. At least until everything else in the play is rehearsed. You can't fight every day or you dissipate your strength and it becomes a way of life. In every play there's one battle you have to win, and when we're in the best position we will do battle." So nothing was done. Everything in the play was rehearsed and when we came to that moment in Mrs. Higgins' house, Moss stopped and moved on past it.

The last day of rehearsal before leaving for the road was devoted to a complete run-through—without costumes and sets, of course. Frequently guests are invited. I was pleased to discover that Moss was as opposed as I to the intrusion of outsiders. The last rehearsal is also always performed without the presence of the conductor. The conductor departs for the road two days ahead of the company to rehearse the out-of-town orchestra and clean up the orchestrations. There is a new orchestra in every city in which one plays. By union rules one is only allowed to carry a half-dozen key musicians. The stage manager has also departed, in order to be present when the scenery arrives and to supervise the impossible task of fitting it into the theatre. Fitting the sets on to the stage is known in the trade as "hanging the show."

The last run-through with the exception of "Without You," which was still without Rex, went extremely well. Fritz, Moss, and I had only one major concern about what we had seen on the stage. Together we represented a sum total of approximately sixty years in the theatre, and it was our collective judgment and sound professional conviction that "With a Little Bit o' Luck" would not work. The song was done twice in the first act and we were convinced that if it was to be sung at all, it could only be done once. It certainly could never hold the stage as the third number in the play. Of course, for the moment it would have to remain as rehearsed, but we agreed that the moment the out-of-town opening was behind us, we would immediately make the change. There is no substitute for experience.

The company left the theatre that evening in good spirits and went home to pack and prepare for the journey into the unknown.

In preparation for the struggle over "Without You," Fritz and I thought it might better be incorporated into the emotional action if Higgins interrupted the song at the climax with: "I did it. I did it. I said I'd make a woman and indeed I did." We had tried to play it for Rex but he would not listen. In the train going up to New Haven, Moss sat down next to Rex and said to him most gently but most firmly: "Rex. Julie is going to sing "Without You" in that scene whether you are on the stage or not. It is my personal opinion you will look like a horse's ass if you leave the stage when she begins it and return when she has finished. However, if you will give me the opportunity, I will show you how it can be staged." No more was said.

The first two days of rehearsal in New Haven were held in a hall as Biff Liff, our incredible stage manager, wrestled with the scenery. The first rehearsal Moss called was to stage "Without You." We waited breathlessly to see if Rex would appear. He did. Fritz and I showed him the end we had written and he decided it made all the difference in the world. The sequence of the scene would not be interrupted by applause, which would have lengthened the time he would have been standing up there like what he said he would be standing there like. Moss staged the scene and the song and that was that.

The company had arrived on Monday. There was to be a preview performance with an audience on Saturday and the following Monday was to be the official opening. By Tuesday morning the orchestra was ready to begin rehearsing with the cast. Far and away the most exciting event for any company in any musical is the moment it hears the orchestra for the first time. Eyes beam and pop, delight is squealed, cheers ricochet from wall to wall and at the conclusion of each number there is an operatic ovation. The composer is rediscovered, hailed, and hugged.

All day Tuesday and part of Wednesday were spent by the principals commuting between the rehearsal hall with Franz and the rehearsal hall with Moss. I stopped in at the theatre on Tuesday, but not for long. The stage looked like the work of a terrorists' gang. The set was conceived on two turntables which were electrically rotated. They did not rotate. Furthermore, there seemed to be no way of making them rotate. Scenery was still piled high, drops were still being hung, Abe Feder's lights were all over the theatre and dangling from pipes, and bodies of exhausted stage hands were strewn about the stage. It looked to me as if it would have been easier to put up the scenery in a vacant lot and build a theatre around it. I saw Biff Liff and said, idiotically: "Hi, Biff. How's it going?" "Fine," said Biff. "Oh good," said I, and started to leave. Biff stopped me. "Oh Alan," he called. "Have you seen Oliver?" Oh my God, I thought to myself, not again. Back across my mind came the ghastly memory of *Brigadoon* and the night before we opened out of town. The forest scene had come down upside down and no one seemed to know how to get the tree trunks back in the ground and the leaves in the air. Oliver knew, but Oliver was not there. Scenically, *Brigadoon* was a one-set play compared to the size and intricacy of *My Fair Lady*. "I'll find him," I called to Biff, knowing full well I would not, and I rushed out looking for Herman.

I found Herman but Herman could not find Oliver. Oliver had two other shows opening that week and each thought he was with one of the other two. Clearly Oliver had astro-projected himself to another plane and taken his body with him.

Nevertheless, by Wednesday night Biff had established sufficient order on the stage to begin what is known in the theatre as a technical run-through. During a technical run-through, no attempt is made to act. Lines are simply mumbled and the actors go through their movements so that the stage hands may familiarize themselves with the flow of the play, and, of equal importance, so the light crew can begin focusing and the stage manager can record the light cues. Every light change calls for a different cue and every light cue and every scene change, down to the smallest cushion, is directed by the stage manager. The first "tech" of a complicated, multi-set musical takes a minimum of two days and I had one experience, *On a Clear Day You Can See Forever*, where it took five days—five days and nights to complete one technical performance of the play!

Without a director in control of himself and the production, and a stage manager with the temperament of a statue and more eyes than a fly, the physical and emotional strain and drain of a technical run-through is enough to drive a Trappist monk from silence to hysteria and leave a marathon runner incapable of walking to the corner. Fortunately we had Moss and Biff. Unfortunately, however, not even Biff could harness the forces of electricity and the revolving stages seemed controlled by static. Sometimes they rotated, sometimes they did not. No one knew why they did and no one knew why they did not. It shredded the nervous system, and at one point even an old campaigner like Fritz demanded that everybody on the stage be fired.

The scenic difficulties multiplied and as the "tech" progressed, the cries of "Where's Oliver?" began to swell to Wagnerian proportions. "This is it," I said to Fritz and Moss. "I'll never work with that son of a bitch again as long as I live." "You won't have to," said Fritz, "because if I ever see him again, I'll kill him!" A moment later we saw him again. Somehow he had come in through the woodwork and was calmly walking up the steps to the stage. He waved and blew us a kiss, then immediately began conferring with Biff. Within ten minutes the scenic problems began to lessen. The builders had been summoned to work on the revolving stages and in the meantime they were moved manually, while some of the sets were relocated on the stage to provide more playing area.

By Friday we had completed the "tech" and that evening the orchestra came into the pit for the first time—and blew Rex sky high. He had rehearsed his numbers in a hall standing next to Franz, with everyone on the same level. Suddenly he found himself on the stage with thirty strange people making strange noises directly below him and no idea at all where the melody could be found. Because we had to go through the play once with the costumes, Moss promised Rex that the following day he could rehearse alone with the orchestra in front of the house curtain for as many hours as possible.

The following afternoon that rehearsal took place. At one

moment when they were going through "A Hymn to Him" Rex suddenly paused. Franz thought he had forgotten the lyric and said, "Let's start it from the top." Again when they came to that moment, Rex paused. I was sitting in the front row and asked him what he was doing. Rex answered, "I'm waiting for the laugh. There's going to be one there, you know." I said to him, "Rex, that's not the way we do it." "I don't care," he replied, "it's the way you ought to do it. What do you expect me to do? Sing through the laugh?" "Exactly," I said. He was appalled, but took my word for it. But his terror of the orchestra did not abate.

Late that afternoon with the house sold out and a fierce blizzard blowing, Rex announced that under no circumstances would he go on that night. He needed more time to rehearse with those thirty-two interlopers in the pit. When all persuasion failed, we realized we had no alternative but to postpone the performance. We decided our excuse would be "technical difficulties," and in order to alert those people who might have left home early because of the storm, there would be hourly bulletins on all the local radio stations.

At this point I think it only fair to say a few words on behalf of temperament. In the theatre it is based on one thing and one thing only: fear. And fear, however outrageously or insultingly it may be expressed, when the tumult and shouting dies remains a very real problem that can only be dealt with by solving the cause of the fear itself. For an actor, especially a star, to walk out on a stage riddled with uncertainty must be like facing a firing squad. To whom and to what does an artist owe his allegiance? To himself and his art, or to the audience? To me they are one and the same.

With the performance cancelled, we decided to use the afternoon and evening to cut "With a Little Bit o' Luck" to one chorus. Leaving Rex at the theatre with his friends in the pit, we retired to the nearby hall to rehearse the change.

Despite the radio bulletins, by six o'clock that evening hundreds of people had braved the snow and were already queuing up at the box office. The house manager was livid. He swore to us all that he would tell the world the truth, and, as far as he was concerned, Rex Harrison could go back to Liverpool. About an hour and a half before what would have been curtain time Rex's agent arrived from New York. Herman filled him in and in tandem they marched into Rex's dressing room. Herman conveyed to Rex in no uncertain terms the house manager's intentions, and his agent told him he was jeopardizing his entire career. No matter what happened that evening on stage, he said, Rex damn well had to go on. Fear of the consequences must have overshadowed his fear of the orchestra because one hour before curtain time, Rex recanted. He girded his loins and agreed that the show would open as scheduled.

It was the custom in those days for agents, actors and various members of all branches of the theatre to attend out-of-town opening nights to "wish you well," which is theatricalese for "hoping you die." They would all assemble for a quick bite before the curtain in a restaurant called Kaysey's, across the street from the theatre. To illustrate the collective attitude, there was one agent who always arrived for out-of-town openings with scripts under her arm and a flashlight so that she could read during the second act. As I was leaving the restaurant, one of the "dear shits," as they were lovingly known, stopped me and said: "How is it, Alan?" I remember my answer distinctly. I said: "I have no idea what the reaction of the audience will be, but I genuinely believe it's the best musical I ever saw." I realized it was a cruel thing to say but I could not help it. That was how I felt.

At eight-forty the curtain went up in the Shubert Theatre in New Haven to a packed house.

The first act ran twenty-five minutes too long. There were technical difficulties—the turntables turned slowly and a few curtains got fouled (meaning caught on a set as they were either coming down or going up). But "With a Little Bit o' Luck" stopped the show! "Come to the Ball," Rex's *pièce de résistance,* was a disaster in three-quarter time and "On the Street Where You Live" was greeted with mute disinterest. The second act played beautifully, but more important, the total effect was stunning and when the curtain came down the audience stood up and cheered. During the cheering, Cecil, oblivious to the reaction of the audience, rushed past me, a look of fury on his face, muttering, "That bitch!" "What bitch?" I inquired. "I told her that hat had to be pulled forward," he hissed, and disappeared. He was talking about the hat Julie wore in "Show Me." We had asked her to pull it back because it was covering her face when she sang.

The other side of the "dear shits" is that whatever they may wish for you, if the play is good their response is immediate, genuine, and enthusiastic. Their comments following the performance were all of that. It was the kind of evening that Oscar Levant used to call "a great night for envy."

The next morning we all gathered to discuss how to cut the first act and what to do about "On the Street Where You Live." The opinion was unanimous—minus one (me)—that the song had to come out. Fritz had never cared for it in the first place and was happy to see it go, but I liked the melody and thought the flagrantly romantic lyric that kept edging on the absurd exactly right for the character. But obviously one cannot leave in a number that dies. I could not for the life of me understand why it failed so dismally. Two or three days later it occurred to me that because it was sung immediately following the Ascot scene, and Freddie Eynsford-Hill was dressed exactly the same as all the other gentlemen at Ascot, perhaps the audience did not realize he was the same boy who had been sitting next to Eliza and talking to her during the scene. Fritz agreed it might be a possibility. So as a last ditch effort to save the song we changed the verse—the section of a song that is sung before the main chorus—and replaced the flowery, romantic one he was then singing with one that echoed Eliza at Ascot, beginning with:

> *"When she mentioned how her aunt bit off the spoon*
> *She completely done me in,*
> *..."* etc.

Fritz changed the music accordingly and the new verse went in on Thursday night. And on Thursday night "On the Street Where You Live" almost required an encore. As Moss used to say (here I go again): "Every show makes you feel like an amateur."

To bring the first act down to size, we cut out Rex's triumphant "Come to the Ball," a ballet that occurred between Ascot and the ball scene, and "Say a Prayer for Me Tonight." (It later emerged from the trunk and was used in *Gigi*.) To replace them, I wrote a brief scene which skipped directly from Ascot to the night before the ball. Moss had had a different idea involving a reprise of "With a Little Bit o' Luck" which, as we had all predicted, was stopping the show regularly. When I showed him what I had written, he read it very slowly and carefully, then looked at me and said: "You son of a bitch! How dare you give me an inferiority complex?" Quite unwittingly, the new scene also solved our one major costume problem. We wanted Eliza to look ravishingly beautiful when she arrived at the ball, and hoped that the splendor of her gown would move the audience to applause. Cecil had designed a most exquisite gown, but she entered to wild silence. Of course, in retrospect, it had to be thus—she was surrounded by two dozen equally exquisite gowns. In the new scene she appeared at the top of the stairs in Higgins' house in her ballgown, and the audience broke into applause. She descended the stairs to the music of "I Could Have Danced All Night" and the scene worked like a charm.

The scene begins with Pickering on the verge of a nervous breakdown and Higgins pacing up and down. Pickering says: "Suppose something goes wrong? Suppose she makes another ghastly blunder?" Higgins answers: "There will be no horses at the ball, Pickering." Big laugh. On the opening night in New York, however, the curtain fouled again and did not completely open until a third through the scene. Rex was not aware of it. It naturally took the audience's attention and the line, "There will be no horses at the ball, Pickering," went by unnoticed. When I went backstage to congratulate Rex on his magnificent performance, the first thing he said to me was: "I knew that horse line was a New Haven laugh."

After a week in New Haven we moved on to Philadelphia.

The reviews were superb. The major changes had been completed and the four weeks in Philadelphia were spent polishing the performances, sharpening a line here, an exit there, making the technical production flow efficiently, and completing the lighting.

For Rex, the major obstacle now was trying to remember the lyrics for "A Hymn to Him." It is the kind of lyric we call in the theatre a laundry list, because it says the same thing over and over again in different ways, and Rex was having the devil of a time memorizing it. In fact, he never once got it right the entire time we were on the road. He used to paste the lyric on his mirror and not only in Philadelphia, but during the three years he was in the play, he would spend every intermission studying it.

One night in Philadelphia, Fritz and I tried to improve "You Did It," which opens the second act. Despite Michael Kidd, it always went extremely well, but both Fritz and I felt there was a section in the middle which did not have a proper climax. Higgins is telling the servants, in lyrics, of Eliza's success at the ball and how another phoneticist had come to the conclusion she was an Hungarian princess. I wrote two lines, which Fritz set, to give the moment an exclamation point. The lines were:

I know each language on the map, said he,
And she's Hungarian as the first Hungarian rhapsody.

We gave them to Rex who loved them. He rehearsed them and the night they went in he forgot every lyric in the entire show. He came off the stage in a screaming rage, and when I went to his dressing room he stuck a finger in my face and shouted: "Don't you dare do that to me again!"

Out went the lines.

Remembering the lyrics of "A Hymn to Him" was not the only problem Rex had in the course of the play. Nothing impresses an audience more or produces a more dependable, spontaneous burst of applause than to see a chandelier appearing from on high. Two chandeliers—ecstasy. Three are a collective orgasm. In the finale of act one there were three. One night, however, after the show had been running a while, they were lowered too far and one of them hooked itself onto Rex's hairpiece. When the stage manager corrected the mistake and raised the chandeliers, Rex's hair went up with them. To his everlasting credit Rex continued as if his hair were still on his head and not hanging from a chandelier like a bird's nest after a storm.

On another occasion, in the fourth scene of the second act which takes place in Mrs. Higgins' winter garden, running across the rear of the stage was a small series of rectangular flowerpots. Rex had no sooner made his entrance one night than he realized he had an uncontrollable desire to relieve a sudden excess of wind that had lodged itself in his lower abdomen. Being an actor of considerable discipline, he waited for the moment when he went up behind the flowerpots to pace up and down in irritation. Once there he let go. Unfortunately, there was more wind in need of egress than he had contemplated and from behind the potted flowers came one of the loudest farts ever heard in the history of the theatre. Despite the unique volume there was no doubt what it was and whence its source. The audience behaved beautifully and bit their tongues. Mrs. Higgins' next line is: "Henry, dear. Please don't grind your teeth." Again the audience held on. Finally—and it was a good minute later—Higgins comes downstage to where Eliza is sitting and says: "My manners are the same as Colonel Pickering's." That did it. The audience could contain itself no longer. The laughter began to roll through the house, and like "Ol' Man River" it kept rollin' right through the entire scene and into the next.

The out-of-town word that a hit is on its way to Broadway travels through the five boroughs of New York as if carried by Mercury himself. Three weeks before the opening, as is the custom, it was announced in the papers that mail orders would be filled. The mail began pouring in. The following week the box office officially opened, and from nine-thirty in the morning to five in the afternoon there was an ever-increasing line at the window. The anticipation began to be frightening. No play on earth, I thought, could equal so much expectation.

We had one preview performance before the official opening, to give the company an opportunity to adjust itself to the theatre and to make certain there were no acoustical pockets. It was a paid preview, meaning that the entire house had been sold to a charitable benefit. After the lights had gone down, I took my accustomed place at the rear of the theatre and limbered up in preparation for an evening of pacing. For me, pacing is not reserved exclusively for previews and openings. I have never been able to sit down at any performance of any play I have ever written. The feeling of exposure is so acute that I would rather stand back and watch the audience than be a part of it. If something goes wrong on stage, be it the fault of the writing, the performing, or the scenery, the only way I can keep my abdominal lining from disintegrating is to know that I am near a door. And so I pace. Back and forth, back and forth, back and forth.

One night out of curiosity I carried a pedometer with me and discovered that I had backed and forthed two miles! Two miles! At least there is some comfort in knowing that while most of me is a withering nerve, some of me is getting a little exercise. Fritz, on the other hand, was not a pacer. He was an in-and-outer. He would usually walk out for a cigarette during the dialogue and walk in when the music began.

At last the overture ended and the play began. The audience was appreciative from the first moment and the cast responded accordingly, giving a splendid performance which was rewarded at the end with a thumping applause. After the final curtain I went backstage, and as usual made my first stop in Rex's dressing room. It was crowded with enthusiastic friends, among them the well-known producer, Leland Hayward, and his wife Nancy, more familiarly known as Slim. Despite the success of the evening, it was still not the opening and my furrowed brow must have revealed my inner anxiety. Slim took one look at me, grabbed me by the arm and led me outside Rex's dressing room. "Alan," she said sternly. "Listen to me, and listen to me well. What is happening in this theatre is incredible. It is something that has happened to few people and will never happen to you again. So for Christ's sake, stop worrying and enjoy it. Do you hear me? Enjoy it!" With that, she gave me a great bear hug and went back to Rex. Oh, how I wanted to take her advice. I tried, but it was simply not within my power. Until that opening night was over my name was angst.

When the curtain rose that mid-March evening, the atmosphere was more ecclesiastical than theatrical. The audience was hushed; staring too hard at the stage to see anything, I thought; listening too intently to hear anything. I felt as if they had all gathered for the second coming of Christ and He was late. The laughs in the opening scene were few and small. The songs were well applauded. (To laugh little and applaud much is typical, incidentally, of an opening night audience in New York, but somehow we did not expect it that night.) I paced back and forth and worried. Fritz stood near me staring at the stage, the picture of satisfaction, not a sign of concern on his face. At the end of the first scene, Moss rushed over to us and it was the first and only time I ever saw him frantic. "I knew it," he said. "It's just a New Haven hit. That's all. Just a New Haven hit." Fritz looked at him with an amused but sympathetic smile on his face. "My darling Mossie," he said. "If you don't know this is the biggest hit that has ever come to New York you had better come with me and get a drink." And he led Moss from the theatre to the nearest bar. When they returned about five minutes later "With a Little Bit o' Luck" was stopping the show. At the end of "The Rain in Spain," the applause exploded like nuclear fission. Walking down the side aisles of the theatre, I saw almost a thousand faces with eyes sparkling with tears, smiling as if it were a contest and applauding like cymbals. I walked to the back of the theatre and stopped pacing. When the final curtain fell, the members of the audience rose from their seats and surged forward down the aisles, crying "Bravo," and applauding with their hands over their heads. There was curtain call after curtain call. It was so overwhelming that I felt lonely. I rushed backstage to Rex's dressing room. The first person I saw en route was Marlene Dietrich who was all in white from top to toe; her face covered in white powder. She embraced me so forcefully that when we separated her face had the normal skin tones and I had the powder. I went around to see everyone to thank them and congratulate them. The stage was filled with members of the audience who were, in some way, connected with the people in the cast. I cannot recall what anybody said to me, nor can I even remember my own feelings. It was too far beyond any experience that I could have been prepared for.

There was no opening night party, and had there been one I would not have gone. I have always avoided them out of self-preservation. One is so easily fooled by opening night applause that every opening night party is high on hopes alone before the first drink is served, and the higher the expectations the shorter they fall. Nothing is more painful than a New Year's Eve atmosphere that comes to an abrupt halt when the first reviews come in and they are bad. To me it is difficult enough to live through an opening night without having to be a good sport afterwards. So I usually sequester myself in some small room with a small group of steadfast chums who will love me in December as they did in May.

On this opening night I had taken a small room at "21" to which, along with my civilian chums, came Moss and Kitty, Rex, the Liebersons and Irene Selznick. Fritz, having not a doubt in the world of the outcome, followed the tradition and went to Sardi's for the standing ovation. The reviews were idyllic, but Rex was Rex to the very end and flew into a blinding rage (which, of course, passed quickly) because he felt the *New York Times* had not given me my due.

By two in the morning I was numb. Not from alcohol—I could not have gotten drunk on a case of brandy. All I knew was that when we separated everyone seemed blissfully happy, and I reacted more to their happiness than to the reviews.

By the time I arrived home I was calm and very tired, but I clearly remember one thought that crowded my mind—or was it a feeling? When I fail I withdraw into myself in search of some place to keep warm. A triumph, as I was fortunate enough to have that night, is quite a different matter. You cannot hide and so you instinctively reach out. If one is alone, one can survive a failure reasonably intact: but success steals your defenses and leaves you on top of the world, stark naked. When you reach out, God help you if there is no one there to reach out to.

Nancy and I got into the elevator. "What a night," I said. "Did you like my dress?" she asked. I looked at it for a moment. "Beautiful," I murmured. "Beautiful."

On the Sunday following the opening, the cast assembled in a large recording studio to make the album. Cast albums are invariably cut the first Sunday following the opening. Many people wonder why they are not made earlier, so that the release of the album synchronizes with the opening of the play. The reason is very simple. Until the opening night one is never certain there will not be changes. In *Camelot*, for instance, which opened on a Saturday night, a new song was added on Friday. The recording begins at nine in the morning and the last song is often recorded well past midnight.

A cast album is not merely a matter of recording what is heard in the theatre. The orchestra may be augmented, a song may be performed slower or faster, the number of verses in a particular song may be reduced, vocal reprises are omitted, and there may even be a change in the running order. The man who makes these decisions is the producer of the album, and the producer in this case was our dear old friend Goddard Lieberson—he of the phone call that led to the $400,000—and, of more importance, the most accomplished and creative producer in the industry and the unchallenged specialist in translating theatrical scores to disc. Goddard was a composer in his own right and his theatrical instinct and knowledge were unerring. He was a firm believer in never, nay never, including any dialogue from the play. His reason was that a recording is for music and lyrics, and that although a few lines of dialogue may fertilize the memory of those who have seen the play, for the rest of the public it will mean nothing and in time it will become a bore to everyone.

In the case of *My Fair Lady* there was an additional problem. The climax of the play, when Eliza returns, happens to be in a line of dialogue. Goddard's solution was to go directly from "I've Grown Accustomed to Her Face" into a dramatic and emotional orchestral reprise of "I Could Have Danced All Night"—Eliza's theme—which then built to a climax. In order to convey to the ear alone the impromptu outburst of joy of "The Rain in Spain," he had Rex, Coote, and Julie perform it before the microphones exactly as they did in the theatre.

The recording was finished shortly after midnight, but because of Goddard's enthusiasm, expertize, and irrepressible humor, the hours were shortened to minutes and hard work came disguised as fun. Yet as I recall that day, I do so with no small amount of pain because as I write these words, twenty-one years later, it is exactly two weeks since I attended his funeral. He was only sixty-six and the villain was a malignancy. Fritz and I had met him at the very beginning of our collaboration and he remained a close and dear friend until he died.

With his passing went another drain on the world's fast-diminishing supply of charm. No computer can replenish it. IBM cannot create another Noel Coward. No electronic adolescent gurgle can turn your entire being into a smile, as could a performance of Maurice Chevalier. I see no one hovering around the diefied age of thirty with the budding urbanity, warmth and wit of Moss Hart, nor the appreciation and joy of life of Goddard Lieberson. Pleasure without joy is as hollow as passion without tenderness, and the pleasure of Goddard's company was the joy he brought to others. We call it charm and I weep for a world without it.

The album jackets had been prepared two weeks earlier and by Wednesday of that week, three days later, one hundred thousand albums were ready for distribution.

The record-buying public in 1956 was quite different than it is today. When the war ended eleven years earlier, several million young men on both sides of the Atlantic came home, took off their uniforms and jumped into bed. By the early 1960s, the issue resulting from that mass display of uninterrupted coitus numbered almost 50 percent of the population of what is euphemistically called the civilized world. In 1956, however, they were still little brats, thank God, whose purchasing power was mainly confined to comics and confectionery. Nevertheless, there was a wave of rock and roll hitting the beaches and show albums seemed to be on the decline.

On Tuesday morning when I heard the completed album, I phoned Goddard and thanked him. I said to him, and I remember this very clearly: "Goddard, it's terrific. If it sells fifty thousand albums I'll be satisfied."

I was no more prepared for what happened to the album than I was for what happened to the play. In fact it was many months before any of us realized at all the full magnitude of what we had collectively wrought. But as spring turned to summer, the lines at the theatre grew longer and the advance sales kept mounting. By September it was almost impossible to buy a ticket without a six months' wait—and by September the album had hopped, skipped, and jumped to the top of the chart, where it remained for the next two years.

In the theatre the only seats that cannot be sold in advance are the nonexistent ones, namely standing room. By law they can only be sold the day of the performance. The Mark Hellinger Theatre accommodated forty standees. For the next three years the lines began to form in front of the box office around midnight, and aspiring standees came with sleeping bags, blankets, and food, and spent the night awaiting the opening of the box office at nine-thirty in the morning.

Fritz's reaction to it all was uncomplicated, total, uninhibited, and enviable. He joyfully flung open his arms, clasped the bitch-goddess to his bosom and danced all night. Shortly after the play opened he departed for Paris. After a fortnight of warming up at the chemin-de-fer table at one of the gambling clubs off the Champs Elysées, he proceeded on to Cannes to spend the summer at the chemin-de-fer table of the Palm Beach Casino. Long separated from his wife, when he was not at the gaming tables, he spent his time proving the accuracy of Marc Connelly's observation that the only known aphrodisiac is variety.

The impact on me was more of relief than ecstasy. I felt an enormous load had been taken off my back. I had, at long last, written something that I truly liked and, by glorious coincidence, so did the audience.

With that kind of encouragement I could not wait to write again. Which, I discovered, was exactly the opposite of how many people expected me to feel. Time after time I was asked by press and public alike: how could I write after a success like *My Fair Lady?* All I can say is, and said was, that it did not compare to the difficulty of writing after a failure. I have never thought I was competing with anyone, much less myself. Unfortunately there is a fact of professional life that exists only in the American theatre. As a man in business is expected to receive a periodic raise and advance to a higher rung on the ladder, so in the American theatre it is expected that each play a man writes is better than his last. Quite a difference from France, for example, where, as a friend of mine in the French Academy remarked to me one day: "A good playwright is a man who from time to time writes a good play." Ever after *My Fair Lady,* no matter what I have written, be it well received or not, there has always been a critic or two who observed that I am not George Bernard Shaw. I could have replied rather smugly that a few years after *My Fair Lady* a musical was made out of *Caesar and Cleopatra* which failed dismally, but I am much too modest and self-effacing. There was one famous actress, however, who believed that I was indeed the reincarnation of GBS and constantly wrote me letters which began, "Dear GBS." I explained to her on many occasions that even if one believed in the "reincarnatory" theory of life, I definitely could not be the shell of GBS's soul because I was alive when he was. But she was in no mood for logic. The poor lady was eventually committed to an institution and from there passed on to the world beyond. If by chance she runs into Bernard Shaw and tells him what she told me, I have a feeling she will be sorry she died.

One of the most gratifying results of my visit to fame and fortune was that I was finally officially graduated from Harvard. As I mentioned earlier, I was in the class of 1940. But there was a rule that if a student owed money around the campus and it was reported to the bursar's office, he did not receive his diploma until his debt was paid. At the time of my graduation one of the local shopkeepers around Harvard Square claimed I owed him sixty dollars. By my reckoning it was forty dollars and as a matter of principle—plus a dash of smart-Alecness—I refused to compromise. He dutifully reported me and when it came to my turn at graduation exercises to march up to the podium and receive my diploma, I was given instead a fleshy handshake. Over the summer I settled my differences with said Uriah Heep and a few months later I received a letter from the university, informing me that they were holding my sheepskin and upon receipt of five dollars they would send it to me. The five dollars seemed entirely reasonable and well within my means, but I forgot about it. Three or four years later came another letter from the university reminding me they were still holding the diploma and were anxious to hear from me. I again forgot about it. Two months after *My Fair Lady* opened and sixteen years after my graduation, lo and behold, I received my diploma in the mail. I was so touched by this obvious demonstration of the university's pride in me, that several years later upon their request I donated the original manuscripts (without tax deduction) of *My Fair Lady* and a few other of my noble efforts, and they were placed on display behind a vitrine in the Widener Library. And thus ended my academic career.

Among the other letters that I received during that first post-natal year was one postmarked Moscow. It was from a gentleman who signed himself Victor Louis. He said that he had just completed a Russian translation of *My Fair Lady* and reminded me that it was the policy of the USSR not to pay royalties, therefore none would be forthcoming. However, said he, he unfortunately did not have in his possession the orchestrations and would I be kind enough to send them to him. The fact that Russia did not pay royalties was not unfamiliar to the authors of all the non-Communist nations in the world. For many, many years the Authors League of America and the Dramatists Guild had tried with zero success to persuade Russia to subscribe to the International Authors Agreement. Because anything connected with *My Fair Lady* was automatically newsworthy, it seemed to me an irresistible opportunity to try and make capital of Mr. Louis' letter. So I answered him, equally politely, saying that merely because he had stolen my money I saw no reason to send him my wallet, and that I had no intention of sending him the orchestrations. Very truly yours. I sent a copy of Mr. Louis' letter and my reply to the Russian Consul-General in New York and to the Soviet Embassy in Washington. I also sent copies to the *New York Times* where it immediately became front page news. The fact that every American author from Twain to O'Neill to Faulkener, let alone every author in England, Spain, France, Italy, etc., had been similarly deprived, was not something deeply embedded in the public's consciousness. But *My Fair Lady* produced a worldwide reaction of outrage.

I heard no more from Mr. Louis. A year later the United States and Russia began the discussions that led to the first inter-cultural exchange. When the Soviets asked the American negotiating team what example of Russian culture they would like, the Americans said "the Bolshoi Ballet." When we asked the Russians what they wished us to send them in exchange they replied *My Fair Lady*. And so it was that a year later the Bolshoi Ballet came to the Metropolitan Opera House for the first time in history, and in 1960 an American company of *My Fair Lady* was despatched to Russia. Unfortunately I was not able to accompany the production that made the journey, but I was told it was a great success—not a howling success—a great, quiet one. There was not a laugh from curtain up to curtain down, but at curtain down the audiences applauded long and vigorously.

The Russian company was the fourteenth production of the play on public view throughout the world. In the spring of 1957 a second company in America was launched in Rochester, New York, starring Brian Aherne and Anne Rogers. Anne Rogers, incidentally, had created the role of "The Boy Friend" in London, while Julie later played in New York. There were also four Scandinavian productions, one in Germany, one in Australia, one in Holland, one in Belgium, one in Mexico and, of course, one in London which opened in Drury Lane in the late spring of 1958. There were later productions in Spain, Switzerland, Italy, Tokyo, Israel, and South America. There was never one in France. Despite repeated requests and a general attitude of "why not?" from all my confreres, I refused, and they were kind enough to go along with me.

My reason was that after living in France on and off for several years, I knew that the French regarded themselves as the cultural Supreme Court of the world, and that nothing irritated them more than to have something become successful before they had had an opportunity to pass judgment upon it. Not only that, but it is a linguistic impossibility to translate lyrics into French, or any of the romance languages for that matter. Economy is the soul of lyric writing and it takes one third more words to say in French what it does in English. (An English novel of three hundred pages, for instance, will be four hundred pages in French.) To my knowledge the only two successful translations of anything in English verse are Baudelaire's translation of Poe, which many consider to be superior to the original, and André Gide's extraordinary translation of *Hamlet*. After years of painstaking labour, Gide produced a translation of *Hamlet* that contains the exact number of lines as Shakespeare's. (God knows I am not putting popular lyrics in the echelon of Poe and Shakespeare, I am simply using them as examples.)

Besides the language problem, there is no musical theatre in France at all, and no audience for it—despite the fact that musical comedy, in a large sense, began in Paris with Offenbach. The French like conversation more than music. Turn on a disc-jockey show in Paris today and a three-minute record will be preceded by a ten-minute discussion. My negative opinion about a French production, I might add, was fortified by several good friends in Paris, including the editor of the leading newspaper and Marcel Achard, one of France's most popular playwrights. Amusingly enough, when *My Fair Lady* opened in London a French newspaper despatched a critic to cover the opening. It was the only bad notice *My Fair Lady* ever received.

The London production was scheduled to open at the end of April in 1958. Because so many of the original cast were English, it would have been theatrical suicide, let alone theatrical madness, for Rex, Julie, Stanley, and Coote not to recreate their original roles. The ensemble and the rest of the cast were to be selected in London and in order to give ourselves sufficient time to prepare, Moss, Fritz, Herman, and I planned our arrival in London for the end of February.

About a week before we left, I was awakened at three in the morning by a telephone call from the night manager at the Algonquin Hotel, where Fritz was staying. He told me that a few minutes earlier Fritz had had severe chest pains and had been taken to the Medical Arts Center on West Fifty-seventh Street. I dressed and cabbed there as quickly as I could, first calling my own doctor, Dr. Milton Kramer, a well-known heart specialist at the New York Hospital. I arrived at the hospital to find Fritz in pain, weak, and a ghastly shade of white. I demanded that he be placed in an oxygen tent at once. The hospital said they did not think it necessary, but I made so much noise they finally agreed. Shortly after, Dr. Kramer arrived and upon examination he informed me that Fritz had suffered a massive coronary. He could not evaluate his chances of survival, but said the first three days would be crucial.

The death of my father four years earlier was the first time I truly realized that life is finite. Dylan Thomas wrote that "after the first death there is no other." Not for me. After my father, death was alive and to be able to face life meant to be able to face death. I believe I can face my own, but not that of others—especially Fritz's—and I was shattered.

When my father was fifty years old it was discovered that he had cancer of the jaw. He told me later he had decided instantly that having spent half a century outwitting life, he would now devote his energies to outwitting death, and he did so for seventeen years and through fifty-seven major operations. Fritz, as I should have known, was made of no less sterner stuff. He had discovered the pot of gold late in life and if he could not take it with him, he had no alternative but to stay. And so he did. And so he has. When the oxygen tent was finally removed, the first question he asked was about the progress of the London production. After being filled in, he thought for a moment and said: "Goddamn it! That son of a bitch Lerner got all my house seats." When I was told that, I knew he was fine.

No play in the history of the West End was ever awaited with more anticipation. It is traditional that when a play is coming to London, the performance of the music is forbidden until the play opens in order to prevent the score from becoming so familiar that it makes the play seem like a revival. Nevertheless, the interest in the show was such that within three months of the New York opening, the black market sale of the American album became a flourishing industry in England. Stewards on ocean liners and airplanes were smuggling them in by the thousands and selling them at twice and three times the original cost.

The first member of the cast to arrive in England was Stanley, who, for reasons known only to Stanley, started things off with a small explosion. In an interview with one of the morning papers, out from behind his Santa Claus smile came an angry lion who tore into Rex and blasted him for being ill-mannered, unprofessional, self-indulgent, and egomaniacally snobbish. He later said that his remarks were misinterpreted and exaggerated, which is quite possible with the British popular press where there is, shall we say, a strong iconoclastic tendency. With some members of the British press, to agree to be interviewed is an act of pure masochism. When such a request was made to Moss, for instance, he used to reply with the most devestating charm that because whatever he said was certain to be misquoted, why did the reporter not make up the interview in the first place and whatever he wanted Moss to say, simply say he said it! It would save him a great deal of time, let alone carfare, and make his job infinitely simpler. Despite all this, and giving Stanley the benefit of the doubt, he certainly must have said something on which the reporter could build, and whatever that something was it could not have been complimentary.

When the interview broke, Rex, now married to Kay Kendall, was in Paris. Rex's recent experiences with the press had been somewhat less than friendly and Stanley's article was a cause for open hostility. I happened to be in Paris one weekend while they were still there, and I received a call from David Lewin of the *Daily Express,* who was and is an old friend of mine, as well as Rex's, and a thoroughly decent and honest journalist. He told me on the phone that he was most anxious to repair some of the damage caused by Stanley's interview, and promised me faithfully that Rex would be treated fairly *if* I could persuade him to see the *Daily Express* correspondent in Paris. So far he had refused to do so.

That afternoon there was a large cocktail party to which Rex, Kay, the *Daily Express* correspondent and I had all been invited. When I arrived I spoke to the reporter who was rather pessimistic about the possibility of my arranging a rapprochement between him and Rex. He said to me: "The moment Rex hears that I'm a reporter, I know he'll turn to me and say 'Fuck off'." When Rex appeared, I immediately sequestered him in a corner and after a comparatively short time persuaded him to trust David and see the chap from the *Express.* Bringing said chap over, he and Rex began to chat congenially. A moment later Kay arrived and Rex introduced her. Said Rex, "He's from the Express." Said Kay, "Fuck off!" End of interview.

Later Rex did consent to be interviewed by the *London Times* and it was, as would be expected, a totally fair and interesting article. That was the article, incidentally, where he said that only six lines in the play were not written by GBS. Some people thought I should have been angry at this, but I regarded it as a testimonial to my gift for deception.

When rehearsals began, Stanley made enough of an apology to keep the peace and whatever Rex's feelings were, or Stanley's for that matter, they were both professionals and it never interfered with the progress of the play.

The excitement in London before the premiere mounted daily. One newspaper ran a small headline each day that simply said: "Five more days." The next day: "Four more days," etc. The demand for tickets was staggering and people were flying in from all parts of Europe and America for the great event. In point of fact, so many people came to see how the British would respond to this Yankee version of one of their popular classics that there was hardly any room left in the theatre for the British. On opening night the streets from Drury Lane to the Strand were lined with people, and it looked more like a Coronation than a premiere.

Although the reaction to the play itself was triumphant, I personally felt that because of the presence of so many people who had seen it before, it was more ritualistic than spontaneous. But my anxiety was not reflected in the reviews. There was a bit of carping here and there, but I suppose there had to be when success seemed so assured with them or without them.

Three nights after the premiere there was a Royal Command Performance attended by the Queen and Prince Philip. Needless to say it was a white tie affair, and I stood at the side of the theatre staring up at the royal box to see their reaction. It seemed to me that the Queen never laughed at all and that Prince Philip was having the time of his life. During the extended intermission, Moss, Kitty, Binkie Beaumont, and I were taken to the anteroom of the royal box where we were all presented to the Queen and Prince

Philip. Moss and Kitty chatted mostly with the Queen and I with Prince Philip, whom I found to be most delightful and most amusing. I remember his telling me how he had learned French from an English nanny with a Cockney accent. Consequently, he learned French with a Cockney accent which he then proceeded to demonstrate for me, hilariously.

During the second act I stood at my post gazing upwards, and the royal reaction seemed the same as during the first act. When the curtain came down a Member of Parliament, who shall be nameless and whom I had known for some time, came up to me and said: "What's the matter, Alan? You look a little pale." I replied that it did not seem to me that Her Majesty had enjoyed it very much. "Well," said he with a chuckle. "Don't let that disturb you. After all, she's more German than English."

The longest running musical that had ever played Drury Lane was *Oklahoma*, which ran three years plus. *My Fair Lady* occupied that most splendid of all theatres for over six.

My Fair Lady was made into a film by Warner Brothers and won the Academy Award for the Best Film. Rex Harrison won an Oscar for the Best Actor. There were many who wondered why Julie Andrews was not asked to repeat her performance on the screen. There was a reason for it which had nothing to do with Julie. By the time the film was made in the mid-sixties, more than half the revenue of any film came from abroad, and musical films, especially those in which the lyrics were an integral part of the story, did not do well outside the English-speaking countries. To protect itself, the studio—meaning Jack Warner—felt that a full-fledged box office draw was needed. I did not have the right to select the cast, but I could approve. In the beginning, Jack Warner wanted Cary Grant to play Higgins. I told him that as much as I admired Cary, there is an unmistakable Cockney strain in his English and the role of Henry Higgins demanded the impeccable. Nevertheless, he invited

Cary to play the role. But Cary was too wise. He told Jack that only a fool would try to follow Rex Harrison.

Jack then called me and suggested Rock Hudson. "A fine actor," I replied, "but all wrong." Why?" asked Jack. "He's not a Cockney." "Neither is Marcello Mastroianni," I said, "but that does not qualify him to play Henry Higgins." Finally, Jack bowed to the inevitable and Rex was signed. The studio then turned to Audrey Hepburn to add the needed lustre to the marquee.

Julie, of course, was heartbroken and the sympathy of the entire industry did little to ease her disappointment. But Disney immediately signed her to play "Mary Poppins," and when Rex walked up on the stage to receive his Oscar for Best Actor, Julie received a standing ovation when she joined him to receive an Oscar for Best Actress.

On September 29, 1962, six and a half years after its opening, *My Fair Lady* gave its final performance on Broadway. On that night there occurred an incident that has haunted me and plagued me ever since. Time has been unable to dilute the pain, and every time the memory of it returns my skin reddens, my heart beats faster, and I feel like throwing my head away in disgust.

The theatre was crowded with well-wishers and as each song began there was a round of appreciative applause. When the final curtain fell, the audience rose, as it did on opening night, and cheers reverberated from wall to wall. Fritz was in Palm Springs, Moss was no longer with us, and so it fell upon me to make a curtain speech. As I stood in the wings and ran over in my head what I intended to say, which was primarily to thank all those involved in the production as well as the audiences who had received it so enthusiastically, I could not quite make up my mind whether to mention Moss's name first or last. At the last moment I decided upon the latter. I thought that in this way I could pause for a moment and underscore his name and still maintain the spirit of the occasion.

So out onto the stage I went. As I began to speak, an unexpected flood of emotion welled up within me and caught me completely unaware. All the memories of that extraordinary experience called *My Fair Lady* suddenly swam before my eyes, and my brief paragraph of remarks seemed like a volume. I thanked everyone, ending with Moss, as I had intended and the curtain came down. As I walked offstage there was a strange look on everyone's face. I assumed it was because everyone had found himself as unexpectedly moved as I. As I was about to exit through the stage door, someone—I do not remember who—said to me: "Alan, why didn't you mention Moss?" "I did," I said. "You didn't," came the reply. The blood left my body and I suddenly felt dizzy. "You didn't hear me," I said. "I mentioned Moss last." Whoever it was shook his head. I turned to two or three other people and asked them the same question. The answers were the same. I had not mentioned Moss. I thought I had, I was certain I had, it was the uppermost name on my mind. But I had not mentioned him.

I finally found Kitty and tried to explain what had happened, but the words turned to ashes in my mouth. I know she understood. She was hurt, but she understood and she forgave me. But I have never forgiven myself, nor have I ever tried. Whoever was in the theatre that night had undoubtedly long forgotten it. I have not, never can and never will.

The closing night in New York was not the closing night of the show. It has never stopped playing somewhere. In Germany, for instance, where every major city has a state theatre, there are over five hundred performances a year, second only to Wagner—much to Fritz's amused satisfaction.

In 1975 it was revived again on Broadway, where it ran for almost a year, and as of this writing there is a company touring the country.

The cast album was made in the language of every country in which the play was performed. There was also a soundtrack album made when the film was released. The total number of cast albums sold, as of this moment, is over eighteen million and the end is nowhere in sight. For the $400,000 investment CBS made in *My Fair Lady*, they have received to date over $42 million.

In 1965, after the film had been running for one year, Warner Brothers, having nothing better to do one day, added up the gross revenue of all the theatres in which *My Fair Lady* had played around the world, the gross revenue of all the albums, cast or otherwise, and the gross revenue of the first year of the film. The total was over $800 million.

But why? Why the universal reception, critically and publicly, eighteen million albums, $800 million? Why? How did it happen? Why was it that in every country in every language, the audience laughed in the same places? Why was it that in every country "On the Street Where You Live" immediately became the number one song, then faded, and "I Could Have Danced All Night" and "I've Grown Accustomed to Her Face" lingered on and became the show's most identifiable songs? Why?

A musical play is a popular art form. I do not believe there is such a thing as an avant-garde musical: it is a contradiction in terms. There are those who in order to avoid the responsibility of memorable melody compose in a musical twilight zone, that is neither popular nor operatic. Critics have grown suspicious of melody, almost as if they say to themselves "if I can remember it, it can't be good," and so there are musicals that receive critical praise, touch no one's heart, and close after a few months. Contrary to this form of perverted snobbery, the fact remains that only what is good survives. The songs that live are good songs. The songs of *My Fair Lady* are good songs, and I know they are, but the quality still falls short of explaining why popularity ascended to such an unprecedented height. I have no answer and I am grateful for my ignorance. It would corrupt my soul and destroy my creative life if I did.

As far as the play itself is concerned, I believe the right people at the right moment in their lives embarked on the right venture—authors, director, costumer, scenic designer, producer, lighting man, choreographer, and actors—and rather than extending their talents to the limit, expressed them to the limit. *My Fair Lady* was the sum total of its component parts. Without one of those parts it would not have been the same.

When contracts were drawn with foreign producers, I insisted that every production be an identical copy of the New York production. "Who knows?" I said to Herman. "It may have been the chandeliers that did it."

Gigi

Among the cluster of city-less suburbs that bear the generic name of Hollywood is a town of well-to-do squalor, gas stations, and oil derricks called Culver City. Amid the polluted opulence is a small street where rises an imposing white-stoned edifice, mounted at the top of two dozen, building-wide steps, still not old enough to be creviced by use. It is the executive office building of Metro-Goldwyn-Mayer, and it stands next to a mortuary. At the far right end of the first floor corridor is a door that once led to crowded sound sets, busy recording studios, a commissary, lusciously-filled dressing rooms, the Mississippi River, a town in the old West, a street corner in Paris, the jungles of Africa, locomotives, chariots, steamboats, and all the other paraphernalia known as "the lot."

MGM was called "The Home of the Stars" and indeed it was. It has always been a paradox to me that as the population increases, the number of stars decreases, not only on the screen and on the stage, but everywhere. Today we have fewer than ever. The last star we had in politics was Kennedy. Nixon was a featured player who tried to steal the show. Johnson was an understudy who almost closed it. Carter, as far as I can tell, is either a character actor or an actor of character.

In 1949, when I first went to Hollywood, through that door

came, among others, Fred Astaire, Gene Kelly, Judy Garland, Mickey Rooney, and June Allyson, on their way to the offices of Arthur Freed, the producer who had taken the studio by the hand and guided it through the bustles and breeches of operetta into the modern world of screen musicals.

MGM had, for years, been the home of Jeanette MacDonald and Nelson Eddy, the powdered wig, the rousing men's chorus, and the fluttering eyelid. Warner Brothers, on the other hand, specialized in the Busby Berkeley backstage story. Those were the films where a Broadway stage would cover half an acre, a scene on a city street would be as long as a city street, a field of tulips would be a field of tulips, and when the chorus sang "By a Waterfall," by God they were by a waterfall. They were something like the stage direction in one of Ring Lardner's one act plays which said: the curtain is lowered for two weeks to denote the passing of two weeks. Paramount had Crosby, and RKO contented itself with the Astaire-Rogers pictures—and never did more grace, charm, gaiety, and elegance light up the screen.

When *Oklahoma* began the new era of musicals on Broadway, Arthur was turning over a new leaf in Hollywood. The list of people he brought to MGM, mainly from Broadway, was endless, but the principal ones were Gene Kelly and Vincente Minnelli who, singularly and together, were the most innovative and moving forces in the changing screen-musical. Vincente Minnelli's *Meet Me in St. Louis* was a step from the past into the present, and Gene Kelly charged the screen with the electricity of his own style of choreography. Arthur, incidentally, also persuaded Fred Astaire to leave his horses and return to films. I once asked Fred what made him decide to come out of retirement, and he replied: "Arthur offered me a picture." Among the films he did for Arthur were *The Barkleys of Broadway, Easter Parade, Royal Wedding,* and *The Band Wagon.*

Arthur was a strange and touching man; filled with contradictions, idiosyncracies, and surprises. By any standard, he was an original. An inveterate collector of any and all objets d'art, every time he went away he returned home with one more suitcase than when he had left, but the contents remained a mystery. As he came through the door, the order went out that the suitcase was not to be unpacked by anyone but himself. But during the ten years that I worked with him he never once got around to opening one of them. They remained like chests of pirate treasure in the attic. He also liked cheese, which he used to bring home frequently and place in the frigidaire with a small banner flying from a toothpick that said "His." It was against the law of the house for anyone to mouse "His" cheese. But his major avocation was orchids. Several miles from his house in Beverly Hills he owned one of the largest orchid farms in the world and his reputation was international.

Socially he was a shy and private man who eschewed the "Hollywood party" and never attended premieres. When he was not at home of an evening, he invariably could be found at Lee and Ira Gershwin's, playing billiards with Ira or laughing at Oscar Levant's endless stream of witticisms. If I also were there, as I usually was when I was in town, the next day Arthur would have forgotten and he would spend the first hour of the morning telling me everything that I had heard Oscar say the night before.

He was a hero-worshipper of talent and if you were one of the fortunate ones whom he respected, his loyalty knew no bounds. He also had the ability to bring out the best in you when you were working; but you had to mete out your ideas with discretion so as not to overwhelm him and at times make him feel your ideas were his. On one occasion Richard Brooks was writing and directing a film for Arthur at the same time as I was working on a script. If either of us had an esoteric notion about whom to cast in a certain role, if it were for Dick's film, Dick would tell it to me, I would suggest it to Arthur and Arthur would then suggest it to Dick. When it was for my film, we went through the same exercise in reverse.

He had begun his career as a lyric writer, being the lyric half of Brown and Freed. During the thirties, each studio had a resident songwriting team—or teams. Warner Brothers had Dubin and Warren, Paramount had Robbins and Rainger and Gordon and Revel, and MGM had Brown and Freed. From time to time, Harold Arlen, Johnny Mercer, Jerome Kern, Dorothy Fields, Irving Berlin, Cole Porter, Rodgers and Hart, and George and Ira Gershwin would also contribute their services to a project they found to their liking. Usually, any picture that involved Fred Astaire was one they found to their liking.

Brown and Freed produced an endless number of song hits, their most famous being "Singin' in the Rain," and they had written the score for the first great musical film ever made, *Broadway Melody*. When Nacio Brown retired, Louis B. Mayer, the Caesar of MGM, thought Arthur had the makings of a producer. So did Arthur. And how right they both were.

At MGM, unlike the other studios, the role of the producer was all important. Mr. Mayer believed (he was always called Mr. Mayer, except by a handful of executive intimates) the order of importance in the making of any film was first, the producer; second, the writer; third, the star; and fourth, the director. His theory was that if a producer had the right script with the right cast, any good director could convert it to film.

This is the way the system worked. The studio would purchase a book or a play or a short story and the producers would assemble to listen to a "reader" recite a synopsis of it. (This technique was primarily for saving time. Most producers, to my best knowledge, could read.) If one of the producers was stimulated by what he heard, he would clutch it to his bosom and it would become his, all his. If, however, it was greeted by a collective yawn, it would be filed under *O* for Oblivion, where it would remain for ever and ever, Amen. Occasionally, as one would expect, the producing body would commit a major goof. Lillie Messinger, Mr. Mayer's favorite teacher and roving assistant, tried devilishly hard to interest the producing muses in a manuscript she had just read called *Gone with the Wind,* but it was the general consensus that civil war pictures were out and it was not even worth purchasing. For some reason, Mr. Mayer's son-in-law, David O. Selznick, later bought it and did rather well with it.

The one exception to this general method of operation was Arthur Freed. Except for the occasions where he would ask the studio to purchase a Broadway musical for him such as *On the Town* and *Brigadoon,* he almost always created his projects from scratch. My own experience was typical. Arthur suggested to me that I come to California for ten weeks, not to work on any particular project, but just to hang around. While I was there steeping myself in the atmosphere, perhaps an idea for a film would develop. If at the end of ten weeks none did, I would return home and so be it. During the first three weeks I was there, Arthur told me he was looking for an idea for Fred Astaire. We began to discuss the days when Fred's partner was his famous sister, Adele. Out of it came the idea of doing a film about a famous brother and sister dance team engaged to perform in London at the time of the royal wedding. And so I went to work. Originally his sister was to be June Allyson, but one day at lunch Arthur, in his own inimitable fashion, mentioned en passant that he had just discovered June was pregnant and obviously in no condition to dance with Fred. About two-thirds through the writing, he mentioned in the corridor one day that Judy Garland was going to play it. I was jubilant. But it was never mentioned again. After I had finished and gone back to New York, he called me again and told me Jane Powell was going to play it. And she did.

Although Burton Lane wrote some spiffy songs and Fred danced in a way that made all superlatives inadequate, my contribution left me in such a state of cringe that I could barely straighten up. Even the one creative moment I liked had nothing to do with me consciously. One night I dreamed that Fred was dancing up the wall, all across the ceiling and down the other wall. I mentioned it to Arthur at lunch the following day and lo, in the film Fred danced up one wall, across the ceiling and down the other wall.

After *Royal Wedding* I did the screenplay for *An American in Paris,* which became the first musical film to win the Academy Award, also netting an Oscar for me. (I know I mentioned it before, but this is my book.)

I then signed a three-picture contract with Arthur, the first of which was *Brigadoon,* starring Gene Kelly and directed by Vincente. It was a picture that should have been made on location in Scotland and was done in the studio. It was a singing show that tried to become a dancing show, and it had an all-American cast which should have been all-Scottish. It was one of those ventures that occur so often where we all knew we were going down the wrong road but no one could stop. I have always believed that only genuinely talented people can create something that is genuinely bad. As Jean Giradoux once said: "Only the mediocre are always at their best."

After *Brigadoon* it was all downhill. Burton Lane and I wrote a musical film based on *Huckleberry Finn,* in which Danny Kaye and Gene Kelly were to play the Duke and the Dauphin, and again Vincente was to direct. Unfortunately, shortly before production began the United States Government, in order to enable American companies abroad to encourage American personnel to move to god-forsaken corners of the world, make a change in the tax law, whereby any American working for an American company overseas who stayed out of the country for a minimum of eighteen months would not be obliged to pay any income tax. Off to Europe went the cream of American stars in pursuit of tax-free loot. Two weeks after *Huckleberry Finn* began shooting, Gene Kelly, with the studio's permission, took a flying leap into the loophole and *Huckleberry Finn* was closed down forever.

But I still owed Arthur one more film.

When *My Fair Lady* was trying-out in Philadelphia, he flew in from California to see it and mentioned the possibility of doing a musical film based on Colette's famous novella, *Gigi*. He, of course, understood that it was hardly the time for me to think about anything other than what I was doing, but I promised that after the dust settled I would be in touch.

My Fair Lady opened in New York in March. By August, relaxation was causing me to lose sleep and I could no longer continue trying to think about nothing. So I flew to California to keep my promised date. It had been almost two years since I had been there and I was astounded and saddened by the change. The huge, white-stoned building seemed more like a hospital and the mortuary next door far less coincidental. The studio was now being run by a polite, soft-spoken gentleman named Benny Thau who had been with MGM for a couple of decades, knew a great deal about the motion picture business, and had become president by not inflicting his knowledge on those less wise, but louder. I was told that he was only to occupy his present position temporarily. I was not certain whether it meant he was temporary or the position was temporary.

The terminal atmosphere was not unique to MGM. It was industry-wide. Somewhere in the early fifties, the movie going habit of forty million Americans had been broken and the crunch was on. The only thing that had not changed was Arthur's enthusiasm.

Rereading Colette's story, I noticed an occasional mention of

Gaston's uncle, Honore Lachailles. It occurred to me that perhaps I could develop Uncle Honore into a role that might be suitable for Maurice Chevalier. I felt that a musical personality, such as Chevalier, was essential to the film: there had to be someone whose singing would be expected. The other characters could sing, but they were not singing roles. Both Arthur and Vincente, who was going to direct the film, were in complete agreement.

One of the reasons that musical films have all but disappeared from the screen is because there are no more great entertainers who can set the film's musical style. One never had to explain why Fred Astaire or Gene Kelly danced, or why Judy Garland or Bing Crosby sang. The fact of their presence automatically meant "a musical." When a stage musical is converted to the screen, the audience is similarly preconditioned. They have usually heard the score and are prepared. But to try to do a musical with legitimate performers whose singing voices are dubbed and who have no reputation in the musical field presents an insoluble problem. Motion pictures are a realistic medium. Musicals are an unrealistic form of expression. It is the performers not the writers who create the atmosphere required to make that form of expression acceptable. As of this writing, there are only two film stars in the world today who can make the unrealistic form of a musical seem realistic. They are Barbra Streisand and Liza Minnelli. But two is not enough to create a trend. If there is ever to be a revival of the musical film, it will have to wait until such time as there is an explosion of performing talent who will make it possible.

The other reason I wanted Maurice Chevalier was a personal one. He had been an idol of mine ever since every little breeze started whispering Louise. In fact, he was one of four stars whom I had always worshipped: Fred Astaire, Katharine Hepburn, and James Cagney being the others. When I entered the theatre and later films, I was determined that somehow, some day, I would work with all four of them. At the time of *Gigi*, only 25 percent of my ambition had been realized: I had worked with Fred. Ten years later I did *Coco* with Katharine Hepburn on the stage. James Cagney has retired, and so I will have to wait for another lifetime. But here, thought I, was a chance to work with Chevalier.

But who would compose the music? Naturally, I desperately wanted to do it with Fritz, but Fritz had always refused to involve himself with a motion picture. Nothing but the theatre was of any interest to him. Nevertheless, on the small chance that he, too, was tired of relaxing I cabled him. He was, to my surprise, at the chemin-de-fer table at the Palm Beach Casino, Cannes. I received a very quick reply: no.

Fritz and I had always had a policy that no matter what either of us was offered, and no matter how unlikely the project, we would always inform the other before refusing. Once, David Selznick called me about doing *Gone with the Wind* as a stage musical. I could not imagine it as a theatre piece, much less see how music and lyrics could enhance what was already there. But I cabled Fritz (chemin-de-fer table, Palm Beach Casino, Cannes). Two days later I received an answer which he must have dictated because it was written in his accent. It said: "Vind not funny. Love Fritz."

On another occasion I was approached on our combined behalf to create a musical out of the story of the Trapp Family Singers. (Later *The Sound of Music* by Rodgers and Hammerstein.) Again I cabled Fritz (chemin-de-fer table, Palm Beach Casino, Cannes). Two days later I received his reply which read: "Dear boy, what do you want me to write—yodel music? Love Fritz."

Arthur was as disappointed as I that Fritz had refused, but I owed him a picture and at that point in the planning I thought there would be no more than four songs. Reluctantly I would have to do them with someone else. So I agreed, on two conditions: the first was that if I created a part that warranted it, every effort would be made to get Maurice Chevalier; and the second, that Cecil Beaton would be asked to design the sets and costumes. Arthur agreed.

I returned to New York and sometime during the autumn completed the first draft of the screenplay. There are a few aspects of motion picture writing that used to appeal to me: one, they are easier because scenes can go anywhere and are not hemmed in by the limitations of the theatre; two, it is less lonely. Once you have embarked on a venture, there are always lots of people to talk to and be with. When you finish a song, you play it for the producer and the director—and sometimes the star—and if they approve, in a way the reviews are in.

Upon completing the first draft, I returned to California for two or three weeks of meetings with Arthur and Vincente. It is impossible to describe a story conference with Arthur. Although he knew perfectly well what he liked and did not like, what he wanted and did not want, his method of conveying it was so circuitous that the mind grew vertiginous with *non sequiturs* and it took patience, respect, and maniacal determination to ferret out nuggets of information.

Sample:

AJL (*to Freed*): Did you read the script?

FREED: Yup. I think . . . I spoke to Oscar yesterday.
    [Hammerstein]

AJL: Do you think the part is big enough for Chevalier?

FREED: I thought you were going to be at Ira's last night?
    [Gershwin]

AJL: I couldn't make it.

FREED: Oscar was in a great mood. [Levant] He has a new
    doctor.

AJL: About Maurice . . . [Chevalier]

FREED: Are you going tonight? [Gershwins]

AJL: Yes.

FREED: I can't make it. That Englishman is staying with them. [Solly Zuckerman]

AJL: Solly Zuckerman?

FREED: I want to buy *Say It with Music*. Christ knows [The Son of God] what he will want for it. [Irving Berlin] He got $600,000 for *There's No Business Like Show Business* and all he did was complain about the taxes.

AJL: I remember. I was there.

FREED: Adolph [Green] said: "Irving, why don't you spread it out? Take a dollar a year for 600,000 years."

AJL: I remember. I was there. What about the script? [*Gigi*]

FREED: Do you want to do it? [*Say It with Music*]

AJL: You have it. [*Gigi*]

FREED: McKenna wants to talk to you. [Kenneth MacKenna, head of the story department.]

AJL: What about?

FREED: Don't pay any attention to him.

AJL: Didn't he like it?

FREED: How about some lunch? I've got some ideas about Maxim's. [Restaurant in Paris. Scene in the picture.]

EXIT from office and pass secretary.

SECRETARY: Mr. Freed, did you see the cable I left on your desk?

FREED: (*Nodding*) Tell Benny [Thau] I want to see him after lunch.

Cut to:

Freed table in MGM commissary. Freed and AJL sit down and study the menu. An agent approaches with Romy Schneider.

AGENT: Arthur, I'd like you to meet Romy Schneider. She's out here to make a picture.

(Freed does not hear and looks up at Romy Schneider)

FREED: I'll have the cheese omelette.

Mistaken identity corrected. Romy Schneider and agent leave the table. Conversation during lunch about Oscar Levant, Haitian painting (Freed had a large collection), and orchids. Nothing said about Gigi. Lunch over.

FREED: (*Rising from table*) I'll be back in my office in an hour. I got to see Benny about making a deal with Chevalier.

AJL: Chevalier?!

FREED: I got a cable from his agent this morning.

AJL: Does he want to do it?!

FREED: Jesus! Why not? It's a great part for him. What do you think of Solly Zuckerman?

Frequently he would begin a sentence on, let us say, Wednesday and complete it on Friday. Yet this same man could look at me and say: "Stop trying to be different. You don't have to be different to be good. To be good is different enough."

As for Vincente, at his best—and his best was with Arthur—he was and is the finest director of musical films since Lubitsch, although their styles are totally dissimilar.

One of the first rules of screenwriting is never use the spoken word when an image can accomplish the same purpose. At that, Lubitsch was the master. Samson Raphaelson, the well-known playwright of the twenties and thirties and the author of *The Jazz Singer* and *Accent on Youth* among others, was one of Lubitsch's favorite screenwriters. He told me, one day, about a script he had written for Lubitsch that began with a husband and wife closing the door of their apartment in the middle of an argument. The argument continued while they waited for the elevator. When the elevator arrived, they stepped in and because there were others in the elevator they held their tongues. The moment they were out on the street, the argument continued. The entire sequence took about three pages. Lubitsch read it, tore it out of the script, and this is what he did: the couple emerge from their apartment in total silence. They ring for the elevator in total silence. They enter the elevator. The elevator is empty. It stops at the floor below and a woman enters. And the man takes his hat off. Antagonism between husband and wife established. End of sequence.

Vincente's genius lies in his faultless sense of style. He had been a set designer and a painter before becoming a director, and each frame of his films is a work of art. Often the realization of his vision could be maddening. He would spend hours during a shooting day arranging the flowers the way he wanted them, while the actors kept awake counting their overtime.

When Louis Jourdan arrives finally at the chorus of *Gigi*, he is sitting on a bench and behind him is a lake. After a few bars, a group of swans suddenly appear and glide across the water. When I first saw the dailies (formerly called the rushes), I was sitting in the projection room with Bill O'Brien, Arthur's production manager. I gasped. "Bill," I said, "where the hell did those swans come from?" "Shhh," said Bill. "What do you mean, shh?" I replied. "I keep looking at the swans instead of Louis. How did they get there?" Said Bill, quietly, "Vincente put them there. In fact, he auditioned swans for four days."

Vincente has a thorough knowledge of music, lyrics, comedy, and drama and there is no one who can photograph a musical number with as much skill and imagination. During the singing of *Gigi*, the camera wanders all over Paris, constantly refreshing the eye without ever interfering with the flow of the song. The night scene with Louis Jourdan pacing up and down in silhouette in front of a shimmering fountain and being shaken into a decision when a horse and carriage, also in silhouette, pull up short to avoid hitting him, is among the most memorable effects ever filmed and uniquely Minnelli.

I am devoted to him and love working with him. His gentleness, however, can be very deceptive. Frequently I would have a suggestion, he would listen appreciatively, nod, agree, thank me—and then shoot the scene exactly as he had intended. And invariably he was right. During *An American in Paris,* we very quickly developed a shorthand communication with each other. He spoke falteringly and often vaguely but in some manner that had nothing to do with logic, I always could feel what he meant more than I understood the words.

The finale of *An American in Paris* is an eighteen-minute ballet to Gershwin's "An American in Paris." He called me from California one day—I was home in New York—and tried to explain that he needed some kind of speech to lead into the ballet that would, in some way, relate the love story to Dufy, Toulouse-Lautrec, and all the other painters whose work inspired the scenic backgrounds of the ballet. "Nothing too long," he reassured me. "Just a short speech. You know." I did not know. "When do you need it?" I asked. Said Vincente: "Not right away. I'll be home tonight. Could you phone it to me? We're shooting it tomorrow."

A short speech to sum up a two hour story that is at the same time an introduction to Dufy and Toulouse-Lautrec and a ballet? I knew he must have thought it possible or he would not have asked me, so I sat down and wrote what I thought he wanted. I phoned it to him that evening. "Perfect," he said. "Thank you, Alan." I have seen the picture many times and I am still not certain what the speech is saying. But Vincente said it was perfect and that was all that mattered, and no one to this day has ever said: "What on earth is that speech all about near the end of the film?"

Come November we still had no composer. I returned to New York determined to have one last whack at Fritz. I told him the least he could do was read the bloody script, and he admitted that sounded reasonable. To add a little seasoning, I said I felt it was essential that the score be written in Paris. It would not only be fun—and this is not an affectation—but unquestionably it was bound to help the atmosphere of the score to write it in the country in which the story takes place. Fritz took the script home with him and bright and early the next morning he telephoned to say he loved it and wanted to do it. I immediately got in touch with Arthur and he and Vincente were jubilant about Fritz's change of heart.

In March, the second company of *My Fair Lady* opened in Rochester and immediately following, Fritz and I took off for Paris—but not without a moment of drama.

The plane was to leave at one o'clock in the afternoon. Fritz is fanatically punctual and we were to meet at the airport at twelve o'clock sharp. For the first and only time since I have known him, Fritz was almost forty-five minutes late. He apologized, but did not explain where he had been and I did not press the matter. Later I found out. The reason was most revealing of Fritz.

He had been with my accountant. Not his accountant, mine, checking the books. We jointly owned half the producing interest in *My Fair Lady* and these rights were held by our music publishing company. During the early days of our collaboration, he was most cavalier about money, the way one is when one does not have a great deal. Frequently he would give me his bridge or poker winnings to hold for him. But the moment the green stuff began to flood the banks, his entire attitude changed. He suddenly became extremely suspicious of everyone who worked for him or with him, primarily me, my accountant, and my lawyer. I was well aware of it, but it never bothered me because it had nothing to do with the rest of Fritz. I have always made it a policy never to judge anyone by his behavior with money and the opposite sex. Money and sex somehow dub in a different voice. Perhaps not to a psychiatrist, but I am a playwright-lyricist. That Saturday morning before we left for Paris, Fritz had made an appointment with my accountant, Israel Katz, to examine our books in order to reassure himself that all was in order, meaning, I suppose, that I had not been raiding the till. The examination took much longer than Fritz had planned, because not finding anything amiss, instead of allaying his suspicions it only increased them. Consequently, he almost missed the plane.

The incident is also revealing of Israel, who has been looking after my affairs (money, I mean) since 1954. Besides being a Merlin in the metaphysical world of the Internal Revenue Service, he is also one of the kindest and most human beings I have ever known. He is bilingual, speaking not only English but "taxasian"—a form of hieroglyphics devised by the corporate slaves who serve on the House and Senate Finance Committees to enable the rich to get richer, the poor, poorer, and to keep the public in a chronic state of confusion.

Israel, one of his assistants and I can be having a chat about my affairs, when suddenly he will turn to his assistant, address him in the language of "taxasian" and I might as well be in Outer Mongolia. His firm is a large one and the sun never sets on his clients. When I call to speak to him, having seen him the day before, he might be anywhere from Berlin to the "21" Club (one of his clients). But he has a profound respect and admiration for the creative person that is never tinged with paternalism. He understood Fritz. He was not the slightest bit upset and never bothered to mention the appointment to me because he did not wish to upset me. Almost a year later he asked me, with a chuckle, if Fritz had made the plane that day, and it was then he told me the whole story.

We arrived in Paris on one of those typical grey, Parisian days which songwriters have always chosen to ignore. From time to time one does see a few sunbeams dancing on "holiday tables under the trees," but not often. One year I spent eight consecutive months in Paris and never saw the sun once. One notices it all the more because the buildings are low and there is no escaping the sky. It also rains a good deal in Paris, but the raincoats are terribly chic. Occasionally, there is a heat-wave and because of the high cost of electricity, there is no air-conditioning, except in a restaurant in the Plaza Athénée, the Relais Plaza, and Maxim's. There was a heat-wave the spring that Fritz and I were there and people were fainting on the streets—and even in Paris there is no chic way to pass out.

We began working on Chevalier's first song, "Thank Heaven for Little Girls." I had given Fritz the title before we left New York. In order to establish the musical style, Chevalier plays the role of narrator or "raisoneur," and in the first scene addresses the audience and introduces Paris, the period, the atmosphere, and Gigi. The style of a film must be established within the first few minutes, as it is in the opening sequences that the audience adjusts its emotional body temperature to the climate of the film.

Arthur had arranged for Fritz and me to visit Chevalier, who was appearing in a nightclub in a town called Le Zout on the Belgian coast. Easter came early that year and we decided to make the great trek over the holiday weekend.

In all the years I had spent in Europe, for some reason I had never been to Belgium, and it was the first time I witnessed at first hand that most lethal of God's creatures, a Belgian behind the wheel. There were no requirements for a driver's license in Belgium at that time. Anyone over fifteen who could see well enough to locate his automobile was allowed to drive. The chauffeur who drove us from Brussels to Ostend was the Blue Max of the limousine world. He could spot a pedestrian a half mile down the road and head for him like a guided missile. Fortunately, Belgian pedestrians are well trained in the art of fender-dodging and there are still lots of Belgians. After a long, harrowing journey, we arrived at Le Zout in time to see Maurice's performance. He was as captivating and adroit as I had remembered him, and although seventy-two years of age, his energy and mobility seemed untouched by time. His one-man show lasted well over an hour.

We met him after the performance expecting him to be exhausted and intending only to pay our respects and make an appointment to see him the next day. Not at all. He showed not the slightest sign of fatigue and we had a long chat about the film. His enthusiasm was high and he could not wait to hear the first song. (Neither could we.) He discussed his age frankly, remarking that being seventy-two was not that bad considering the alternative. He also said something else that stuck in my mind. "At seventy-two," he said, "I am too old for women, too old for that extra glass of wine, too old for sports. (He had started his life as a boxer and was always very athletic.) All I have left is the audience but I have found it is quite enough." Months later his words returned to me and undoubtedly led me to the idea for "I'm Glad I'm Not Young Any More."

The next day we found the Blue Max and heavily sedating ourselves for the trip, returned to Brussels and then Paris to continue working.

Two weeks after we had been there, I received a phone call from Arthur, saying that Audrey Hepburn was at the Hotel Raphael and would I call her, go to see her, and talk to her about playing Gigi. Audrey had originated the role on the stage. In fact it was the part that launched her career. I strongly doubted she would be interested in doing it again, but nevertheless I went and had a chat with her. She could not have been more gracious, but she did not want to do it again. I reported this to Arthur. He then told me that Leslie Caron was living in London with her husband, then Peter Hall (he is still Peter Hall but), and would I mind going there and talking to *her*. I did not mind, I told Arthur. It had been in the back of my mind that the ideal man to play Gaston was Dirk Bogarde, who also lived in London, and I would be able to see him at the same time.

Besides being a good friend, Dirk happens to be one of the best screen actors alive who, to this day, has never received, in this country at least, the recognition his talent deserves. Unfortunately, he bears the cross of good looks and all too often American critics find themselves incapable of believing depth and artistry can thrive behind a handsome face. A tortured life properly publicized will sometimes remove the stigma. A severe accident or a prolonged illness will also help. Suffering somehow assures them that he is not a photograph. If, by any chance, he is English and his accent is not laced with Cockney, then he is apt to be further handicapped. Any sign of education is regarded as a perversion of the truth. Generally speaking, the more an actor resembles a New York cab driver, and the more difficulty he has with the English language, the better his chances are of receiving critical praise. The attitude seems to be that the lowest common denominator and the most common denominator constitute reality.

In the theatre, give the gentlemen on the aisle a play riddled with profanity, ungrammatical sentences, and a fair amount of stuttering and mumbling, and the author will be extolled for his splendid ear for speech. The actor will also receive his share of acclaim for bringing real, honest to God life to the stage. The private lines of critics must be utterly fascinating.

The role of Gaston was not a simple one. It takes considerable style and skill to play a bored man and not be boring. Dirk, I knew, had and has all that skill and I also knew that he had, and I presume still has, a very serviceable singing voice. I had mentioned all this to Arthur and he gave me his blessing to try and interest him in the role. I saw Dirk and spent some time with him, and he reacted most favorably. He was under contract to J. Arthur Rank at the time, but he thought he would be able to obtain a release.

I then made an appointment with Leslie. She had been living in London ever since she had married Peter and I had not seen her since *An American in Paris*—when she came to Hollywood equipped with one of those adorable French accents that everyone is always so mad about. I was astonished to discover that she now sounded more English than the English, a disease that often afflicts Americans who move to London. I did not think the French were as susceptible. We had a rather tense meeting, not unfriendly, but definitely not relaxed. She asked me how I intended to interpret the role of Gigi. I was perplexed. "Why?" I asked. She explained that she understood Gigi thoroughly because she had played it that year on the stage in London. It came as a complete surprise to me. I asked her how it had been received. Unabashed, she told me it had been a failure. "Well," said I, "I think you had better tell me how *you* interpreted it." She did not. I explained it was my intention to concentrate dramatic attention as much on a girl becoming a woman as on a girl becoming a courtesan. She thought for a moment and said, "Oh!" Rather than exploring the "Oh!", I thought I had better ask the pertinent question. "Are you available?" I enquired. "Yes," she replied. "Good," said I. "I'll see you in Paris."

Back I went to Paris and to work. I soon finished the lyric of "Thank Heaven for Little Girls" except for the few lines in the middle, professionally known as "the bridge" or "the release." I had written pages and pages, but none of the versions seemed right.

One evening Fritz was going out, as was his wont, and said that when he returned he would call and if I was still awake come up to see how I was doing. If I had gone to sleep I was to turn off the phone. He returned about six in the morning, as was his wont, and I was still up. I read him everything I had, which he liked enormously. I then told him what I had been going through with those damn middle lines. Said Fritz: "What are you trying to say, dear boy?" Said I, picking up a piece of paper I had written some twenty-four hours earlier: "I am trying to say something like this:

> *Those little eyes so helpless and appealing,*
> *One day will flash*
> *And send you crash-*
> *Ing through the ceiling . . ."*

Said Fritz: "What's wrong with that?" I replied: "You can't crash through the ceiling. You crash through the floor." Said Fritz: "Who says so? It's your lyric and if you want to crash through the ceiling, crash through the ceiling!" At six in the morning I was easily persuaded. And so I crashed through the ceiling.

It reminded me of a daydream I have often had about lyric writing that goes something like this. I am locked in a hotel room for three days working on a song. Suddenly the door opens and there stand all the members of my family and my closest friends. One of them says: "What have you been doing in here for three days?" I reply: "Writing." One of them says: "What have you written?" I reply: "I could have danced all night, I could have danced all night, And still have begged for more." They look at each other hopelessly, call the appropriate medical authorities and I am put away for the rest of my natural life.

With "Thank Heaven" out of the way, we went on to "I Remember It Well," and when it was finished we telephoned Maurice at his house in Marne-la-Coquette, a small village just outside Paris which I later discovered he owned most of. We told him we had two songs to show him. He was delighted and made an appointment to come to see us the next day at three o'clock.

The following afternoon as the clock struck three there was a knock at the door. This I later found to be typical of him. Maurice was the infinite professional: always punctual, always courteous, always frank, always encouraging, always working harder than everyone else. He had no illusions about his vocal capabilities. He honestly believed—and he told me this himself—that God had given him a talent and that he owed it to himself and his Creator to take care of it to the best of his ability.

In the thirties, when he first arrived in Hollywood to appear in his first American film for some astonomical figure, he felt he had to make some sacrifice to pay for his good fortune. So he stopped smoking. He was also one of the most tightfisted gents in the history of the profession. There was a parking lot outside Paramount where, for ten cents in the meter, one could park all day. However, five blocks away there was another parking lot that only cost a nickel. I believe his salary was around $20,000 a week. His parking bill was five cents a day.

His house at Marne-la-Coquette was less of a residence than a museum of Chevalier memorabilia. There was no phase of his career that had not been photographed extensively, and the walls were like the pages of a photograph album. I am not too familiar with his early romantic life, but whoever the ladies were they were not prominently featured, except Mistinguette—who had discovered him and with whom he had a long affair. In the thirties, while his popularity in America and the rest of the world was in the ascendancy it was on the decline in France. The French detest any Frenchman who becomes a success outside of France. As Marcel Achard said to me one day: "In France they sometimes forgive you happiness, but never success." During the war, like so many other French entertainers, he was forced to perform during the German occupation. The French, who have never quite forgiven the Allies for winning the war, like to pretend that only a handful of performers and very few others cooperated with the Germans. Anyone who has seen the film *The Sorrow and the Pity* knows what a lot of foie gras that is.

But Maurice bore the stigma of being pro-Nazi and was not allowed into America. For whatever reason, he later signed the Stockholm Peace Petition which was considered (and may have been) Communist inspired, and suddenly he was no longer a Nazi but a Communist. A short time afterwards, it dawned on the French and the Americans (who were being equally ridiculous at the time) that what Chevalier really was was an entertainer. So he eventually was allowed to return to New York where he did his one-man show to wild acclaim, and all was forgotten.

Despite his egomaniacal devotion to his work and his career he was not at all conceited, in fact quite the reverse. When we played him the two songs he listened politely, thanked us, and took the music and departed. Fritz and I had no idea if he liked them or not. The next morning he called and asked if he could come and see us again at three o'clock. I said to Fritz: "Oh, Christ! What's wrong?"

As the clock struck three, in he came. "I love the songs so much," he said, "that I worked on them all night long." He turned to me. But he said, "Alan, would you sing the middle part of 'Thank Heaven' again for me? I like the way you phrase it better than the way I do."

By no stretch of anyone's imagination could I be termed a singer. I considered it a triumph when I did not sing in the key of F while Fritz was playing in the key of G. But the idea that Maurice Chevalier wanted to listen to *me* sing would have moved me to tears had it not seemed so absurd. We did the song again for him, he listened intently, again thanked us profusely and off he went into the grey, Paris afternoon.

Arthur and Vincente arrived towards the end of April. The plan had been to shoot some exteriors in and around Paris, but the bulk of the film was to be made at the studio. By then, Fritz and I had become convinced that the entire film should be made in Paris. For some unfathomable and marvellously mysterious reason, even if one is shooting an *interior* scene, if it is in its authentic setting something of the outside atmosphere creeps through the woodwork and on to the film. *An American In Paris* had been made at the studio, but the sets had been designed to give an artist's impression of Paris. It had never been the intention to hoodwink the audience into believing it was actually Paris. But *An American in Paris* was anything but a French story: *Gigi* was. Paris was as much a character as Gaston and Gigi themselves. Vincente spontaneously agreed. So did Arthur, but he was worried about the cost of the studio. In the few months since I had been in Hollywood, the tide of accounts receivable had been rising to the point of panic, and if there had been any question in anyone's mind that the Hollywood studio was about to join the lost continent of Atlantis, there was none now. Budgets were being slashed, pictures and contracts were being cancelled, and salaries squashed. In typical Hollywood fashion the first people to receive the pink slip were the secretaries, the parking attendants, the elevator men, the waitresses in the commissary, and the night-watchmen.

Nevertheless, Arthur was persuaded that location was essential to the film and somehow he was able to induce the studio into approving. Among the reasons for Arthur's preeminence as a producer was his unshakeable faith in the people with whom he had selected to work, and his passionate determination to do everything in his power to create the conditions in which they would best function.

One night Fritz and a few of us were sitting in a bistro talking about him, when someone said: "I don't understand Freed. Why do you all think he's such a great producer?" Fritz looked at him and replied: "We're all here, aren't we?"

So the film would be made in Paris, but there could be no dawdling. Every day on location is prohibitively expensive. After trying in vain to persuade Yvonne Printemps to return to the screen to play Aunt Alicia, the retired courtesan, Vincente thought of Isabel Jeans who could not have been better. Eva Gabor would play Gaston's mistress, Hermione Gingold, Gigi's grandmother Mamita. Because of "I Remember It Well" it was vital that Mamita did not have a trace of sentimentality, and there was no danger of that with Hermione. But J. Arthur Rank became the face on my dartboard. He refused to release Dirk. Everyone was deeply disappointed, but no one as much as I. Only I, who knew him well and knew his voice, had been sitting at the typewriter seeing him and hearing him every time I wrote a speech for Gaston.

Arthur suggested Louis Jourdan, who certainly looked the part and was certainly French. But could he sing? Fortunately, he was in London and Arthur arranged for him to come to Paris and give us the opportunity to find out. To our delighted surprise he was not only extremely musical, but had a most charming voice. But could he play boredom without falling into the trap? Louis is a very serious fellow, usually more serious than the topic of conversation. He is not without humor, but his humor does not include a twinkle in his soul. The more time we spent together the more my anxiety grew. Finally I decided to play safe. I rewrote the boredom and made Gaston constantly angry that he was bored. To drive the point home, Fritz and I wrote a brisk, buoyant duet for him and Chevalier called "It's a Bore."

While Fritz and I were rummaging through our minds looking for words and music, Arthur, Vincente, and Cecil were rummaging through Paris looking for locations. Instead of the usual Eiffel Tower/Arc de Triomphe/sidewalk café view of the city, Vincente had decided that what he wanted to put on film was the green of Paris—the parks, the trees, the gardens. There were only two Parisian interiors of consequence indicated in the script: one was the Palais de Glace, where the very, very rich of the Belle Epoque used to go ice-skating; the other was Maxim's. Fortunately, Maxim's had not changed. Unfortunately, the Palais de Glace had. It had become as tattered a relic as the hotels on the boardwalk of Atlantic City. Despite the limitations of the budget, Vincente and Cecil somehow were able to restore it sufficiently to give an illusion of its former glory, and it became one of the loveliest sets in the film. As for Maxim's, Arthur convinced its owners, Louis and Maggie Vaudable, to close the restaurant for five days so that the scenes in Maxim's could actually be filmed there.

The song that was to be performed in Maxim's was written to be sung in Gaston's head. It is called "She's Not Thinking of Me" and its intention was to prevent Gaston from looking foolish. Gaston's mistress had made a rendezvous with her ice-skating lover for the following day, and it seemed to me vital that Gaston reveal enough sensitivity to be aware that hanky panky was afoot. It is a waltz and as I have mentioned before the interrhyming that is needed to make it sing is fiendish. I made reasonable progress, however, and after five days and nights it was completed, except for the last couplet. The couplet that ends the first chorus is:

Oh she's shimmering with love!
Oh she's simmering with love!
Oh she's not thinking of me!

Try as I may, I could not find two similar lines with which to end the second chorus.

Four days passed and by now the open window began to look inviting. There was no emotional reason for it: I could not blame it on Mary Martin and Richard Halliday—I was simply stuck, that's all.

During the first five days the technical entourage began to arrive from MGM: the set decorators, some of the camera crew, the sound technicians, and André Previn.

André had been conducting and arranging at MGM since he was sixteen and he had been selected by Arthur, with Fritz's whole-hearted endorsement, to wield the baton for *Gigi*. Now a celebrated conductor in his own right, André is one of the most gifted musicians I have ever encountered, one of the most amusing, and also one of the most mysterious. A graduate of the Paris Conservatoire at the age of eleven, he is not only a concert pianist but equally skilled as a jazz virtuoso. He is mysterious because when he is at the keyboard his facial expression never changes, and one has the feeling that someone else's arms are reaching from behind him and doing the playing. His hands seem totally disassociated from his body. He also has the extraordinary ability to carry on a conversation, to which he is giving his complete attention, and compose music at the same time. Many years later I wrote a musical play with him, *Coco,* and one day we were sitting together discussing the kind of song required for a particular scene. As we talked, our conversation being punctuated from time to time with a non sequitur story or a bit of humor, André seemed to be doodling. Suddenly he rose from his chair and handed me the piece of paper containing the doodling. It was a complete piano part for a song which he had composed during our conversation. There would be no point to this story if it were a bad song, but it happened to be a very good one and became one of the highlights of the play.

I am always reluctant to hand in a lyric until I am as satisfied with it as I think I am able to be. Certainly, if there is a line missing

I keep it to myself. While we were working on "Gigi," there were many instances when I told Arthur of a lyric I was writing but would not show it to him. I did not realize that I was fanning the flame of curiosity of Arthur the ex-lyric writer. André later told me that during the second week of my agonizing over "She's Not Thinking of Me," Arthur came to him one midnight and surreptiously handed him a key. He told André in a hushed voice it was the key to my room. He knew I was not in and he wanted André to go up and steal the lyric. André refused to do it. "I can't do that, Arthur," he said. "If you want it, you steal it." Arthur became furious and said to André: "It's not my department. You're in charge of the music." But André was adamant. It was typical of Arthur that despite his frustration he never once asked me when the lyric would be finished.

On the ninth day I finally found the missing couplet. As I look at it now, it seems hardly worth the effort. It is:

She's so ooh-la-la-la-la,
So untrue-la-la-la-la,
She is not thinking of me.

I passionately wish I could say that outside of "Wouldn't It Be Loverly?", "She's Not Thinking of Me" took me longer to write than any other lyric. But it would not be "the vrai." Six years later I sat down to do the lyric for "On a Clear Day You Can See Forever." After two weeks of the usual run-of-the-mill torture, I realized that if I were ever to finish the rest of the score and complete the play I had better move on. So I decided to allot the first three hours of every morning to working on that lyric and I did. Seven days a week. I finished it eight months later. During the eight-month period I wrote ninety-one complete lyrics and discarded them all. Several years ago a friend of mine who lives in Bar Harbor, Maine, in the summer wrote me a letter and told me that the minister at the local church had used the lyric as the text for his Sunday sermon. I wrote back and told him to tell the minister not to wait for the second chorus.

Arthur may have been patient with me, but no one was ever more so than Fritz, and for a composer it is the rarest of virtues. I once tried collaborating with Richard Rodgers, who had been spoiled by Larry Hart. Larry could write a lyric in the middle of a cocktail party while a band was playing. Dick could never even understand the time it often took Oscar Hammerstein. In fact he said to me one day: "Do you know what Oscar used to do? He would go to his farm in Bucks County and sometimes it would be three weeks before he would appear with a lyric. I never knew what he was doing down there. You know a lyric couldn't possibly take three weeks." I should have realized at once our collaboration was doomed. Ira Gershwin is another of the sweat and stew club. When he was writing the lyric for "Embraceable You," he told me he got completely hung up on one line and finally, to escape the pressure, he took a room in a hotel where no one could find him. After a few days he finished the lyric. The missing line was: "Come to papa, Come to papa do."

One of the great joys of working with Fritz was his understanding of my own creative process and not once, no matter how long the lyric may have taken, was he ever anything but sympathetic and encouraging. In Paris, the longer I took the better he liked it. It meant that he was free until I was finished, and he could devote his creative energy to the chemin-de-fer table and other more basic sports—all of which he infinitely preferred to composing. As he would leave the hotel, if someone from the picture asked where I was, Fritz would always reply: "The poor little boy. I have knocked him up!"

By the end of April Fritz and I had finished our musical blueprint:

there were to be eight songs. By the beginning of July, five had been completed. The actual shooting was scheduled for the first of August, when "the little people of Paris" close up shop and depart for the beaches, mountains, and countryside that make France the most beautiful land in the world. For one month Paris is veritably empty, and therefore it is the ideal time to film. Of the remaining three songs, only one had to be finished by the time shooting began. Vincente and Arthur had decided that Gigi's apartment would be constructed at the studio, and therefore two of the songs were not needed until the company returned from Paris in mid-September.

The missing song was the most important in the film, the title song "Gigi." During the intervening three months Fritz and I had attempted it several times, without success. The melody Fritz eventually found, sometime in July, is one of the most rapturous he ever composed and it happened exactly in the way one always expects beauty to be born.

Paris was in full bloom. It was a clear, sunlit day, Sacre Coeur in the distance seemed like a creation of Turner against the soft blue sky, and I was sitting on the john. Fritz was at the piano in the living room, dressed in the Byronesque costume in which he always works—his baggy underwear. Suddenly an exquisite melody came wafting down the hall, causing me to drop my newspaper. "My God!", I yelled. "That's beautiful." Leaping from my perch with my trousers still clinging to my ankles, I made my way to the living room like a man on tiny stilts. "Play that again," I said. He did. I started to walk up and down with excitement and almost broke my jaw on the coffee table. Assuming that having fallen down I would get up, Fritz paid no mind and continued playing. Within an hour he had finished it—except for the last two lines. For once, the last two lines took the composer three days to write.

While I was in lyrical solitary confinement, Arthur and Vincente were making the necessary preparations to begin shooting. After much searching, Jacques Bergerac was cast to play the skating instructor who is having an affair with Gaston's mistress. Arrangements were made with the "petits functionaires" of the civil service to allow Vincente to film in the Bois de Boulogne. Although the French civil service does not run France, it does keep it running. During the fifties, before the reascendancy of de Gaulle, governments rose and governments fell with the swiftness of a soufflé—and with about as much substance; but the civil service remained above or beneath it all. Corrupt, but only slightly so, they kept the water flowing, the phones ringing, the trains running, and collected enough taxes to keep the country reasonably solvent. In France the latter is not an easy task because the French regard paying taxes as a character flaw. Hanging in the wardrobe of most French men is an outfit of rags known as tax clothes, which they wear whenever they are called before the collector to explain the difference between what they have paid and what they owe. It is also someone in the civil service from whom one rents a few acres of the Bois, which is accomplished not at a table but under it.

Also during this period "pre-recording" began. In a musical film all the songs are recorded with an orchestra before the filming begins, and an actor mouths to his own voice during the scene. In the case of *Gigi*, because it would have been impossible to orchestrate, pre-record, and be ready to shoot by August, the songs were pre-recorded with a piano only and the orchestrations were added in Hollywood after the filming had been completed. In order to achieve the proper balance, the actors were required to sing everything over again in Hollywood and synchronize each word frame by frame. In cinematic language this process is called "looping." The dialogue of all outdoor scenes in any film almost always has to be looped because of interfering noise. In Italy, they shoot everything, be it exterior or interior, without any sound at all and all the dialogue is added later.

(When the film of *My Fair Lady* was made, pre-recording became an immense problem for Rex. He called me on the phone one day, his voice rising as it does when he is upset, and said: "Alan! Do you know what they want me to do? They want me to stand up in front of a bloody microphone and sing like a bloody singer. I can't do that! I have to be on the stage. In make-up. With an audience. And frightened!" In the end they only pre-recorded the orchestra and he sang the songs during the scenes as they were being filmed.)

Fritz and I had arrived in Paris in mid-March with a first draft of the script, no songs and no cast, except for Maurice, no sets and no costumes. Four and a half months later a finished screenplay with six of the eight songs, a complete cast totally costumed went before the cameras. Not only went before the cameras, but with everyone exuberant and optimistic.

The night before the first day of shooting, Arthur gave a launching party upstairs at Maxim's. Everyone in the cast was handed his script for the first time. I could not help but notice that only Maurice took his and immediately found a quiet corner and began to read it. Everyone else put his script aside and continued with the festivities. The next morning the only actor who called to tell me how much he liked the script was Maurice Chevalier.

The first few days' shooting was in the renovated Palais de Glace. Filming begins at nine o'clock and those involved in the first scene of the day assemble at seven for costumes and make-up. At nine o'clock, Vincente began rehearsing the scene between Eva Gabor and Jacques Bergerac, as the assistant director decorated the hall with several dozen magnificently costumed skaters and patrons. But the cameras never turned. No filming began.

Unfortunately, no one had asked Jacques Bergerac if he knew

how to skate. Because no one had asked him if he could, Jacques never asked if he had to. If they had or he had, they would have discovered that the closest Bergerac had ever been to ice was opening the frigidaire. In motion pictures you can dub a voice, but not a pair of legs, so a contraption was devised to keep him from falling on his face, the scene was photographed from the navel up and a two-page scene was cut to a few lines. Such are the hazards of art.

The following day Fritz and I left Paris and headed for California to write "I'm Glad I'm Not Young Any More" and "The Night They Invented Champagne," the two songs to be filmed on the coast in September. On the way we stopped in London for a few hours to have lunch with Binkie Beaumont, to discuss the London production of *My Fair Lady* which was to open the following year. After lunch, I persuaded Fritz to allow me to make one stop on the way to the airport.

A few weeks earlier while we were in Paris, as I walked out of the hotel I saw the most extraordinary automobile I had ever beheld. I had never been, and am not now, a car buff, but this was something celestial. It was a convertible Rolls Royce. I had never seen one before and I later discovered it was the first of its kind Rolls had made. When we finished lunch with Binkie, we had about one hour to get to the airport to catch the plane. The stop I made was at the Rolls Royce showroom on Conduit Street. Rushing up to a tall, reserved, middle-aged salesman, I quickly asked him if he knew about that car I had seen in Paris. He did indeed know all about it. I said I wanted one. He said it would take a year to make. I told him that would be quite all right and could I please see the color chart. I immediately picked out a dark, royal blue with a beige hood. Fritz stared at me, dumbfounded. I was so enthusiastic I said to him: "You must get one, too." Fritz replied: "What for? I don't want one." To which I answered: "Maybe you don't now. But when I have one and you don't, you'll be sore as hell. Pick out a color!" By this time Fritz was as dazed as the salesman. He pointed to a battleship grey and I said to the salesman: "That's it. The grey one for Mr. Loewe and the blue one for me. We have no more time to discuss details. We have to catch a plane. Louis Dreyfus (the co-owner of Chappell Music, our publisher) will be in touch with you tomorrow to confirm the order." With that I grabbed Fritz by the arm, ran out of the showroom and off we went to the airport. The entire transaction had taken less than five minutes. When we arrived in California, I called Louis Dreyfus who thought the whole story was very amusing and said he would follow it up.

The story of the two Rolls Royces made the rounds and, as usual, became distorted. One day I picked up a newspaper where it was reported that we had bought two Rolls Royces in five minutes, and that when I reached for my checkbook, Fritz took out his and said: "I'll get this. You paid for lunch."!!

We later found out that the other salesmen in Conduit Street thought the man who had taken our order had suddenly gone crackers. Two wild Americans dashing in and buying two Rolls Royces in five minutes? It was a prank! When Louis Dreyfus confirmed the order, our salesman was promoted to manager.

The following May, two weeks after the opening of *My Fair Lady* at Drury Lane, the cars were ready for delivery. Fritz was not in London at the time, but I was. My plans were to proceed to Paris for a few weeks and then to Switzerland for the rest of the summer. Rolls suggested to me that I would be wise to hire a Rolls chauffeur to tend the car until it and I went to America.

A Rolls chauffeur, I was to discover, is not only thoroughly trained in the care and feeding of a Rolls, but also receives a special graduate course in snobbery. The chap assigned to me was named MacIntosh and he was an honor student in all departments. He was, without question, the most outrageous snob I have ever encountered. Sample: One day he told me that Prince

Philip had seen the car just before it was delivered to me and had expressed a desire to have one. I replied that if he wanted one, I was certain he would get one. "Why should he?" said MacIntosh. "After all, before he married the Queen what was he? Nothing but a penniless Greek."

A day or two after MacIntosh and I arrived in Paris, I had a date for lunch with Art Buchwald, who was then working on the *Paris Herald*. I was a moment or two late coming downstairs and I found Art standing outside admiring the car and discussing it with MacIntosh. He told me during lunch that he had asked MacIntosh if he might see the motor. "No," said MacIntosh, "you cannot." "Why not?" said Art. "Because," said MacIntosh, "if I raise the bonnet (hood to us) someone might think there was something wrong with the car." After lunch, Art and I got back into the car and I said to MacIntosh that Mr. Buchwald was most anxious to see the motor, that we both appreciated his strong feelings about raising the bonnet on a public street, and therefore, I suggested, we should go to a quiet spot in the Bois de Boulogne and while I stood guard, perhaps he would condescend to expose the engine. MacIntosh thought that was satisfactory and off we went to the Bois. We found a secluded spot and after I had cased the area and made certain there were no nurses with baby carriages in the vicinity, MacIntosh allowed Art to put his head in and look at the engine.

For the next two weeks, MacIntosh became one of Art's favorite companions. He even extracted permission from him to write an article on the subject of Rollsmanship, without mentioning, of course, MacIntosh's name. Before I left Paris, he and MacIntosh had a farewell chat and Art said: "MacIntosh. You and I have become pretty good friends, and I think you know you can trust me." "Oh yes, sir," said MacIntosh. "Then tell me something," said Art, "and I promise it will go no further. In your opinion is Mr.

Lerner worthy of a Rolls?" "Yes, indeed," said MacIntosh. "Why?" asked Art. "Because," replied MacIntosh, "he is so careless with it."

In Hollywood, Fritz and I began working on the two missing songs. After we had been there for two weeks, the dailies began to arrive from Paris and we had a chance to see the progress of the filming. Besides Bergerac's rubber legs, there had been one further disaster. It happened at Maxim's. Among the splendors of its decor is a tinted glass roof. Vincente had arranged for a boom to be brought into the restaurant which would give him the height to shoot down on to the dance floor. One afternoon he got a little carried away and he and the boom went "crashing through the ceiling." So I guess Fritz was right.

The dailies looked beautiful. The scenes in Maxim's were shot with all of Vicente's customary flare. He has a special fondness for rooms with mirrored walls and in Maxim's he had a field day. There was only one disturbing omission: there were no close-ups of Louis singing "She's Not Thinking of Me." And how can an audience know a song is being sung in someone's head if one cannot see the head? Facial expressions definitely demand a face. Without a close-up of Louis, all one heard was a disembodied voice which, for all anyone knew, could have been coming from the bandstand, and the whole scene made no sense at all. It was inconceivable that Vincente had overlooked it and we assumed the shots had simply not yet arrived. When Arthur returned, which he did about a week before the shooting in Paris was completed, we asked him about the missing close-ups. He was certain they had been made and were on their way. And so we waited patiently. But the next footage that arrived was only that of Leslie doing "Say a Prayer for Me Tonight."

When the song had been dropped in New Haven, I was not sad to see it go. I never liked it. Fritz did. I told him I thought it sounded like a cello solo. He said it did sound like a cello solo, but a very nice cello solo. It would never have found its way into *Gigi* except Fritz, that dirty dog, played it one night for Arthur and Vincente when I was not around, and the following morning I was outvoted three to one.

Vincente decided that Leslie was to sing it to her cat. Leslie did not have a cat, but after extensive auditions Vincente found one to his liking. I do not know the sex of the poor beast, but it was soft, sweet, and gentle. Gentle, that is, until Leslie picked it up to sing to it. Pussy took an instant dislike to her and the moment Leslie's hands touched it, it turned into the werewolf of Paris and began not only clawing at her face but, of much greater concern to Cecil, her dress. It was suggested they find another cat, but Vincente wanted that one and so onto the set came a bottle of phenobarbitol and poor pussy was drugged until it was a fur piece. When I heard about the incident I told Fritz it was not Leslie's fault, it was because of the song. The cat obviously had good taste. (It pains me to admit it, but I was wrong: it was one of the most touching moments in the film.)

At the end of the first week in September, filming had been completed in Paris and the members of the company were given eight days off for traveling and relocating themselves in California. They were all grateful for the time and disappeared. All but Maurice. The day after shooting closed down, he flew to California and bright and early the following morning he called Fritz and me to begin work on "I'm Glad I'm Not Young Any More." Naturally.

By mid-week all the dailies were in—but still no close-ups of Louis. It was bewildering. Somehow Vincente had forgotten to shoot them. Without them the scene in Maxim's was beautiful but pointless, and Arthur was left with but one choice. After the expense of five days' shooting in Maxim's, plus the cost of repairing the ceiling, Maxim's had to be rebuilt on the MGM lot to film Louis in close-up. But by the time the set was built and Vincente had finished shooting the scenes in Gigi's apartment, he had no more time to give *Gigi*. He was obligated to return to Paris to begin *The Reluctant Debutant* starring none other than Rex Harrison. It could not be postponed as Rex had to be finished in time to go into rehearsal with *My Fair Lady* in London—which is the sort of coincidence that may delight the Hindu mind but drives the Occidental out of his. To shoot the close-ups of Louis, Arthur called in Charles (Chuck) Walters, a well-known director of MGM musicals who had directed *Easter Parade* for him. Chuck filmed that scene and later on "The Night They Invented Champagne."

Because we were in Hollywood and had the luxury of time, both "Champagne" and "I'm Glad I'm Not Young Any More" were pre-recorded with orchestra. When Maurice did his, he asked me to come with him and sit in the control room. After the first take, I went out into the recording studio and congratulated him. I told him it was perfect. He said to me: "How was the accent?" I said: "I understood every word." Maurice said: "That's not what I mean. Was there enough?"

Leslie had recorded "The Parisians" and "Say a Prayer for Me Tonight" in Paris and joined Hermione and Louis in doing "Champagne" in Hollywood. Leslie is not only a superb dancer but a fine actress, and so it is not a criticism of her talent to say that her singing voice is not up to scratch, or, if you will, too much up to scratch. To put it bluntly, it was not a pretty noise. Unfortunately she did not hear it that way. In the land of the stars, the gift for auditory illusion is not uncommon. Some of the most discriminating and perceptive artists I know, Audrey Hepburn for example, can sit in a control room, listen to a sadly inadequate singing voice, and somewhere between the inner ear and the cortex convert it to Joan Sutherland. Leslie heard Edith Piaf. There was no question she had to be dubbed and Fritz and I mentioned it, somewhat vehemently I might add, to Arthur. Arthur was in complete agreement but like so many executives he was incapable of telling one of his stars something he or she did not wish to hear. André found a girl who sounded like Leslie and a recording date was made for her to dub the songs.

I was on the set the day before, talking to Leslie about something inconsequential, when she mentioned in passing that she would be busy all the following day recording. Mon Dieu! I thought. Arthur has not told her. Back I scurried to Arthur's office.

AJL: Arthur! Did you tell Leslie we're not going to use her voice?

FREED: I spoke to Oscar this morning. [Who cares?!]

AJL: Arthur, you've got to tell her. She's going to turn up at the studio tomorrow morning and it's going to be mayhem.

FREED: Don't worry. Are you going to the Gershwins tonight?

AJL: Would you like me to tell her?

FREED: Tell who?

AJL: Tell Leslie she's going to be dubbed.

FREED: I've bought the kids' play. [*The Bells Are Ringing* by Adolph Green and Betty Comden]

AJL: She's *got* to be told.

FREED: I'm going to use Judy. [Holliday]

AJL: What about Leslie?

FREED: She's not right for the part. How about some lunch?

WE exit from his office and pass his secretary.

FREED (*To Secretary*): I'm going to have lunch and then I'm going down to the set.

(*To AJL*): Somebody better tell Leslie she's not singing tomorrow.

Nobody told Leslie she was not singing tomorrow.
The following morning Marne Nixon, a talented singer with a

chameleon voice, appeared at the studio to begin recording under André Previn's supervision. Twenty minutes later Leslie Caron appeared at the studio to begin recording under André Previn's supervision. It fell upon André to tell Leslie the news. She was furious and doubly so because she had not been forewarned. She immediately called Arthur. There was no escaping it this time. Arthur had to tell her the painful truth.

Back went Leslie into the studio. She was there, she told André, to supervise the recording and to make certain that every line would be sung with her intention and her motivation. By mid-afternoon, Marne Nixon was on the verge of hysteria and André halted the session out of concern for her health. By the following day the worst was over, and at sundown Marne under Leslie's direction completed the dubbing.

"I'm surprised she took it so hard," said Arthur.

Many years later I wrote and produced *Paint Your Wagon* for Paramount. Jean Seberg was the leading lady and she was required to sing one song. She had a nice voice—almost good enough, but not quite. Remembering the incident with Leslie, I immediately went to her and told her she would have to be dubbed. She was unhappy, of course, but she understood. I was again working with André Previn, only this time we were collaborating. *Paint Your Wagon* was originally a play that Fritz and I had written in 1951. Additional songs were needed for the film, but Fritz, long retired, was unwilling to undertake them. With Fritz's approval, André agreed to do the few extra songs with me.

Who would sing for Jean Seberg was of special interest to him because it was one of his songs. One day he said to me: "You know, there's a girl I used to work with years ago named Rita Gordon. I have no idea where she is or what's happened to her, but as I remember, she sounded very much like Jean." "Let's try and find her," I said. André called around to no avail. He finally checked with the Screen Actors Guild who had an address for her, but no telephone number. André decided to send her a telegram asking her to get in touch with him. He picked up the phone, asked for Western Union and began to dictate his message. "I want to send a telegram," he said "to Rita Gordon." He gave the address. There was a long pause, then the girl at Western Union said: "I'm Rita Gordon." It was Rita Gordon. Unable to find work in her own field, she was now a Western Union operator. The following day she came in to see us: her voice was perfect. And Rita Gordon sang for Jean Seberg in *Paint Your Wagon*. Such are the miracles of art.

Gigi was finally finished in October and the next two months were spent orchestrating, recording, cutting, editing, putting in the titles, and all the other work that goes into the final print of a film. By the end of January (1958) it was ready for preview.

The first preview of any Hollywood film is called a "sneak" preview. I do not know how much the preview custom has changed in recent years, but at that time a theatre was selected in some small town within reasonable distance of Hollywood, preferably a theatre that was showing a film not too dissimilar to the picture being previewed. Quite obviously, an audience that arrives expecting to see "Godzilla" knocking over some miniature buildings is not the ideal audience to react to a film about the education of a young courtesan at the turn of the century.

Our preview took place in Santa Barbara before a substantially human audience. The heads of all the departments associated with the film were there, except Vincente who was in Paris, and the actors who had gone home. The picture was twenty minutes too long, the action was too slow, the music too creamy and ill-defined, and there must have been at least five minutes (in the theatre that can seem like five hours) of people walking up and down stairs. To Fritz and me it was a very far cry from all we had hoped for, far enough for us both to be desperate. As was the custom, the audience was asked to fill out cards in the lobby at the end of the film, which contained astute, psychologically disguised questions such as: What did you think of the film? How did you like Maurice Chevalier? Etcetera. The cards, on the whole, were quite good, which confounded Fritz and me, but did not change our opinion. We could tell that Arthur was as disappointed as we were. The ride home from Santa Barbara was not unlike the ride home from any funeral, and as I sat in the back of the car I suddenly realized for the first time the full implications of the demise of the motion picture studio.

In the halcyon days of Hollywood, stars were under long-term contracts. They were always there. If a picture were previewed and needed work, one could easily reassemble the cast and changes could be made. But with *Gigi* (and all pictures since) the cast was signed for a precise period of time. When that period of time expired, they departed to the four corners of the world to do other films. In other words, once the film was shown, changes could only be made in the laboratory—by the editor, the sound department, the music department, and all the others involved in the technical production. But no changes of dramatic substance were possible.

Fritz and I, following our usual habit whenever there was trouble, did very little talking that night, got a good night's sleep, arose early in the morning, ordered breakfast and four pots of coffee, opened up the cigarettes, and began the dual assault on our lungs and the problem. There was no doubt the pitter-patter of little feet running up and down stairs had to go. But we felt that some scenes not only needed cutting, but rewriting. There was no doubt that "I Remember It Well" did not come off at all and had to be reshot. There was no doubt in Fritz's mind that the orchestrations were far too lush and Hollywooden and did not have the sharp, brilliant tone of a smaller orchestra—something that sounded more like the theatre than motion pictures. The orchestrations could be done again. But what about the scenes? Where were the actors? Could they come back? Could we re-shoot? How much would it cost?

Over to MGM we went. We found Arthur trying to be optimistic, probably to keep our spirits up, but obviously as depressed as we were. There was little disagreement between us what had to be done. Arthur had even totted up the bill and the repairs came to $330,000, which was 10 percent of the budget. In no way did he believe the studio would cough up one more dime. But he made an appointment for all of us to meet with Benny Thau at noon.

Fritz and I went out for a walk to decide on some plan of action. We had no financial stake in the film: we had both been paid a salary. But we were determined that the picture not be released the way it was. We finally decided on a strategy.

CUT to Mr. Thau's Office.
CAST: Benny Thau, Arthur, Fritz, and AJL.

We read off the list of artistic ills and Arthur mentioned the figure required to cure them. Mr. Thau did not say no, but the way he did not say yes meant no. It was time for the pre-arranged strategy. Fritz and I spoke up—not in unison, of course, but in alternate sentences. We said: "Benny, we would like to buy 10 percent of *Gigi* for $300,000." Arthur was astounded. So was Benny. He thought for a long moment and finally made a decision. His decision was to call Mr. Joe Vogel in New York, the head of the company, and let him make the decision. Mr. Vogel said he would come to the coast to discuss the matter, but first he wished to see a preview himself.

While awaiting his arrival, fifteen minutes or so were cut and we had another preview with Mr. Vogel present. The picture was obviously better, but to Fritz and me still not good. But Mr. Vogel liked it, and everyone else was pleased with the improvements. Fritz and I were fearful that our little group was about to fall into one of those traps we knew so well from the theatre. When something is bad and gets better, one begins to think it is now good, when all it is is less bad.

The next day we met with Mr. Vogel and told him of our continuing concern and repeated our offer. He told us that it was against studio policy to allow outside financial participation and that, furthermore, he did not think any reshooting was necessary. The picture was good and it was to be released as it was. Fritz and I disagreed and asked if we could continue the discussion after lunch.

Out on to the MGM lot we went again. What to do? Finally, I asked Fritz if he were willing to gamble on a grand gesture. The key word here was gamble, something Fritz could never resist.

CUT to Mr. Vogel's office—after lunch.
CAST: Joe Vogel, Benny Thau, Arthur, Fritz, and AJL

"Joe," I said. "Fritz and I would like to buy the print of *Gigi* for $3 million." "I beg your pardon?" said Vogel. Fritz repeated it. "We would like to buy this, what-do-you-call-it? . . ." "Print," I said. "Yes," said Fritz. "This print for $3 million."

Vogel, Thau, and Arthur turned to stone. During this petrified silence I think it only fair to mention that Fritz and I did not have $3 million, did not know where we would get three million dollars, and if Joe Vogel agreed, had no idea what in God's name we were going to do. When Vogel at last spoke up, he asked if he, Mr. Thau, and Arthur could be excused for a few moments to confer. Fritz and I graciously agreed and exited.

CUT to men's room.
FRITZ: (At the washstand, following nervous relief) Dear boy, where the fuck are we going to get $3 million?

AJL: We don't know. Don't you remember?

FRITZ: Don't remind me.

AJL: What about Bill Paley?

FRITZ: Bill Paley?! Put $3 million in a picture which isn't very good? My boy, he's not an idiot. Who would make such an offer?

AJL: *We* just did.

FRITZ: That's because we don't have $3 million. Bill Paley has. That's a big difference.

Washing up continues in troubled silence.

CUT to Mr. Vogel's office—five minutes later.

(Same cast)

Joe Vogel spoke immediately. I do not remember his actual words, but I do remember the essence of what he said and it was this: he was deeply impressed by our sincerity and faith in the film. He was also deeply impressed with the success of *My Fair Lady*. And if we both felt as strongly as we did, the studio had no alternative but to put up the necessary $300,000.

CUT to Men's room—for further relief.

Fade out.

Maurice was in Paris. Hermione was in New York. Leslie was in London. And Louis, Arthur, Fritz, and I were in California. Maurice and Hermione returned and "I Remember It Well" was reshot by Chuck Walters against a rather badly painted sunset drop, which did not matter at all and which proved again that the close-up, not scenery, is motion pictures' greatest individual contribution to the dramatic arts.

Two key scenes in Gigi's house, which involved Hermione, Louis, and Leslie were rewritten, sharpened, and trimmed, and when Leslie arrived from London Chuck Walters reshot them.

Fritz went over all the orchestrations with André from the lion's roar at the very beginning to the final frame before "The End." André was in total agreement with Fritz's concept of a small orchestra, and the entire film was re-orchestrated.

The picture was gone over inch by inch in the projection room and every unnecessary line or visual effect was deleted: and the ice-skating scene in the Palais de Glace was vastly improved by finding other angles that had not been used. For that kind of painstaking work I have never known anyone with better judgment or a more unerring eye than Arthur Freed. It was here that he was at his most creative and most positive.

Several weeks later the picture was ready to be previewed again. It was a memorable evening. By the grace of God, all the steps we had taken had been in the right direction. The reaction of the audience dramatically changed from appreciation to affection. The studio still passed out those demented cards in the lobby, but it was not necessary to read them. We had all been a part of their spontaneous involvement. We had seen them with tears in their eyes at the moment there should have been tears in their eyes. And we had heard their applause at the end.

Being relative neophytes, Fritz and I had no idea what the universal reaction would be. All we could say to each other was that it was at long last *Gigi*.

Gigi opened in New York in the spring of 1958. It had been decided to treat it more as a theatrical event than a motion picture. Consequently it did not open in a motion picture theatre but a theatre theatre, the Royale, with reserved seats only.

I was not present: I was in London preparing for the opening of *My Fair Lady* at Drury Lane. The first review I saw was published two days before the film opened. It was in *Time* magazine and it was dreadful. Fritz was in New York, still in an oxygen tent, and when I read it I wished I were there with him. Fortunately it was the last bad review the film received. The New York press embraced it warmly and *Gigi* began its long and happy life.

From the late winter to the early spring of every year, it is award time in the motion picture industry. Among the most prominent are the Screenwriters Guild, which gives an award for the best dramatic screenplay, the best comedy, and the best musical screenplay; the Directors Guild which gives an award for the best direction; the Foreign Press Association which gives a series of awards (known as the Golden Globe because it is a golden globe) for excellence in almost every branch of motion picture production; and in New York, the New York Film Critics vote on the best film, the best acting, and the best direction.

Finally, with the first blush of spring, the voice of the Oscar is heard in the land.

Officially its donor is the Motion Picture Academy, and it is the most widely known of any accolade bestowed in any country upon any branch of the performing arts. Besides the artistic recognition, the fame of the Academy Award is such that it has been estimated it adds a minimum of $1 million to the gross revenue of the winning film.

The Oscar season begins about six to eight weeks before the fateful night with the announcement of the nominations. The announcement is immediately followed by a series of advertisements that appear in the two Hollywood trade papers, *Daily Variety* and the *Hollywood Reports*, in which the studios of each nominee or nominees congratulate him or them. This is followed by another series of advertisements in which the producers of the various films congratulate the actors, directors, creators, and technicians who have been nominated. Following that comes another set of advertisements in which the nominated actors, directors, creators, and technicians thank the studios for the opportunities they have been given. In the final series, the various recording companies who have released the soundtrack albums and the music publishers congratulate the composers who have been nominated—and the composers and lyric writers then thank the studios and the producers. Simultaneously with the well-advertised congratulations and gratitude, the Directors Guild, which has its own theatre, shows on successive nights every film that has figured in any of the various nominations. Press agents work overtime, scheduling interviews with the newspapers for their nominated clients and arranging personal appearances on radio and television. Behind the scenes, friends of nominees call other friends to solicit their votes, and each studio which has any-one nominated lets it be known that it expects every man on the lot to do his duty.

Despite all this huckstering, the ballot is a secret one and no one knows who votes for whom, much less who is the winner. When the envelopes, sealed by the accounting firm of Price Water-house, are opened on Academy Award Night, there is no one con-nected with the motion picture industry who knows the names contained therein.

It is bromidically simple to be cynical about all the shenan-igans leading up to the awards—if one is not among those com-peting. But for those who have been nominated, cynicism is only a form of self-protection that wears thinner and thinner as The Big Night approaches, and disappears completely when the hour arrives and one enters the arena.

The nominations for the Best Picture of 1958 that were announced in the closing days of winter 1959 were *Cat on a Hot Tin Roof, Auntie Mame, The Defiant Ones, Separate Tables,* and *Gigi.* Besides the nomination for Best Picture, *Gigi* also was nominated in eight other categories: for Direction, Costume Design, Editing, Scoring, Best Song, "Gigi," and Best Screenplay and Best Sound. Oddly enough, not one actor was nominated.

On the night of April 6, the Academy Awards took place at the RKO Pantages Theatre. During the day all the nominees were assembled at the theatre and given minute instructions about how to reach the stage, where the microphone would be placed and on which side of the stage to exit. We then all returned to our respective dwellings to slip into the black tie and shimmering gown. Fritz and I were staying at the Beverly Hills Hotel and there is no sense in pretending that I was not excited. I was. Fritz, however, because of his recent coronary, was determined to stay calm and somehow he managed to do so, assisted either by something given him by his doctor or something given him by the bartender.

We returned to the theatre at the appointed hour. The streets were lined with fans, the Klieg lights were shining from across the street, and for all the world it could have been one of those famous Hollywood openings about which one used to read in the twenties and thirties. The ceremony was being televised by NBC and inside the theatre its cameras lined the walls. We made our way to our seats, which happened to be in the second row. To my great delight, André was sitting on the other side of me. Finally the lights dimmed, the overture began, and I started preparing myself to be a good loser. Fritz had decided to be a very old and wise man that night and said very little, but at the last moment he, André and I quietly wished each other good luck.

After the usual fanfare, the speeches of welcome by the master of ceremonies and the president of the Academy, and the expected monologue by a comedian, the evening settled down to business. One by one the envelopes were opened, and in the categories for which *Gigi* had been nominated, one by one the winner was *Gigi*. After the first three, one can feel a sweep in the making and despite all my efforts to remain detached and pessimistic, I could feel my metabolism begin to change, my hands grow colder and the rest of my body warmer.

It has always been the custom for every winner to thank everyone from the head of the studio to his uncle Julius in Pittsburgh. I made up my mind that if I were included in the landslide the best way I could thank the Academy was to spare them that endless list, say my thank you in one sentence and get off. When my name came up for the Best Screenplay (based on material from another medium, as opposed to Best Original Screenplay), I did just that. A few moments later when *Gigi* was announced for the Best Song, back I went and simply added an "again" to whatever I had said before. I could have taken more time, however, because Fritz, still playing old and wise, came up the steps very, very slowly, and when I heard what he said I could have crowned him with the Oscar. Said Fritz, after a long historic pause: "I want to thank you all from the bottom of my somewhat damaged heart."

We had been told to exit stage right, meaning audience left, and I had done so a few minutes earlier. I was so rattled by his acceptance speech, however, that I began to exit in the wrong direction and had to be pulled back and re-aimed. Fortunately, the prickle left my skin when Vincente won for best direction and my teeth stopped aching when I heard the name *Gigi* announced for the Best Picture. As if nine Academy Awards were not enough, Maurice Chevalier was given a Special Award for all the joy he had brought to the screen during his lifetime. *Gigi* won ten Oscars, the largest number ever received by any film in the thirty-one years of Academy Award History.

It was also the first time in the thirty-one years of Academy Award history that the singer (Tony Martin) chosen to sing the winning song forgot the lyrics. To the vast viewing audience, the second half of the best lyric of the year went: "Gigi, la-la-la-la-do-do-do-do, la-la-la la-do-do-do-do, la-la-la-la, Oh Gigi, la-la-la" etc.

It was very avant garde.

By 1958 the war babies were barely reaching the age of puberty, and the days of instant art and the broken eardrum had still not descended upon the land. Melody and the English language had not yet been outlawed and a cast album could still find favor in the public marketplace. The soundtrack of *Gigi* soon rose to number one and remained among the top three best-selling albums for over a year. Its total sale to date is somewhere north of two million albums. The title song survived the adolescent, gorilla warfare of rock and roll and remains to this day among the fifty most played songs in the world. It is worth noting, incidentally, that a goodly number of the permanent members of that honored list are not, as one might expect, of recent vintage, but were written by such composers as Gershwin, Rodgers, Berlin, and Porter.

As for the financial fate of the film itself, it cost a little over $3 million to make and as of this writing has returned to the studio something in the vicinity of $16 million. But before one leans against the wall to keep one's balance as the vision of a $13 million profit swims before the eyes, allow me quickly to correct this altogether reasonable assumption.

A finished film is called "the negative." Why it is called the negative I do not know. It is obviously not a negative, but a developed print. However, we humans seem to enjoy the dim view. We prefer to "descend" from the ape rather than "ascend." The cost of the negative is multiplied by 250 percent to cover the costs of advertising, prints, and distribution, and this figure becomes the official studio cost of the film. In other words if the negative of *Gigi* cost $3 million it would be multiplied by 2.5 and the studio would record *Gigi* in its books as costing $7.5 million.

How, you may ask, does the studio arrive at this fascinating figure? After all, no matter how much the film may have cost, the advertising rates are stable: so much per line; so much per half page or full page. The factory that manufactures duplicates of the negative charges the same per foot if there are two people on the film or two hundred thousand.

And what exactly are distribution costs? Well, let us say a motion picture company has an office in Chicago, whose business it is to supervize the advertising of the picture in that area and keep a watchful eye on the way it is presented in the local theatres. The people in the office must be paid. The landlord will insist upon his rent. The telephone company will not permit the use of its services without remuneration. All of that is part of the cost of distribution in the Chicago area. All well and good, yes? Ah, but suppose the film company has five films to be distributed in the Chicago area. Is the cost of the office divided by five, with each film donating a fifth? No, no, no, no. The cost is *multiplied* by five because each film is charged with the entire cost of the office. Well then, you say, where goeth the extra four salaries, four rents, etcetera? Into whose pocket do they fall? The answer to that and all other baffling questions concerning advertising, printing distribution can only be found in the I Ching Division of the motion picture company's accounting department. I say the answers *can* be found, not that they *will* be found. The accounting departments of motion picture companies are the moors of high finance, the quicksand of profit.

The purpose, however, is simplistically clear. It is to reduce the profit—on paper, that is—thereby trimming the taxes and reducing to the shadiest possible minimum the money that is owed to those who have percentage of the film. In the case of *Gigi,* Arthur had a percentage.

Today, every star, well-known director, and frequently the author of the book or play on which the film is based, have participating interests. So one can see the incalculable benefit it is to a motion picture company to have a well-trained corps of bandits in the bookkeeping department. Warner Brothers, for instance, purchased the film rights to *Camelot* and Fritz and I own a percentage of the profits. The financial statement included the usual fee for prints, advertising, and distribution, but because there was still a possibility the film might somehow emerge from the red, there appeared on the statement of the cost of the negative an additional item. It said: Miscellaneous—$2 million. The studio adds 25 percent to the cost of each film for the use of its facilities. So the $2 million became $2.5 million. When it was multiplied by 2.5 it became $6.25 million. Ergo, no profits for Fritz and Alan.

Ah, Willie Sutton! Ah, Bernie Cornfield! Had you only known that there is a place in this world where your genius would be appreciated! Where your unique gifts could thrive with complete immunity—in the bright sunlight of respectability—without fear of penalty, punishment, or prison!

Arthur Freed produced one more musical, *The Bells Are Ringing.* Closing his eyes to the crumbling reality around him, he continued planning and dreaming as some men must. But time and change are invincible foes. Metro-Goldwyn-Mayer, the home of the stars and the fountainhead of screen musicals, passed to different management who auctioned off every costume, portable artifact, and memento, and within a few years all that remained of its once royal past was the roar of the celluloid lion, occasionally heard on a film made for television or one whose destiny it would be.

MGM was not alone. The legendary Hollywood studio slipped into history. The backlot of Twentieth Century Fox became a housing development for high rise office buildings. RKO was sold to Lucille Ball and Desi Arnaz for television production. All the great sound stages, recording studios, and scenic facilities of all the studios were ignominiously reduced to the mass manufacture of living room entertainment. Even the Hollywood gossip columnist died from malnutrition.

For so many years the most derogatory critical epithet that could be hurled at a film was to call it "Hollywood." It still happens, but to do so today is like joining a protest march against Pompeii.

I entered the Hollywood scene shortly before its demise, but I saw enough to make me wish it were still there. I wish there still were talent scouts combing the country in search of a pretty face or a handsome profile to bring to Hollywood, train and educate, give continuity to a career until one day a new name might appear above the title of a film. I cannot find it in my heart to despise glamor. I cannot forget a day when I was having lunch with Arthur Freed in the vast MGM commissary. It was filled with cowboys, Roman soldiers, ladies in hoop skirts, and technicians from all departments. Arthur's table was against the farthest wall and I was sitting with my back to the distant door. Suddenly, for a reason I cannot explain or identify, an impulse compelled me to turn around and look toward the entrance. Clark Gable had just walked in.

Arthur died in the spring of 1973. It was a small funeral. Not many of the old unit were there. He had wanted desperately to produce the film version of *My Fair Lady,* but the studio, or what was left of it, was in no position to undertake it. There is no doubt in my mind it would have been a far better film had it been an Arthur Freed production.

Camelot

By the summer of 1958 Fritz had been released from the hospital and was allowed to resume his normal life—in moderation. So off he went to the French Riviera where he spent the summer doing a little less of everything he had always done. By October, he, Moss, and I were once again in New York.

One Sunday, while reading through the book section of the *New York Times,* I came across a glowing review of a book about King Arthur and the Round Table called *The Once and Future King* by T. H. White. It looked interesting, but I did not make a mental note to buy it. The following morning, Bud Widney, our production manager, came into my office and placed the review on my desk. "Lerner," he said, "here's your next show."

When I describe Bud as "production manager," it is like calling a bottle of Dom Perignon a cold drink. We had met in Los Angeles in 1951 shortly after his graduation from UCLA, where he had majored in drama and had begun directing local productions. As occasionally happens in life, we began as old friends. Fritz and I were about to go into rehearsal with *Paint Your Wagon,* and I suggested to Bud that if he really intended to make the theatre his career, the place to be was New York and the way to start was as assistant stage manager on *Paint Your Wagon.* He agreed instantly and we have been working together continuously from that day until the present. Not only is he now a professional and skilled director, but his knowledge and experience in the "steak and potatoes" of putting together a musical production is as thorough as anyone I know.

But over and above that, he has been invaluable to me when I am writing. Most writers, when in the process of creating, find that if they discuss what they are doing with anyone, their ideas are dissipated by exposure. However, because I am used to collaboration, I am also accustomed to talking things out, provided there is someone with whom I feel that compatible. I always felt it with Fritz, later with Moss, and always with Bud. He has always understood me well enough to know what I have been searching for, and the kind of theatre I am trying to create. He also has no inhibitions about criticizing me, and that alone makes him indispensable.

In this success-blinded country, anyone who carves out a small measure of it is apt to be regarded as all-wise and omniscient. It is especially true if success brings with it a respectable amount of coin of the realm. It is only since the forties, when hit plays began running for years and there were countless road companies and productions abroad, that authors began entering the higher income brackets. It is not a coincidence that, simultaneously, their status radically rose in the eyes of the public. A long accepted national axiom has been that money equals wisdom. Never mind that some of the most narrow-minded idiots I have ever encountered are successful businessmen. To the rest of their fellow men a millionaire is a genius. A misanthropic millionaire is called eccentric. An inventor is only crazy until his invention becomes a household essential. (In America invention is the mother of necessity.) It so happens that as it is possible to have a talent for playing the tuba and nothing else, it is also possible to have a talent for making money and nothing else.

In the theatre, fame and fortune can become artistic hazards and I have always feared that in the preparation of a play those associated with me will forget that I am as apprehensive and as uncertain as I ever was and not tell me the truth. Bud Widney has always been my most reliable iconoclast.

When he told me this was my next show, I immediately sent out for a copy. Before it arrived, Moss rang up and asked me if I had happened to read a review in the *Sunday Times* of *The Once and Future King.* He said he thought it sounded like a possible project. So I sent out for a copy for him. A little later in the day, Fritz popped in and I read him the review. "You must be crazy," he said. "That king was a cuckold. Who the hell cares about a cuckold?" I answered that people had been caring about Arthur for over a thousand years. "Well," said he, with a hopeless sigh, "that's only because you Americans and English are such children."

It must be remembered that Fritz is Viennese and in Europe, especially in France and Vienna, a cuckold is a figure of fun and a play about one is invariably a comedy: while a play about a woman whose husband strays is the stuff of drama. In England and America it is the reverse. A play about an unfaithful wife is a tragedy and one about an unfaithful husband is a comedy. But then again, it must be remembered that in America virility is so touchy a subject that it even invades the court, and we have a monstrous piece of absurdity called "the unwritten law," to wit: if a man's wife is unfaithful and in a fit of pique he shoots the lover, not only will he evoke the sympathy of the jury but, by the unwritten law, he will receive a very light sentence. What makes it so absurd is that if the husband feels compelled to shoot someone—which is uncivilized in the first place—he ought to shoot the wife. After all, she had to say "yes." How ludicrous the last act of *Carmen* would be if Don José stabbed the bull-fighter instead of Carmen! It would reduce passion to adolescent jealousy.

In spite of his strong feelings Fritz agreed to read the book and so I ordered a third copy. Moss and I fell in love with it. Fritz could not even finish it, but he was swept along by our enthusiasm and after much persuasion agreed to do it. When the doctor had given him permission to work again, he had said to me: "My boy, I'll try it one more time. But if it's too tough or if I start to worry so much I can't work the way I want to, the next will be my last."

The first decision Fritz, Moss, and I had to make was which producer we should approach. After careful consideration, we opted for greed and decided to produce it ourselves. The next step, of course, was a phone call to Irving Cohen to acquire the rights. Tim White was alive and in robust health. There were no banks and no estates with which to contend and we were certain it would only be a question of negotiating with White's representative. How wrong we were!

The Once and Future King is actually four books published in one volume. The first book deals with the boyhood of King Arthur and it is called *The Sword and the Stone*. Tim White had published *The Sword and the Stone* many years earlier and Walt Disney had purchased the rights for an animated film. Although he had not made the film, he still owned those rights. Irving wrote to the Disney Studios to inquire if Disney would be interested in a sale. We heard nothing for a month, then a letter came back with a very polite, but very definite "no." By this time, however, Fritz, Moss and I had come to the conclusion that the story we wished to tell did not require the dramatization of Arthur's boyhood, and therefore we did not need it. So Irving proceeded to make the necessary arrangements with White giving us the rights to the remaining three books of the quartet.

The question of cuckoldry that so concerned Fritz was not without merit. I remembered in *Gigi* we were so concerned about Gaston and the skating instructor that we wrote "She's Not Thinking of Me." Lancelot's love affair with Guinevere was invented by the French four hundred years after the fact, if fact can be applied to Arthur at all. It was somewhere in the twelfth century, for reasons now lost in time, that the cuckholded husband became a standard prop in popular French literature. Still, no one, not even T. H. White, decisively explains why Arthur countenanced it. As I began thinking about the dramatization of this monumental tale, it seemed to me that the play demanded, almost depended upon, finding a reason, and that once found it had to be the turning point in the drama.

All the great love stories that have endured through the ages have ended tragically. Arthur is the only tragic hero to survive the indignity of a faithless wife. But the legend of King Arthur is far more than a mere love story. I believe it is the idealism expressed in the concept of the Round Table that accounts for the indestructability of the Arthurean legend. Stripped of its tales of derring-do, its magic, love potions, and medieval trimmings and trappings, there lies buried in its heart the aspirations of mankind, and if Arthur lived at all, he was a light in the Dark Ages. If Arthur is pure fantasy, it is even more significant. To me, the greatest contribution of Jesus Christ is contained in three words, the "Brotherhood of Man." Arthur is more related to that dream than to the monarchial pageantry of English history. Even the many versions of his death include one that faintly echoes Isaiah's ancient prophecy of the coming of a Messiah. It was the Welsh who created the belief that Arthur and his knights did not die, but lie asleep in a cave in Avalon and will once again awaken when the world is ready for a Round Table.

All of this may seem far removed from the light entertainment of a musical play. It is not. It is the hidden guide, the silent voice that is heard when creative decisions are made.

The cuckoldry issue dictated the kind of situation, music, and lyrics required to introduce Arthur and Guinevere. What was needed was an all-pervasive innocence in order to make Arthur so ingenuously charming that one would fall in love with him, forgive him anything, and follow him everywhere, even over the hot coals of tolerating his wife's infidelity. Innocence was no less essential for Guinevere, to present her in the most appealing light and, one hoped, to explain her future transgression. Fortunately, there is no composer in the modern theatre with the gift of pure classic melody comparable to Fritz's. One would have to reach all the way back to Jerome Kern to find anyone who lived in the same neighborhood. So Arthur's first number became "I Wonder What the King Is Doing Tonight" which shows him shy and frightened at meeting his bride. It is immediately followed by the entrance of Guinevere and "Where Are the Simple Joys of Maidenhood" which reveals the bloodthirsty, romantic yearnings of an adolescent girl longing for knights in armor to woo her with feats of heroism. Arthur's second song in the same scene is the title song, "Camelot," pure romantic whimsy. The contrast in the lyric and melody between Guinevere's first song and her last song, "I Loved You Once in Silence," is striking. The music is more sophisticated, more harmonically complex, and the lyric a sad reflection of a woman whom guilt and grief has aged. We intentionally wrote it "unpassionate." I have always thought that song is one of Fritz's most haunting creations. Almost Schubertian. To present Lancelot, Fritz very rightly felt the melody should have a strong, French feeling, which it does, and the lyric, "C'est Moi," is an almost comical exaggeration of his overblown dedication to righteousness, chivalry, and chastity. As the Round Table progresses from idealism to decay, the music also journeys from innocence to sophistication, and the beginning and end of the journey are clearly signposted by "The Lusty Month of May" in the first act and "Guinevere" in the second. The one detour in the second act is when Arthur and Guinevere wistfully wonder "What Do the Simple Folk Do?" as they try to relieve their heavy burdens.

By the middle of the first act, Guinevere has met Lancelot and has begun behaving in a manner that is to Arthur both perplexing and maddening. Alone on stage, he musically soliloquizes his confusion and out of desperation resolves it for himself in an uncomplicated reaffirmation of love in a song called "How to Handle a Woman." I had had that idea for two or three years, but I cannot claim sole inspiration for it. My silent partner was Erich Maria Remarque.

He had just married an old friend of mine, Paulette Goddard, all woman, magnificently distributed, as feminine as she is female. One night when we were having dinner, I said to Erich (not seriously): "How do you get along with this wild woman?" He replied: "Beautifully. There is never an agrument." "Never an argument?" I asked incredulously. "Never," he replied. "We will have an appointment one evening, and she charges into the room crying, "Why aren't you ready? You always keep me waiting. Why do you . . . ?!" I look at her with astonishment and say, "Paulette! Who did your hair? It's absolutely ravishing." She says, "Really? Do you really like it?" "Like it?" I reply. "You're a vision. Let me see the back." By the time she has made a pirouette her fury is forgotten. Another time she turns on me in rage about something, and before a sentence is out of her mouth I stare at her and say breathlessly, "My God! You're incredible. You get younger every day." She says, "Really, darling?" "Tonight," I say, "you look eighteen years old." And that is the end of her rage." I was as amused as I was admiring and I said to him: "Erich, one day I will have to write a song about that." The song was "How to Handle a Woman" which ends:

The way to handle a woman is to love her,
Simply love her; merely love her,
Love her, love her.

The first person we thought of for the play was Julie who was still doing *My Fair Lady* in London. We spoke to her about it and she loved the idea. Julie was then married to Tony Walton. She had been in love with him long before *My Fair Lady*. During the early months of the production he was still in England and they communicated by tape recordings. While we were in New Haven and Philadelphia she was forever in her room with her little machine. The day after we opened in Philadelphia she became so involved describing what had transpired the night before that she forgot to read the reviews.

Not long after she agreed to play Guinevere she appeared by chance on a television program in London with T. H. White. White lived an ascetic existence on the island of Alderney. Julie and Tony fell so much in love with him that they bought a little house near his on the island. By the time the rehearsals of *Camelot* began I think Julie was more familiar with *The Once and Future King* than was I.

To play King Arthur, Moss suggested Richard Burton. Moss had written a screen play several years earlier in which Richard had starred and he knew him well. Richard was still in his early thirties but his theatrical experience belied his years. His family name was Jenkins and he came from a large coal mining family in Wales. While still in his teens his inexplicable talent came to the attention of Philip Burton, a theatrical coach in London. Philip undertook the responsibility of Richard's education and training and in return Richard took Philip's name. In his early twenties he joined the Old Vic and at the age of twenty-three became the youngest Hamlet in its history. When he was twenty-five he made his debut on Broadway in *The Lady's Not for Burning*. A few years later he starred with Helen Hayes in Anouilh's *Time Remembered*. Between his career in London and frequent visits to Hollywood he had not suffered from inactivity. He was married at the time to a lovely lady, Sybil—as the world was soon to know—and they had two children. I happened to have heard him sing. One night at the Gershwins he and Sybil did some charming Welsh folk songs together. But even if I had not, we would not have been concerned about his voice. Not only is his speaking voice one of the rare instruments in the contemporary theatre but he is Welsh; and at birth when a Welshman is slapped on the behind, he does not cry, he sings "Men of Harlech" in perfect pitch.

Richard was in California when Moss called him. Some time later we had a meeting and Richard expressed genuine interest, promised to think about it, thought about it, and eventually agreed to play the part for one year. (Contracts are always based on the naive hope that the play will be a success. If the play is a failure and closes in two weeks, quite obviously an actor who has signed for a year does not continue playing the part in his bedroom until the year is up.)

Robert Coote, the master of bumble and blimp, was obviously ideal for Pellinore, the King who had lost his kingdom and could not find it again. We reached him in London where he was still playing Pickering. Coote maintained a rigid regime which included fresh air in the afternoon followed by a lie-down, as he referred to it, before the performance, so we called him in the late afternoon. Moss and I were both on the phone. "Cooter," one of us said "did you ever hear of a book called *The Once and Future King?*" "Got it by my bedside," said Coote. "My favorite book. Want me to play Pellinore?" "Yes," we said. "Love it," came the reply. "Absolutely love it. All that rusty armor. Couldn't be better." And that was that.

Not too much time was spent discussing who would play Mordred, the evil, bastard son of King Arthur, because two weeks after it had become known we were doing *Camelot*, Roddy McDowall telephoned Moss and insisted upon playing the part.

We told him that, of course, he would be marvellous, but Mordred did not appear until the second act and it was not the kind of star part befitting a man of his stature—and salary. Roddy said he did not care, that he would make every concession he could, but he *must* play the part. And he did. And by skill and the sheer weight of his personality, he made it a star part.

The theatre, as I previously mentioned, creates instant friendships that occasionally continue past the life of the play. So it was with Roddy and me, and for many years we saw a good deal of each other. Unfortunately, it is also idiosyncratic of our profession that because of commitments, it often becomes a long time between drinks. After *Camelot*, however, there was a period when both of us were in California. Roddy was doing a film and I was writing the musical about parapsychology and reincarnation, *On a Clear Day You Can See Forever* and it involved hypnosis. One night Roddy took me to see an extraordinary hypnotist called Pat Collins (female). She did an act—and still does—in which she brought ten or twelve people to the stage, hypnotized them and had them perform some amazingly funny stunts. Roddy had gone to see her privately to see if hypnosis could cure his fear of flying. He had been in the middle of a film and had to fly to New York for twenty-four hours, return, and continue shooting. By post-hypnotic suggestion she not only cured his uneasiness about the air but enabled him to make the trip without fatigue.

It occasionally happens that when trance has been induced by a particular hypnotist, if someone is unusually susceptible he can be hypnotized again unintentionally. While Roddy and I were sitting at the table having a drink and Miss Collins was hypnotizing her little group on stage, Roddy went right under with them. I had to interrupt Miss Collins to bring Roddy out of his trance otherwise he would have done everything at the table that was occurring on stage.

Two or three days later I invited Miss Collins to lunch at the Beverly Hills Hotel to discuss hypnosis and I also invited Roddy. The sound of her voice ordering lunch put him under again and again she had to bring him out of it. Throughout the rest of the meal Miss Collins and I had our discussion in whispers in order to keep Roddy's head out of his Caesar salad.

By mid-winter the only part left to fill was the all-important role of Lancelot. He was French and the best place to look for a Frenchman is France. They seldom leave it. With few exceptions the French do not like to travel because they find all other countries inferior, especially at meal time. I have a dear friend named Charles Gombault who for many years was the editor of the newspaper, *France-Soir*. Shortly after Israel established her independence and before many outsiders had been there, Charles went on behalf of the newspaper. When he returned, I said to him eagerly: "Tell me about it. How was it?" He replied: "The food was terrible."

There is, however, one major obstacle in searching through France for an actor who can speak English and has a large baritone voice, and that is there is none: with the exception of Yves Montand, of course, who is one of the best singing actors alive. Unfortunately, neither in character nor size was it a role that would have enticed him.

Therefore, we began to audition Lancelots in New York. Around that time the English motion picture, *Room at the Top*, opened and Laurence Harvey became a star. He arrived in New York to publicize the film and immediately called us. To our astonishment he said he wanted to play Lancelot. Moss knew him. I knew him slightly. We met with him and naturally we were all intrigued. But, we told him, he would simply have to sing for us. Larry said he would be delighted to do so. He warmed up for a few days with the assistance of Kitty Hart and finally he came to the theatre to do his stuff. He did indeed have a voice, but surprisingly enough he was a basso profoundo, not at all like his speaking voice. The problem with a bass voice is that it must be a trained and developed one in order to project at all, and Larry's, good as it was, was certainly not that. After listening to him, we explained the situation and he understood. But he was still determined. He asked us if we knew a good singing coach in England. We did and gave him the name. He said he intended to return to England after his press tour and would work on his voice for the next few months. If, by the spring, we had not found anyone in America, would we then come to England and hear him again? We agreed. So off he went to England where, upon arriving, for reasons I will never know, he announced to the press he was going to play Lancelot in *Camelot*.

We auditioned all through the winter and found no one. On the very last day of the auditions as we were about to leave the theatre, a young man suddenly appeared on the stage in blue jeans. (Unfamiliar garb at that time.) He was from Canada, had been in Bermuda and was on his way back to Toronto, but had stopped off in New York to audition. He had lost his luggage en route. He came on stage and Moss and I paused at the end of the aisle. Fritz was coming up the other aisle and also stopped. The young man began to sing and the three of us quietly returned to our seats. When he finished the first number, Fritz asked him to sing another, which he did. He then launched into a speech or two from Shakespeare, and one hour later Robert Goulet was signed to play Lancelot. Because of his name we thought he was a French Canadian and although he had no accent it was not implausible for us to believe he could assume one. We found out later that he was from Lawrence, Massachusetts, had only gone to Canada to work and spoke the barest smattering of French. But it did not matter. He had a superb baritone voice, was undeniably handsome, and he looked like Lancelot.

A month after we announced that Robert Goulet had been signed, I received a letter from England from a gentleman named

Lloyd, who identified himself as Laurence Harvey's business manager. It was a very polite note, one of those "enclosed please find. . . ." What I was supposed to be pleased to find enclosed was a bill for eight pounds for Mr. Harvey's singing lessons. After Moss, Fritz, and I had a good laugh, I answered Mr. Lloyd saying that he seemed to have a misconception about the function of our office. We did indeed do a certain amount of charity, but we had no actual program for student training and I suggested he get in touch with the Ford Foundation who did that sort of thing rather extensively. Some days later my letter was sent back with a message scrawled across it in large, red letters. It was from Larry. He said he was returning my letter as he was certain I would wish to keep it for my memoirs because it was so (underlined) witty (underlined), exclamation point.

Well, thought I, that is the last I will see of dear Larry. Not at all. A few months later I ran into him at an auction at the Parke Bernet Galleries in New York. I did not have to wait cautiously too long to see how he would behave because the moment he saw me he crossed the room, threw his arms around me, and we embraced like long lost friends.

The theatre plays with its own deck of tarot cards that no gypsy can read. Three years later Larry Harvey appeared in *Camelot* at Drury Lane, not as Lancelot but as King Arthur. He gave a stunning performance which Harold Hobson of the *London Sunday Times* called one of the five great performances of his theatregoing lifetime. By some mysterious vocal alchemy he was no longer a basso profundo and sang with a charming, light baritone voice, which made Fritz and me feel foolish and the audiences ecstatic.

The last time I saw Larry was a year before his untimely death. It was at a party in California. He was alone, having recently been divorced from his wife, Joan Cohn, the widow of the founder of Columbia Pictures. He was, as we say, smashed. He came over to me and said: "Alan, I have a splendid idea. Why don't you arrange for Fritz to marry Joan and when they die, leave me everything in their wills." I said I would mention it to Fritz, but that anything less than total pessimism would be optimistic.

The writing of *Camelot* took twenty-one months and twenty-one thousand miles. Fritz had developed a passion for Palm Springs. He regarded it, as do most of the inhabitants, as America's Valhalla for the living, where life is preserved ad infinitum and health abounds. It no doubt is. But every time I go there someone has just put up a brand new hospital, until today Palm Springs has more hospital beds per capita than almost any area in the country—a paradox that can only be explained by the quality of the restaurants. So the first winter we spent working in Palm Springs.

When spring came Fritz felt that from July to September the most beneficial place for his health would be the chemin-de-fer table at the Palm Beach Casino in Cannes, and would I mind joining him there for the summer. "Of course not," I lied, and took a "cottage" at Antibes large enough to house four children, nurses, wife, etc. And the writing continued. When the summer was over, it was back to New York until the first, sharp wind of winter, and then off again to Palm Springs. Finally, that spring, the caravan came to a halt. Rehearsals were scheduled for the beginning of September and we each rented a house at Sands Point, Long Island, within an hour of New York City.

In between transcontinental and transatlantic zig-zags, Oliver Smith had once again been signed to do the sets, Abe Feder lights, Hanya Holm the dances, and our redoubtable Franz Allers to conduct the orchestra. But what of the costumes? No designer shining in armor came readily to mine.

One day Moss called us and said he had what he thought was a brilliant idea. The most famous costume designer in Hollywood during the thirties and forties was Adrian. When still a comparatively young man he had retired, because of ill health, and he and his wife, Janet Gaynor, had been living in Brazil. (Near Mary Martin and Richard Halliday.) He had recently returned to New York, had had dinner with Moss and Kitty, and had expressed an interest in returning to work. Moss had encouraged him to make a few designs at random, inspired by White's book. When we saw the sketches were jubilantly impressed. They were original and beautiful and as fanciful as the book. We all agreed that Adrian would do the costumes. Eight months later we had our first taste of the tragedies that were destined to befall *Camelot*. Adrian died of a heart attack. In order to preserve what he had already done, Janet Gaynor suggested that a disciple of his in California named Tony Duquette be called in to complete the job. Both Moss and I knew him and liked him and a short time later Tony became the official costume designer of the play.

During March of that year (1960) it became dramatically clear to us that *Camelot* was not going to be a "sleeper." On the fourth anniversary of *My Fair Lady* a multi-paged advertisement appeared in the *New York Sunday Times*. Part of the copy was an announcement that *Camelot* would open late in November of that year—eight months away. Within the next four weeks we received over three-quarters of a million dollars' worth of mail orders. The general reaction other than that at the box office served to remind us all of one of the theatre's most bizarre idiosyncrasies. The theatre, as Moss often pointed out, "is a mild form of insanity" that claims both "inpatients" and "outpatients," i.e., the theatrical press. The paranoia is that once one has written for the theatre from then on only what one writes for the theatre is of consequence. If a playwright, after a play or two, publishes a novel that wins the Pulitzer Prize and a book of poetry thus wins the Bollingen Award and then returns with a new play, to the citizens of the theatre the new play is the first thing he has done since the last play. If Churchill had written historical drama instead of historical prose his leadership during the war years would have been regarded as his dry period. Since *My Fair Lady* Fritz and I had written *Gigi* and Moss had published *Act One* but the announcement of *Camelot* meant that at long last we had gone back to work.

I think it necessary at this point to mention that CBS was again playing Big Daddy and was putting up the needed $400,000.

To understand what happened during that summer and subsequently on the road during the tryout period, it will be necessary to mention a few details concerning my health.

To understand the details concerning my health, it will be necessary to mention a few details concerning my private life. Which I shall now do with a minimum of detail and a maximum of generality.

I have been married repeatedly. I am not proud of it, nor am I ashamed of it. If anything, I am astonished. It may seem hard to believe, but having come from a broken home I was determined it would never happen to me. The first time I married, the ceremony was performed by a monsignor of the Catholic Church and I thought it was irrevocable. My younger brother had married at nineteen, my older at twenty-two. Being in the middle, I faced the altar at twenty-one. Three years later our daughter, Susan, was born. (Thank Heaven for little girls.) Although our marriage was not a happy one, it never occurred to me it would end in divorce. When it did, at her request, it was under the friendliest of circumstances. The word friendly has a special meaning when it is linked with the word divorce. In relationship to divorce it is a financial term meaning economic parity and no alimony fight.

Ruthie was a lovely woman. All my wives were, with one aberrational exception. Her name will not appear in this book, but the havoc she wrought that summer must.

The causes of so many marital misadventures may have varied but to my best knowledge none was because of my profession. I have made my own personal survey of the matrimonial record of the contemporary writer and I do not find the divorce rate higher than it is in any other trade. Nevertheless, I am the common denominator and if it cannot be blamed on me, the writer, mathematically that leaves me, Alan. I am not, however, about to spread a guilt-ridden soul across these pages. It would be chivalrous, perhaps, but false. Of more importance, it would be totally irrelevant to the matters under discussion. All I can say is that if I had no flair for marriage, I also had no flair for bachelorhood. Marriage, as someone said, is often like a besieged fortress. Everyone inside wants to get out and everyone outside wants to get in.

Nancy and I were divorced in 1957 but I had two more daughters to thank Heaven for, Liza and Jennifer. I remarried (the unnamed wife) and we had a son, Michael. The summer we moved to Sands Point he was two years old and I treasured being with him. At that time the cacophonic willfulness of my wife was such that I had already begun to abandon any hope of domestic bliss. Whether it was her aim to make my life so unbearable that I would pay any price for peace, or it was merely the uncontrollable manifestations of a nasty spirit, I do not know, but life at Sands Point during June and July would have attracted the professional eye of any passing exorcist. My nerves were beginning to fray at the edges and the writing was bogging down to the point of panic. In mid-July she announced that she could not tolerate Long Island one more moment and that she would like to take Michael to Europe for a short spell. As she told me, the trunks were already coming down the stairs. I agreed, thinking that perhaps a few weeks of monasticism would free my mind and enable me to regain the momentum needed to finish the play.

She departed and within two days I was writing away furiously.

A week later I received a phone call from her in which she announced that she was never coming back and that if I wished to see our son I would have to visit him in Europe. The impact on me was devastating. For three days I could not move out of the chair by the telephone. I felt torn, trapped, and helpless. I lost all control of my tear ducts and other bodily functions and still could not get out of that chair. I realized that I must be having something akin to a nervous breakdown. In an imagination warped by depression I was reacting as if I were never going to see my son again.

During those three days Fritz never called, because he thought I was working on a lyric and was waiting to hear from me. On the morning of the third day, I screwed myself together sufficiently to pick up the phone and call Moss. I was determined not to admit to anyone what was happening to me because, right or wrong, I was fearful it would shake everyone to the roots and endanger the entire production. I said to Moss, as calmly as I could, that I was having a bit of trouble working. I knew that he had once gone to one of the most famous analysts in the country, Dr. Lawrence Kubie, and I asked him if he happened to know where I could reach him. "Perhaps," I said "he might know someone in the neighborhood whom I could visit from time to time." Moss told me Dr. Kubie was now at Johns Hopkins in Baltimore and gave me his phone number. I called him and by the grace of God was able to reach him immediately. I did not lie to him and told him as much as I could. He said he would get back to me before sundown. Within half that time he called and told me he knew a first-rate psychiatrist whom, he had discovered, was vacationing in Great Neck, twenty minutes from Sands Point. He had already spoken to him and the doctor was waiting for me. Somehow I extricated myself from that grisly chair, showered, got into the car and drove to Great Neck. How I got there without killing half the population en route was a miracle. When I arrived the doctor took one look at me and shrewdly observed that he could tell by my eyes, which had now sunken back into my head well past my ears, that I was in a depression. I wholeheartedly agreed but told him that I had no time for any psychoanalytical examination of my psyche. It was now the last day of July, rehearsals were to begin on September third, and I had not written page one of the second act. What I needed, I said, was medication with a capital *M.* To this *he* wholeheartedly agreed, and proceeded to prescribe for me some pills of unusual potency. He said I was to begin with four a day and gradually build up the dosage to twelve a day, and that it would be necessary for me to see him every three days to make certain my head was still on.

Off I went to the local pharmacy to procure the magic capsules and inside of two days I was back at work. I finished the lyric, called Fritz to come over and apologized for having taken so long. The lyric, ironically enough, was "If Ever I Would Leave You."

Depression, I discovered, tosses all problems, great and small, into one foul pit of despair. The most trivial inconvenience can seem insurmountable and the road to reason becomes "the tanglewood of Weir." I remember a winter some time ago when the city was smothered by a heavy snowfall, and I was standing on a corner of Madison Avenue waiting for the light to change. There are those curbs in New York City that have false bottoms. One expects to step down three or four inches to the street only to find it eight or ten. There was a small, wan, sallow-faced, middle-aged man standing next to me. The light changed. He took one step down on to the street and ended in the snow up to his knees. He stood there for a moment in total resignation, then looked up at me and said: "What the fuck are they doing to us now?" That's a depression.

By week's end perspective had begun to return and I was able to separate the problems. The first order of business was clearly to give my full concentration to the play. In proper time I would turn my attention to reclaiming my son. By week's end plus three I was also up to full dosage. I worked day and night with the minimum of sleep and on the last day of August the completed script was sent to mimeo. On September third rehearsals began.

A company of sixty-one assorted talents and sexes assembled on stage for the first reading. There were twenty-four singers who had been selected from thousands of candidates and I cannot remember a finer singing group in any musical play. Several have since become featured and leading players. One, John Cullum, is now a star and another is a leading tenor in Europe.

Moss, as usual, had arranged to have the sketches of the sets and some of the costume designs on display. Oliver had decided, after much trial and error, to use height to achieve grandeur and there was not only more scenery than Switzerland, but the canopy of the royal bed and the height of the throne were Alpine.

The first reading gave us all serious pause. It lasted well over three hours. Clearly we would have to make extensive cuts as we went along, but no one fully realized the extent of the problem. The following day the company fragmented, the singers in one hall, the dancers in another and the actors in still another. At the theatre where Moss was rehearsing the book, Julie immediately opened up her old tea stand and at four o'clock everyone knocked off for the customary bit of old England. Everyone, that is, but Richard, who retired to his dressing room for more stimulating refreshment.

It is no classified secret that Richard's devotion to the bottle was almost religious, and his capacity was one of the wonders of the twentieth century. If the Atlantic Ocean had been made of whiskey, Richard would have been able to walk across. But never in all the time we worked together did I ever see him show any sign of intoxication. He was not only always compos mentis, but at no time did it impair his memory. When any normal man would have been placed on the critical list, Richard could stand firmly in the centre of the room, recite Dylan Thomas from "hello" to "goodbye" and rattle off any Shakespearen part he had ever performed. From time to time his voice was a little croaky, but only in the wings. The moment he set foot on stage, by some occult magic, all traces of alcoholic wear and tear disappeared, his voice rang forth with its customary majesty and when he sang every note was hit squarely in the middle.

One day when the play was in Boston, I was discussing it with a doctor friend of mine. The doctor said he had run across it before. "Welsh livers and kidneys," he said "seem to made of some metallic alloy, quite unlike the rest of the human race. One day, like aeroplanes, they eventually show metal fatigue." But having seen Richard in the play, he thought he still had thousands of miles to fly.

I developed a fondness, admiration, and respect for Richard that runs deep indeed. For reasons that I shall come to, *Camelot* might have never reached New York were it not for his high degree of professionalism, courage, and decency. He is a driven man, but a remarkable fellow and a remarkable actor and anyone who ever counts him out will grow fat on crow.

I never appreciated him more than when Richard Harris did the film. Harris is an extremely likable fellow and in the past had proven himself capable of giving a first-rate performance. I was hopeful when I saw him drink that perhaps we had an Irish Richard Burton. Not at all. First of all, he got drunk. Secondly, he could not remember his lines. Thirdly, when he did remember them it was by chance rather than conviction.

In films, when a performer is faking he can give the illusion of acting by whispering and the illusion of passion by shouting. Harris, being Irish, added the illusion of depth by having a far-off look in his eye. But he sang very well and although I was not around, I understand he was terribly amusing on the set. There was one scene when he was sitting in a tub and Vanessa Redgrave, who played Guinevere, was scrubbing his back. As she began to play the scene her eyes dropped and then bugged. Richard was stark naked. The shock blew the lines clear out of her head. Which made two of them. But everyone laughed and a jolly good time was had by all.

Richard, Julie, and Bobby got along famously. But as so often happens to an actor playing his first major role, Bobby developed a wild crush on his leading lady. He got nowhere. At times the clinches seemed to last a few seconds longer than planned, but it was probably due to muscle more than reciprocal desire. In the parlance of the playing fields of Ebbets, he struck out consistently. In despair he went for advice to the master, Richard, hoping to receive a few directions that would lead him to the gates of paradise. His hopes were dashed. Richard had no pointers or potion to give him and said so rather gruffly. After Bobby left the room, Richard turned to me and said wryly: "Why did he come to me? I couldn't get anywhere either."

When Bobby first auditioned we did not notice that he had a rather peculiar walk. He was not bowlegged, but somehow it seemed as if a horse was missing between his legs, and his entrance in the forest scene where the Queen had gone "A-Maying" was more like the last scene of *High Noon*. We tried everything to correct it without making him self-conscious. One day I happened to glance down at Fritz's shoes which he had made for him in London with lifts so high that, as the old jokes goes, when he took them off at night his ears popped. "Eureka," I thought, "I've got it!" We told Bobby to go around the corner and buy himself the highest pair of elevator shoes he could find, which he did. Until he got used to them he walked like the leaning tower of Pisa. But he soon straightened up, and if his gait was not completely aristocratic, at least he never more appeared to be the leading dancer in a ballet choreographed by John Wayne.

Richard had a magnetic effect on the cast. He had played with almost every great actor and actress in England, had a huge bag of

stories about them all and was a spellbounding raconteur. Both
on stage and off he was the king in every sense of the word and
he soon had an entourage of dedicated worshippers who followed
him everywhere. Bobby was one, John Cullum was another. By the
time rehearsals were over, Cullum, who was a native of Tennessee,
sounded like an Oxford graduate. In all fairness, he had done some
Shakespeare in the park, but he studied Richard so assiduously
that he became his understudy: and, in fact, on one or two occasions during the run went on for him.

There were two or three scenes in the play where King Arthur
stands silently, lost in his own thoughts, while the action swirls
around him. At least it was written to swirl around him, but for
some reason the stage turned to waxworks. It soon became apparent why. One of the most extraordinary facets of Richard's talent
is that when he withdraws into himself, unconsciously he takes all
the energy on the stage in with him. Nothing moves. Even when
one is not looking at him one feels it. Consequently, I had to rewrite
those moments and bring him articulately into the scene in order
to keep it alive.

Moss, of course, was in complete control of every phase of the
production. It is one thing to make a decision and quite another to
execute it, especially when it means cutting someone's good work.
Moss was always able to do it without creating a ripple of hard feelings. One of Hanya Holm's most brilliant choreographic creations
was a ballet she had designed for the magic forest in the second
act. It was a dance of animals and it was enchanting. Every animal
was characterized by movement but when Tony Duquette added
the actual animal costumes the choreography simply disappeared.
Because of the excessive length of the play, Moss, very rightly, felt
that it was not a matter of discarding the costumes, but discarding
the entire ballet. And so he did.

He was more tolerant with Fritz and me, presumably because

we were the authors. We had written a twelve-minute interlude of Lancelot's "quests," all done in music and lyrics. Moss felt very strongly that they were an unnecessary intrusion, but also felt that Fritz and I should at least see them in front of an audience before a final decision was made. The final decision, I might add, was made after one performance.

After five weeks of rehearsal and a brilliant last run-through (we thought), the company went home, sang a chorus of "I'll See You Again" to friends and family and departed for the road. In heaven the gods assembled, looked down on our band of strolling players, unpacked a few clouds of trouble, trauma, and tragedy and decided to remind us they were still up there.

We were opening in Toronto and we were to inaugurate a new theatre. There is a law in Canada that prevents the advertising of alcoholic beverage (this may have changed). There are many ways, however, a brewery may publicize its name and one of them is by "good deeds and public welfare." The O'Keefe Brewery Company had chosen the good deeds route and proceeded to adorn the city of Toronto with an enormous theatrical and concert auditorium called, quite naturally, the O'Keefe Center. A gentleman named Hugh Walker was appointed manager and a few months earlier he had approached us about *Camelot* opening the Centre.

To open a new theatre is a hazard to be fanatically avoided. A new theatre is always, without exception, filled with devastating flaws. For instance, one can absolutely depend on the acoustics not working. Strangely enough they may work in a month or two, but never at the beginning. The walls of a theatre, and I mean this quite literally, are quasi-human. They need to absorb life in order to become alive. It is a well-known fact that when one plays a theatre that has been dark for a long period, it is difficult to induce laughter for at least three performances. *My Fair Lady* reopened the Erlanger Theatre in Philadelphia when it had been closed for many months. It was a brilliant opening, but the laughs were a quarter of the size they became a few days later.

André Previn once told me an interesting story that is obliquely related. Before he became chef d'orchestre of the London Symphony, he conducted the Houston Symphony. Houston is the control centre of the American space program. André met several of the astronauts, including Walter Shirra who was one of the first Americans in orbit. He told André that while they were passing over the United States, they suddenly picked up a disc jockey playing four or five records. Shirra thanked the base by radio for the entertainment and was told, to his surprise, they were not responsible for it. Somehow the spacecraft had picked up on its own. Shirra made a list of the records that were played and when they returned to Houston a check was made throughout the country to see who was playing those records that day. Not only was no one playing them, but all the records were over twelve years old. End of story. In other words, there is a "livingness" to sound.

The inevitable acoustical problem is only one of the land mines. There is also a stage crew for whom all the technical equipment is virgin territory. "Hanging" the show, always chaos under the best of circumstances, with a new crew in a new theatre is a season in hell. Anything mechanical will not function. The orchestra pit, never tested before, is seldom the right depth. The list of known potential disasters is endless. Then there are the ugly surprises. Many years ago when the Forrest Theatre in Philadelphia opened, it was discovered at the last moment that the architect had made a small oversight: he had forgotten to put in dressing rooms.

Clearly, based on the accumulation of our collective experience, it would have been utter folly for Moss, Fritz, and me to accept Hugh Walker's offer to open the O'Keefe Centre. And so we accepted it.

We did so for two good reasons, both bad. The first was

"money." Hugh made a spectacular offer and because we knew *Camelot* would be a costly venture, we thought it might lighten the financial load. (The cost of out-of-town openings is one of the major items of any production. The hauling in and out of the scenery, the traveling and living expenses of the company, the out-of-town rehearsals run into the six figures. Lately it has become so prohibitive that many shows have abandoned the road completely and simply give extended previews in New York.) The second reason was a total vacation from common sense. We thought that by opening so far from New York we would not be descended upon by all the "dear shits" and would be able to work in reasonable peace. We should have realized that the O'Keefe Brewery Company and the city of Toronto did not intend to allow their new toy to be unveiled in secrecy. It was a national event. Planes were chartered to fly people in from all corners of Canada and the United States. Not only did we not escape from the theatrical horde of "well wishers," but they were cordially invited, all expenses paid.

The company arrived in Toronto a week before the opening. There were dressing rooms. *But,* the stage crew was unfamiliar with the technical facilities, the orchestra pit was too deep, and the acoustical system, which consisted of a complicated set of sliding panels that lined either wall of the theatre, had been so devised that the forty-piece orchestra in the pit sounded as if it were in Montreal. (All of this has been corrected since.) Etc., etc., etc.

During the rehearsal period the doctor had placed me on a withdrawal plan and I had been warned to eat often and slowly. The last two days before the opening I was down to about four a day. In the mayhem of those last forty-eight hours, I completely forgot about the pills, never took them, and returned to the normal, pre-opening diet of black coffee in soggy containers and infrequent, indigestible sandwiches.

The pre-opening exhaustion and anxiety became more complicated by the unexpected re-appearance of my wife and son. I can only assume that because I did not immediately fly to Europe in hot pursuit she had decided to return to fight another day. Which she did. I confess, however, that I made this assumption long after the fact, basing it entirely upon future events. I was overjoyed to see my son but his traveling companion added considerably to the tense and nerve-wracking atmosphere.

On the opening night, parties had been planned all over Toronto. The curtain rose at eight-fifteen. Normal show time is two hours and forty minutes, and the early curtain had been scheduled to allow the festivities to begin a little earlier. They thought.

The show ran four and a half hours! The curtain came down at twenty minutes to one! Only *Tristan and Isolde* equaled it as a bladder contest. The quality of the show, if any, was completely fogged by time. And any humor was nonexistent.

As for the visiting crowd from the bar at Sardi's, not since Rodgers and Hammerstein's first failure had I seen so many smiling faces. The agent with the flashlight and scripts was able to do a whole week's work during the second act. And what does one say to you after an event of such delicious calamity. Some will come up and say: "I liked it." Or you will get a smile, a pat on the back—and silence. Or "It needs work." Or—and this is the most common one—"Well, that's what you're out of town for." What they really mean is that is what *they* are out of town for. Two days later we heard that the word in New York was that *Camelot* had been officially designated a "disaster area."

The next morning while the city of Toronto was recovering from a wave of low back trouble, Moss, Fritz, and I met to begin surgery. Fritz was desperate about the nonexistent sound from the orchestra pit, as were we all, but the first problem obviously was the length. Any play will pick up ten to twelve minutes if you leave it alone, but we needed to lose a minimum of one and a half hours.

Out went the "quests," along with about twenty minutes of other redundent material. It was Sunday and we could not rehearse until the following day.

The Monday morning reviews were not good but not as bad as they could have been and reflected a genuine desire by the critics to be as constructive as possible. As a rule, dancing on a grave is how a critic gets his exercise. It provides him with the irresistible opportunity to prove how witty he is and show that he can write, too. One Toronto critic, however, found the temptation too delectable and referred to *Camelot* as "Gotterdammerung without laughs." Obviously he had not seen some of the "Gotterdammerungs" I had. The joke-and-dagger impulse is most uncontrollable with a new and/or young critic. In New York, because of the prestige and power of the *New York Times,* its critic enters the arena like a Roman emperor with a thumb that determines life or death. Therefore, every time the *Times* changes its drama critic a shiver runs through the theatrical body. Authors, actors, and directors spill a good deal of blood while learning their craft. Now they must do it all over again while the new man is learning his. Although the gentlemen in Toronto were far from inexperienced, Toronto had not been a tryout town and their restraint was all the more admirable and, I must say, appreciated.

On Monday we rehearsed the cuts and that evening the curtain came down at around midnight. The man who had installed the acoustics had also adjusted the sliding panels and about fourteen of the forty men could now be heard playing—a little closer to Toronto.

While having supper after the performance I suddenly began to have dizzy spells. Returning to the hotel as quickly as I could, I called a doctor. He came at once and after a brief examination he informed me that I was haemorrhaging internally and whisked me off to the Wellesley Hospital. There it was soon determined that it was caused by an ulcer, undoubtedly the result of the conglomeration of events of the previous three months plus my careless behavior before the opening. I was furious with my abdomen for deserting me in my hour of need and told the doctor it was absolutely essential I be mobile in no more than three days. He nodded sympathetically, filled a syringe, and that was the last I remembered until Saturday, five days later. On Saturday I asked the doctor how long it would be before I could return to work and he replied that it could not possibly be before the following Saturday and only then if I behaved myself and obeyed his instructions implicitly. His instructions included no visits by anyone connected with the play. However, he did give me a message from Moss telling me not to worry and that all was going as well as could be expected. I am rebellious by nature but I have a great respect for stone walls and so I followed his instructions to the letter. I was allowed a phone call or two a day and so a minimum of information about the play filtered through. I learned that Moss, being the theatre man that he was, refused to touch the writing of the play until I returned. So during the two weeks following the opening the curtain continued to come down closer to midnight than eleven thirty. I also learned that somehow Moss was managing to keep the company together and the spirits from falling. How he did it I will never know.

On Thursday the doctor told me that my exemplary conduct had been rewarded and I would indeed be discharged on Saturday. On Saturday afternoon I dressed and packed, said my thank-yous to the members of the staff who had been so kind to me and walked down the corridor to the elevator. My nurse was with me. While waiting for it to arrive, I happened to look back and I saw a hospital bed, obviously occupied, being wheeled into the room I had just vacated.

As we rode down in the elevator the nurse told me who it was. It was Moss.

That morning he had had a heart attack. I could not believe it. I went weak in the knees and for a few minutes I could not get my bearings. When someone has a heart attack, for some reason people always ask: "Was it a bad one?"—as if there is such a thing as a good one. This was a bad one because it was not Moss's first. He had had one ten years earlier. He was not placed on the critical list but he was a very sick man and there was no doubt he would be a very sick man for a very long time. *Camelot* was taking its toll.

By the time I had reached the hotel and settled in, it was too late to go to the matinee. Fritz, however, did and very wisely assembled the company immediately following the performance. He gave them the precise details of Moss's illness before the facts of his condition could be distorted by rumor. He also told them that I was being discharged from the hospital that day and that we would begin work immediately.

When I saw him that evening he was as shaken as I, perhaps even more so, because of his own recent coronary. I was going to the play at night so we agreed to table our discussions until the following day in order to give me a chance to digest the performance. But needless to say, all that was on our minds was Moss. How would we manage without him?

The *Camelot* I saw that evening was indeed better than the one that had opened but only because it was shorter and the performances were more polished. But stripped of an hour, the blemishes were all the more apparent. And it was still more than a half hour too long. After the performance I went backstage to see the company in order to assure them that I was indeed alive. I told them there would be no rehearsals until there was something new to rehearse and suggested that while Fritz and I were writing, instead of dissipating their energies on fear and anxiety they shore them up in preparation for the vast amount of work that had to be done.

Fortunately, we were playing to packed houses and a packed house is a great tranquilizer.

The following morning, before Fritz and I could meet, I received a phone call from Kitty asking me to come see her. I did. I found her pale but clear-eyed and in full possession of herself. Kitty is one of the few all-woman women I have ever met, the rare mixture of little girl and a grown-up strength that is never hard but always feminine. She told me that Moss was resting comfortably but a prognosis was not possible as to when he would be able to leave Toronto. The chances were that he would be there for many weeks. She also told me that before he was placed in the Oxygen tent he gave her a message to give to me. The message was that he did not want another director called in and that whatever additional direction was necessary when new scenes were added, he wished me to do it. I told her that if it were humanly possible I would try to abide by his request. Perhaps he thought he would be out of the hospital in time to rejoin the show before it opened in New York and thus be able to polish the play himself. I did not know. Nor did I ever know. I never asked him.

I then went to see Fritz. He was obviously weary. At that point neither of us had a clear idea about how to fix the play. I repeated to him the message that Kitty had given me. It added greatly to his concern. He said it would be impossible to do the amount of rewriting that was required—especially since we did not know what that re-writing would be—without directorial assistance. Besides, he said, we needed a fresh mind to help *us*. There was no question that he made good sense and I found myself being pulled in one direction by my promise to Kitty, in another by Fritz and in still another by what I truly believed was best for the play.

Nevertheless, I told Fritz that we should both immediately start thinking of a director but that it must be someone with whom we had some kind of shorthand, someone who would not try to remake the play in his own image of it but would help us perfect *this* play. It also would have to be someone satisfactory to Richard and Julie. To all that Fritz was in agreement. Furthermore, I said, it would not be possible for a new director to take over until after we had opened in Boston. We had one more week left to play in Toronto and that week had to be devoted to cutting the play down to size. Not only that, only someone totally familiar with the vast scenic problems would be able to supervize a technical run-through in Boston. Therefore, I said, I *must* open it in Boston myself and by that time we would have found, I hoped, a director.

Fritz was not happy about this and said so. He insisted that we find a director that week if possible. I refused. And left his room.

I left with more troubles than when I had entered. It was the first time in all the years we had been together that we were not indivisible in the crunch. It was the first time the seams of our collaboration had begun to pull loose.

It was my first day out of the hospital and I was not exactly in olympic condition. So I went back to my room for a little "lie-down" and thought-collecting. There were several telephone messages waiting. Most of them were from the press. I had forgotten what a fish bowl we were swimming in. My sojourn in the hospital and now the tragic illness of Moss and the automatic question of who would succeed him served to attract even more attention. If that were not enough, *Time* magazine was doing a cover story on Fritz and me and had assigned several investigative reporters to track our movements and interview not only us but as many of the company as possible. The press is an organic part of theatrical life. Before I went into the hospital the company was taking it in its stride. It was not to last long.

There is nothing more debilitating and more confidence-shaking than to be on the road and alone in a hotel room with a million insoluble problems. I did not stay there long. I called Richard and went to see him.

I did not tell him about Moss's request, but simply said that I would have to scale the play down for the Boston opening, that I would direct the new scenes myself, and that within the next two weeks we would find, we hoped, a director. I asked him to give it some thought because whomever was selected had to be someone with whom he felt comfortable. I asked for his support, both on stage and off. I told him the morale of the company trickles down from the star. An unhappy and nervous star makes for an unhappy and nervous company. A confident star in a play in trouble goes a long way toward creating confidence in the company. Even though Julie was also starring, I went to see Richard first because he was much more intimately involved in the life of the cast and commanded their affection and respect.

He listened carefully and then said: "Don't worry, love. We'll get through." I thanked him and as I was about to leave he said: "Why don't you direct it yourself? Anybody else who comes in is liable to muck it up." He had no idea of the relevance of what he had said as I stared at him for a moment both in surpise and, I confess, gratitude. I said I would think about it.

Later in the day I went to see Julie, told her that I had seen Richard, and repeated what I had said. She understood thoroughly and she could not have been more sympathetic or encouraging. In fact, she reflected so much confidence that she almost made me believe it myself.

We had one more week in Toronto. *Camelot* needed a massive reconstruction. Excessive length is not a disease. It is a symptom. If the steps required to reach the dramatic conclusion take too much time then either other steps must be found or the dramatic conclusion is unachievable. I have always thought of the characters in a play as being on an emotional journey. In a legitimate play (one without music—one with music being something else) the emotions can follow a more winding road with more side paths of nuance and inferential action. In a musical the journey has to be taken with bolder steps and with fewer incidents along the way. A considerable number of musicals, like operas, are based on plays. None is based on a bad one. As a rule, the plays that best serve as vehicles for music are those with almost classic construction. (I have noticed, incidentally, that in a genuinely good play if, as you watch it, you think of it as an opera, it is always clear who is the tenor, who the baritone and so on. In *A Streetcar Named Desire,* for instance, Blanche is obviously a dramatic soprano, Kowalski is a baritone, the brother-in-law is a tenor, and the sister a lyric soprano. There is even a quartet of card players. In *A Long Day's Journey into Night* the father is the bass, the wife a lyric soprano with a coloratura range and the sons are a well-defined tenor and baritone.) Thinking about *Camelot* I could not tell at that point whether there was too much story to tell in order to reach the end of the journey, or if the same story could be told with fewer incidents, or if the journey was simply too long in the first place. There was, however, one thing I did know. When it opened in Boston the curtain had to come down before eleven-thirty. Therefore, no time could be spent in Toronto recreating or attempting to solve major problems. I also remembered a remark Richard had made one day in rehearsal. He had just finished a scene and as he sat down he turned to me and said: "You know, love, it takes me about two hundred performances before I really get into the role." "Richard," I said "This ain't the Old Vic. This is Broadway and you'd better plan on cutting that number by a hundred and ninety-nine." Although he was only half serious when he said it, I realized he was speaking a truth born of repertory experience. Many of the scenes were playing well despite the need for linear cutting and I decided for the sake of the actors not to touch them. Instead, I would apply a cleaver to the second half of the second act, leaving the very last few pages alone.

There was a scene that took place in Arthur's study in which Arthur and Mordred gaze from the window into the courtyard where Guinevere is being tied to the stake and the executioner awaits a signal from Arthur to ignite the flame. There was also a number sung by the full ensemble in which they grieve for Guinevere and wonder if Lancelot will come with his army and rescue her.

Out went the scene in the study and I rewrote the lyrics of "Guinevere" and told in quasi-oratorial fashion how Lancelot came and rescued Guinevere. All that was left of the scene in Arthur's study were two lines, one by Arthur and one by Mordred, interspersed into the choral number. Mordred was in one tower and Arthur was in another looking down on the embattled courtyard. Arthur's line was: "Merlyn, Merlyn, make me a hawk and let me fly away from here." When we had the first reading, Richard said the line, smiled, looked over at Roddy and said: "well, love, it's every man for himself." He knew perfectly well what he was going to do with that one. With that incredible voice of his the line exploded with a cry of anguish that almost cracked the rear wall of the theatre. In the rewriting of "Guinevere," with Fritz's permission, I was able to eliminate some of the verses.

There were no rehearsals at the theatre Monday and Tuesday while I was writing except for one cast replacement. To change a member of a cast is ordinarily not a geographic problem. One finds him in either New York or California but in *Camelot* nothing was simple. The little boy with whom Arthur plays the last scene had to be English and we had opened in Toronto with a twelve-year-old American boy. It did not work. While I was in the hospital Bud was dispatched to London in search of a replacement. He found a splendid young lad named Peter DeVise. Peter's mother was dead and he lived alone with his father. When Bud told Mr. DeVise that he wanted to take his only child all the way to America the poor man almost broke down. But then he decided he could not deny his son the opportunity to play a scene with Richard Burton. And so he gave his consent. Bud had returned to Toronto with Peter the day before I left the hospital.

And on Monday and Tuesday he rehearsed with him. During the week the gulf between Fritz and me seemed to widen. On Wednesday I thought of a director we both knew and both respected. It was Jose Ferrer. Fritz agreed and I called Jo in Hollywood. He was in the middle of a film and was disconsolate that he could not come to help. I told Fritz, hoping that even though Jo was not available the fact that I had called him would at least demonstrate that I was not opposed to a new director. He was not appeased.

The Wednesday matinee brought the only moment of comic relief of the entire week. Richard had a cold which developed into a mild case of laryngitis. I doubt if the audience was even aware of it. At the end of Act One he is alone on stage and has a rather lengthy soliloquy (for a musical) in which he reveals the knowledge of the passion of Lancelot and Guinevere and decides because he loves them both he will do nothing and with God's help they will live through it. It was the moment in the play when the full power of his voice rang through the theatre. When he reached that point during the matinee he realized his voice was tired and so he did the soliloquy almost in a whisper. It was deeply moving, so much so that an elderly lady in the front row felt an uncontrollable desire to comfort him. She lifted out her arms to him and began to climb over the orchestra rail in order to reach him on stage. Fortunately, Franz Allers saw her coming and gently restrained her before she took a header into the pit. Richard also saw her coming and somehow was able to control himself. But when the curtain fell the people in the front row heard the tortured King Arthur roaring with laughter from behind the curtain.

On Thursday and Friday the company rehearsed the changes. None of them was seen by the tolerant people of Toronto. To the very end of the run that Saturday night the curtain kept coming down at ten-minutes-to-twelve.

By the end of the week Fritz and I were seeing less and less of each other. Irritations and differences between us that had been long forgotten and were of little consequence at the time had now become the subject of questions by interviewers. Our replies traveled from mouth to mouth and by the time they reached us they were unrecognizable distortions. If we had stayed steadfastly and constantly together as we always had in the past we would have laughed, rowed, or shrugged but in the end gone on about our business. We did not. I do not know why we did not. I may have thought I knew then but whatever I thought, I am certain I was wrong. I have a feeling the reason was something far more insidious, something of which neither of us was aware and which affected each of us in different ways. I have a feeling it may have been too much success.

Success, as I mentioned earlier, can be a creative stimulant. It encourages reaching in and reaching out. But it also can take the concessions of collaboration and call them compromise. It can embitter as often as it elates and inflates and it can weaken as much as it toughens. It can magnify faults and unearth a few new ones and its only virtue is when it is forgotten. Perhaps I was too disdainful of the words of others and Fritz too vulnerable. Perhaps I misinterpreted our differences as lack of support and he misinterpreted mine as heroics. Perhaps. Perhaps not. I will never know. Too much was never said. In the end we were a little like the couple being discussed in one of Noel Coward's early plays. "Do they fight?", said one. "Oh, no," said the other. "They're much too unhappy to fight."

It would have been easier to move Toronto to Boston than *Camelot* to Boston. The scenery went by van and from the air it must have looked like the opening of the West. It had been designed for the Majestic Theatre in New York, which was a good deal larger than the stage of the Shubert Theatre in Boston, and much of the scenery that had been built to move offstage instead had to be attached to pulleys and lifted into the air.

Meanwhile, the newspapers, not only in Boston but in New York and elsewhere, continued to be filled with day-by-day accounts of our trials and vicissitudes and we began to be known as a "medical," not a musical.

A technical run-through in a new city after one has been running is not as chaotic and time-consuming. Even though there is a new stage crew in every city, the stage manager and his assistants are now familiar with the play. Lights have to be re-focused but the cues are in the stage manager's book. There is, of course, a fair amount of disorder. I ran the "tech" with Biff's, Abe's, and Bud's assistance and it went fairly well but Fritz did not sit beside me. He stayed in the back of the theatre and left early.

When we left Toronto the unhappiest actor on the stage was Robert Coote. His role and his ineffable humor had been greeted with almost total silence during the three weeks in Canada and I had promised him faithfully he would have first attention when I began the rewrite.

A preview had been scheduled for the night before we opened and I awaited it with all the eagerness of a trip to the dentist. The curtain rose and within two minutes laughs we had never heard before began to fill the theatre. Julie's first song, "Where Are the

Simple Joys of Maidenhood?", not only got laugh after laugh but it stopped the show cold. Fritz, Bud, and I looked at each other in astonishment, the same thought on our minds. Had the O'Keefe Centre been so large that the audience saw the entire play through the wrong end of a telescope? Had the new theatre done the play in? Laughter, after all, implies involvement and interest. We waited. The scenes began to play for the first time. Coote entered and every line he said was a cue for laughter. The audience was so caught up in the play that even the patchwork cutting in the second act caused no restlessness or coughing in the audience. (Coughing in the theatre is not a respiratory ailment. It is a criticism.) The reaction and the laughter added several minutes to the running time and the curtain came down at eleven-thirty-five. But no one cared. It was time for champagne.

The following night we opened and put the cork back in the bottle. The play went far better than it ever had in Toronto. Cooter got all his laughs but "Where Are the Simple Joys of Maidenhood?" evoked only smiles. The length began to show again and when the curtain came down we realized that what had happened in the Shubert Theatre the night before was some sort of joyous excursion from reality and the play did indeed need as much work as we had thought.

The reviews ran the gamut. Boston critics, however, are seasoned out-of-town reviewers and have the ability to gauge what the play might be, could be, or will never be. In making this judgment, they also consider the experience of the people involved. So the reviews were respectful and all but one optimistic.

Oliver Smith not only did not disappear, but realizing that with Fritz unable to burn the midnight oil with me, and Moss still in hospital in Toronto, let all his other shows wonder "where the hell is Oliver?" and stayed with me for several days to comfort and contribute. He felt very strongly that the second act had to be cut in its entirety and that the first act should be extended and end with the shadow of the doom that was to come. He said there was no other way to solve the discrepancy in style between the two acts. Thornton Wilder once said that more plays fail because of a breech in style than any other reason and it is undoubtedly the easiest trap to fall into I know.

Many years earlier when Kurt Weill and I opened *Love Life*, Moss came up for the opening in New Haven. After the show he told us the trouble was that we had two plays. The first act was a satire and in the second act satire was abandoned and the play was solved realistically. All quite true. Six months later Moss opened a play called *Light Up the Sky* and Kurt and I went up for the opening. In Moss's hotel room afterwards, Kurt said, quite innocently, that the trouble was Moss had two plays. The first half was a comedy and the second was a drama. Also quite true. In *Camelot* the first act was joyous and romantic. But the second act told the story of the disintegration of the Round Table and it became pure drama. Unfortunately, there is no way to making a downhill story go uphill. Many years later when the film was made, I tried to solve the breach in style by beginning with the end and then flashing back to the first scene of the play. At least it warned the audience of the tragedy to come. The same thought had occurred to me in Boston but we were all afraid to touch the beginning which was playing so well.

After three or four days of discussing every conceivable drastic change I sat up one night alone and tried to determine for myself once and for all why I had wanted to do *Camelot*. Most authors, I believe, before they begin to write have a very clear idea what it is they are trying to say and why the story they have selected is the best way to say it. For some reason it has always happened to me after the fact. Only after the play is written, sometimes many months later, do I really see it for the first time and understand what drove me to write it. It is never a profound discovery, just a surprise, and usually something that was perfectly obvious to everyone but me.

When Cheryl Crawford, the producer of *Brigadoon*, sent Bobby Lewis the script with the hope that he would direct it, Bobby came to see me and asked me what I thought I had written. I was startled. It was the first time anyone had ever asked me that. I said, rather glibly, that I had written a fantasy about a town in Scotland that returns to life one day every one hundred years, that during that one day's existence in the twentieth century two Americans stumble upon it, that one of them falls in love with a Scottish girl, that he finally decides he cannot give up his life for her and returns to New York. In New York he discovers that his life is empty without her, returns to Scotland and by a "miracle," whose possibility is indicated earlier in the play, is able to restore the town long enough to disappear with it.

"No," said Bobby. "That's not what you have written at all. What you have written is the story of a romantic who is searching, and a cynic who has given up. The cynic talks him out of his romantic notions and forces him to leave Brigadoon. In the end, cynicism is proven wrong." The moment he said it I realized he was right. And after having struggled with the imperfections in the script for many months, I was able to complete the final draft within a week.

I began to see clearly that what motivated me was in three pages, the last three pages of the play. For me, the raison d'être of *Camelot* was the end of the journey when Arthur has lost his love, his friend, and his Round Table and believes his life has been a failure. Then a small boy appears from behind a tent who doesn't know the round table is dead and who wishes to become a knight. Arthur realizes that as long as his vision is alive in one small heart he has not failed. Men die but an idea does not. To me, that scene was the play and somehow the steps had to be shortened so the journey could be made.

I went to see Fritz and told him what I wished to do. He still did not think that either of us was in a position to judge what was best for the play and again we had a tussle about the director. Again I said that I would gladly call in anybody we could both agree upon. I made one other suggestion that Fritz rejected. So in the end we were arguing in a vacuum. And in a vacuum we remained.

During the first week in Boston T. H. White arrived from England to see the play for the first time. He was a large, shaggy man with a great white beard. Julie was overjoyed to see him and the cast was enchanted to meet him. I myself have always been a little cautious about large authors with white beards. The combination of writer, weight, and whiskers automatically creates the image of "sage" and makes the most ordinary conversation glow with warmth and wisdom. Tim was gentle and engaging and had the far-off look in his eye of a poet—a poet who wishes he were somewhere else. The company was spellbound by every word he uttered, but it is my respectful and affectionate opinion that splendid writer though he was, in conversation it was the beard.

He was most generous to me, however. I had forewarned him by mail that the task of converting his beautiful six-hundred-page book to a form whose dimensions had to be limited to two and a half hours, was less a matter of dramatizing incidents than capturing the spirit.

After recovering from the first shock of seeing it on the stage in a shape that must have seemed light years away from what his imagination had envisioned, he was enthusiastic and encouraging and magnanimously gave me free rein to do whatever I thought was best for the play.

And so I went to work. Eliminating some of the steps meant creating others. It meant that more than half of the first act had to be rewritten and most of the second. A new set was required to open the second act and Guinevere would require an additional song in the first act in order to condense the emotion.

The daily and nightly schedule went something like this. As each new scene was completed, I would read it over to the cast after the performance and they would take it home to study. I would rehearse it, with Bud's assistance, for the next two afternoons and then it would go into the play. I would go to the theatre and watch the performance, give notes after, let it settle in for two performances, and after the second night's performance there would be a reading of the next new scene. And so on and so on and so on.

Oliver Wendell Holmes once said: "I have had a thousand troubles in my life, most of which never happened." In the theatre the trouble that never happens is called rumor. Where they come from no one knows. Perhaps from the same mysterious man who writes dirty jokes. But suddenly, from nowhere, a story would fly around the company: that after Boston we were going to Cleveland: that such and such a director was coming in tomorrow; that a new book writer was arriving at the end of the week; that we were closing after Boston. It was endless. But each one had to be dealt with. The worst way is to assemble a company and make an announcement. It protests too much and gives it so much attention it seems true. The best way is to mingle with everyone after a performance in the best of spirits and sooner or later someone will "casually" mention it. One then laughs at its absurdity or dismisses it equally "casually" and gracefully changes the subject to something pertinent to the performer. The answer flies around the company and half an hour later the rumor is dead. Until the next one.

At the beginning of the second week it became apparent that it would not be possible to keep our opening date in New York and so we postponed it one week. This, of course, became the subject of a new rumor which was disposed of in the customary fashion.

Whether or not the company sensed the tension between Fritz and me I do not know but there seemed to be no evidence of it. But the endless stream of visitors from the press and the stories in the newspapers, through no one's fault, began to make the company feel like a patient on an operating table in a crowded, glassed-in rotunda. The interviews and interviews and interviews with the resulting "Do you know what *he* said?" added to the gossip and kept feeding the rumor factory until the company became a forum of misquoted questions and misquoted answers.

God knows what would have happened had it not been for Richard Burton. If ever a star behaved like a star in every sense of the word it was he. Whatever doubts he may have had about the future of the play were his secret only and throughout the four weeks in Boston he radiated a faith and geniality which infected the company and for which I shall be forever grateful to him. He accepted the cuts and changes necessary to open the play in Boston without a word, and two weeks before the play opened in New York he began rehearsing almost a brand new second act—except for the last scene—and launched into it with gusto and diligence. It was inevitable that from time to time one of the actors would have a sudden fit of despair, inevitably overstated and inevitably due to the fear that he was being overlooked, or that his part was not being honed or improved. Richard always stepped in, calmed him down, and reassured him all would be taken care of in good time. In simple language he kept the boat from rocking and *Camelot* might never have reached its final destination on Forty-fourth Street had it not been for him.

Or had it not been for Julie. Julie Andrews is a professional in the proudest sense of the word. In the theatre since she was a child, she meets any challenge with a smile and an unbatted eyelid that makes you wonder how Britain ever lost the Empire. Always gracious, always willing, an amazingly quick study both musically and dramatically, I cannot remember one moment in the almost seven years we worked together that was anything but joy. Nevertheless, I cannot say in all honesty that I knew her any better at the end of those seven years than I did at the beginning, or know her now. As my regard and respect for her climbed and climbed, so did my frustration, but somehow it never influenced my affection. I occasionally wondered whether Julie knew Julie any better than I did. Obviously she did and obviously she does. The years have revealed her to be very much her own person, aware of where her happiness lies and not easily affected by the heady wine of the fame she achieved. Somewhere along the line she decided it did not lie in the theatre and the theatre is the poorer for it.

As we began the third week in Boston my principal concern began to centre on the new song for Guinevere in the first act. Fritz saw as clearly as I that the way the play was being reshaped the song was essential. There was a long scene of farewell between Lancelot and Guinevere before his departure for the unseen "quests." One of the great functions of music is that it can do in a few bars what would normally take a dramatist a few pages. To cut the scene there had to be a song that dramatized emotionally Guinevere's feelings. I gave Fritz the title, "Before I Gaze at You Again," and he wrote the music. But how long would it take me to write the lyric? Suppose I got hung up (not unusual) and three or four days went by? The play had to be in its final form by the middle of the fourth week so that I could "freeze" it. It is an absolute necessity the company perform the same play without change for a few consecutive nights before the Broadway opening. The only time I could figure out that I would be able to write the lyric was while the caravan was traveling to New York and the scenery was being hung in the Majestic Theatre. I went to Julie, told her my problem and asked her if she would bear with me and consent to perform a brand new song at the first New

York preview. "Of course, darling," she said "but do try to get it to me the night before."

I can say unequivocally that there is no star in the theatre today, nor perhaps has there ever been one, who would have agreed to that outrageous request, but Julie Andrews.

The one scene in the play that I knew was a breach in style was the penultimate scene involving the song "Guinevere" in which the story of Lancelot's rescue is told. I improved the lyric but I could think of no other way to impart that information to the audience. It was not only a stylistic change, but it was breaking a second major theatrical law: it was describing events that took place offstage. I hoped against hope that Fritz's music, which I thought was marvelous, would throw smoke in the critical eye and get us through.

By Thursday of the fourth week everything that was going out was out and everything that was going in was in—except, of course, Julie's song. I now was on the edge of exhaustion and Fritz seldom left his room. Sometimes I would not see him for two or three days and then only at the back of the theatre during a performance. Oh, my God, why did we let it go on so long? It must have been as much agony for him as it was for me but by now we were too far away to find the road back.

The last weekend in Boston my friend, Lars Schmidt, came up to see the play. Lars, who had begun his career producing in Sweden, had recently become one of the leading theatrical entrepreneurs in Europe. By recently, I mean ever since *My Fair Lady*. I had met him many years earlier at Oscar Hammerstein's. Over lunch one day he said to me that it was a pity he had never produced anything of mine in Sweden. I said to him, offhandedly: "all right, old boy, you can have the next one." The next one was *My Fair Lady*.

It was only a matter of days after *My Fair Lady* opened that we were swamped with offers for foreign productions including, naturally, Scandinavia, and including, naturally, Lars. I told Fritz and Herman of my promise to him and they had no objections. So he was given the rights. No fool he, he immediately aligned himself with Binkie Beaumont for all other European productions and before you could open and close a cash register, Lars had become the official producer of *My Fair Lady* on the continent. And a good producer he was. In between openings he also became the husband of Ingrid Bergman.

He had moved his base of operations to Paris by the time Fritz and I were there writing *Gigi* and I used to see a good deal of him. He is a most charming fellow, professed great friendship, and I deeply appreciated his coming to Boston. I was anxious to get his reaction. He came back to the Ritz with me after the performance and told me he thought it was an awe inspiring undertaking, certainly not without its faults. But he loved it and he wanted me to know that no matter what happened in New York, he would do it in Europe. It was a good omen, I thought, and I was vastly encouraged.

I am glad I am not clairvoyant or the momentary exhilaration of his promise might have been dissipated by the knowledge that he would never mention it again.

When we closed in Boston, besides "Guinevere" one cloud continued to hang over the play. It was still too long. The curtain came down before eleven-thirty, but just barely.

During the road tour, the only mishap that had not befallen *Camelot* concerned King Pellinore's sheepdog, Horrid. It was the only time in the history of the theatre that an animal had appeared in a play and never once left a pile in the middle of the stage. As we headed for New York, I hoped I would be able to say the same.

We closed in Boston on a Saturday night. We were scheduled to begin the first of two previews in New York on Thursday night and open on Saturday. My first move upon arriving in New York was to lock myself up in a hotel and begin work on Julie's lyric. Leaving

Bud to keep an eye on the technical progress at the Majestic The-atre, I finished it on Tuesday. Fritz had wisely gone ahead and had had the song orchestrated even before the lyric was finished. Tuesday afternoon at the theatre, Fritz and I showed it to Julie. She sang it through and thanked us profusely. I could have kissed her.

Despite the prophets of doom and the discouraging reports from the hinterlands, the advance sale had continued to mount. By the time we arrived in New York it was close to the two million dollar mark.

During the four days it took to hang the show, we continued to rehearse bits and pieces in empty theatres and on Wednesday evening, there was a performance that lives with me still. After all those weeks of sets, costumes, and lights, where so often the technical problems "take over" the play and the meaning becomes diffuse, I thought it would be a good idea to have a complete run-through on a bare stage and give the play a chance to become private and personal again. Free of the trimmings and trappings, the company was unprepared for the rediscovery of intimacy and intention. The result was a most moving experience for everyone, both on stage and off, and when I think of *Camelot* today it is that performance that remains most vividly in my mind.

Thursday night was the first preview with a New York audi-ence. Preview audiences are in a difficult position. They come into the theatre not quite knowing what to expect and uncertain whether it is permissible to like the play or not. If that sounds like a cynical observation it is not. The fact is that if one knows one is about to see a hit play, one automatically enters the theatre in a hit mood, ready to applaud the ushers. A preview audience, how-ever, is more curious than expectant—unless, of course, it is a very expensive benefit, in which case half of them are there under duress and totally unpredictable.

I assembled the cast before the performance, made a little

speech about preview audiences, advising them to be prepared for anything—or nothing—and no matter what the reaction, play the play.

After delivering my "words of wisdom," within ten minutes after the curtain rose, I was proven totally wrong. Whether the audience had expected something far worse or whether it was simply captivated, I do not know. But the first preview was a joy. Everything one could hope for happened. And Julie sang the new song as if it had always been there.

The next night I again assembled the company and warned them not to expect a Xerox of the Thursday reception. I knew this Friday benefit, I told them. They were appreciative, but quietly so. Where others laughed, they chuckled, and where others chuckled, they smiled. Where others smiled, they coughed.

The curtain rose and within three minutes it was obvious that the Friday night audience was even better than Thursday night's. It was Bastille Day and the Fourth of July plus. As I paced back and forth I kept wishing with all my soul that Moss were there. But Moss was still in that hospital in Toronto.

The following day I spent at the theatre. Naturally, Abe Feder was still lighting. Around four o'clock he finished and the stage crew was dismissed until that evening. The opening night curtain was six-forty-five and at four-thirty I was still sitting in the theatre, too tired to move. I finally pushed myself out of the seat and walked up on the stage to leave. One of the stage hands, I believe his name was Johnny, was sweeping the stage floor. As I passed him I touched him on the shoulder and said: "Good luck, kid." He stopped sweeping and looked at me. "Mr. Lerner," he said "you don't need any luck. There's too much love on the stage." I thanked him, walked out of the theatre and standing in the alley outside I began to sob.

I again assembled the company to do my speech. *This* time

I warned them about opening night audiences. I told them how they laughed little and applauded much and repeated again that no matter what happened, play the play. With my record for predictions, I do not think my words carried much weight, but I thanked them all and told them if ever a company deserved a success, they did.

No one can ever accuse an author or a director of slaving selflessly with concealed halos under their hats. But on an opening night, shortly before the curtain rises, standing in front of a group with whom one has shared the lifeboat for so many weeks, at that moment you do indeed think of them only—gratefully and affectionately. A few moments later when the curtain rises and you are standing at the rear of the theatre it is, as Richard said, every man for himself.

The opening night audience was an autograph hunter's paradise. As the lights dimmed I walked down the side aisle and there was no one in the first twenty rows whom I either did not know, or know of. Just as the lights went out I saw Noel Coward sliding into his seat, exactly on time.

I took my place at the rear of the theatre. Overture. Curtain up. After one has watched a play for a certain amount of time there is usually a line or a song early on that tells one exactly the mood of the audience. In *Camelot* my barometer used to be a couplet in the second chorus of "I Wonder What the King Is Doing Tonight." I knew I was among friends if there was a warm, shall we say, chuckle on the lines

You wonder what the king is doing tonight.
He wishes he were in Scotland fishing tonight . . .

There had been a reaction at the previews. Not tonight. The audience just listened. I began to shrink. All through the first act the audience laughed a little and applauded much, but not as much as hoped for. The cast was caught off guard and the scenes played without the verve of the previous two nights. Richard sensed the audience and kept driving the play forward. He performed his soliloquy at the end of act one magnificiently but the applause was perfunctory.

I never mingle during intermissions and usually hide out in the manager's office waiting for someone to bring me news of the word-of-mouth. No comment is as bad as bad comment. That night no one came to report.

At the opening of the second act Bobby Goulet stopped the show with "If Ever I Would Leave You" and it was the one life-saving moment of the evening. Despite the absence of the usual laughter and applause the show did not gain in time. Running time remained the same. The curtain calls were well-applauded but it was all too clear there was no excitement in the house.

After the final curtain call I went backstage. The first person I saw was Noel Coward and he, bless him, broke the tension. Richard used to give impersonations of what various theatre people say to you after an opening. Noel, according to him, invariably came up to you, patted you on the shoulder and said, veddy, veddy softly: "Mahvellous, darling, mahvellous." I met Noel in the alley just outside the stage door. He came up to me, patted me on the shoulder and said veddy, veddy softly: "Mahvellous, darling, mahvellous."

I made my dressing room journey to thank everyone. I sensed their disappointment and reminded them—and it is the truth—that the reaction of an opening night audience is often no indication of the reviews. At the opening of *Brigadoon* people kept walking out through the second act and the play received a unanimous rave. On the opening night of *Love Life,* the musical I had done with Kurt Weill, the audience stood up and cheered at the end and the press was very mixed indeed.

I said all this with as much underplayed conviction as I could and I have no idea how many were convinced by it. The one person I did not convince was myself. I had already begun to prepare for the worst. Although I have never had a play where bad notices made the actors turn and point an accusing finger at me, nevertheless, I have always felt a certain sense of guilt as if I had failed them. It takes much more work to produce a failure than a success, and the feeling of "us against the world" can be very strong indeed: so I inevitably feel I have let them down.

As usual the stage was crowded with friends, agents, and relatives of members of the cast. The general mood was neither festive nor funereal, and I found myself instinctively preparing to submerge, leaving about an inch of periscope above water for observation.

After the play I did the one thing I always swore I would never do: I went to an opening night party. Luchow's restaurant had offered to throw a bash and the press department had persuaded us to agree. I felt battered by my own emotions and given the choice would gladly have been back in that hospital in Toronto. But everyone connected with the play would be there and I had no alternative.

When I arrived at Luchow's, it was gaiety unlimited. One of the benefits of a Saturday night opening is that the reviews do not appear until Monday. The critics for the morning papers write their reviews after the performance, but under less pressure. Usually the *Times'* review becomes available to the press department within two hours of the curtain coming down. On a Saturday night opening, it is at least three hours. As a result, a good deal of concern is filtered out of the atmosphere and everyone can forget about the show for a while and enjoy himself. Unfortunately, it is no longer true today. We now have television critics. (Not really critics—in most instances news reporters professionally moonlighting.) They appear during the eleven o'clock news, thus enabling Saturday night parties to die just as quickly as they do during the week.

Luchow's is a very large restaurant with a very large number of tables, and I covered them all, radiating goodwill and good cheer, and then sat down to cushion myself with a bit of booze.

Finally the excruciating moment arrived. It always happens the same way. Someone from the press department comes to the table and touches you on the shoulder and whispers in your ear to come to the telephone. You casually rise, as if on your way to the men's room, and make your way to a telephone somewhere in the front of the restaurant. The press agent is on the telephone, the review is being read to him and he is jotting down as many lines as he can. You wait. You look in his eyes for an indication. He is too busy to notice. A year goes by. He hangs up.

"The *Times* isn't good," said the press agent "but I think there's enough stuff to quote." (They always say that.) The *Times,* incidentally, was Howard Taubman.

AJL: What didn't he like?

PRESS AGENT: The second act.

AJL: Did he like the first act?

> PRESS AGENT: Oh, yeah. He loved the first act and he loved the music and lyrics, Burton and Andrews, the sets and costumes and everything else. He just didn't like the second act. But I think it's good enough to get by.

(They always say that, too.)

I accepted it stoically, which means I did not burst into tears. I looked at Fritz. He was staring down thoughtfully. I touched him on the shoulder. He looked up at me and shrugged, which meant, "Too bad," or "Who cares?", or probably both. A second later the telephone rang again. The press agent picked it up. I waited.

Another year went by. He hung up smiling. "The *News* is a rave. Chapman loved it," he said. I felt better. I looked at Fritz again. He shrugged. A different shrug. It could have meant "That's better," or "I knew Chapman would like it," or "Too bad it wasn't the *Times*." A Viennese shrug is the crossword puzzle of body language.

I went back to my table. I do not remember who was sitting at it, but I told them the *Times* was mixed, the *News* was wonderful and that I was tired and I thought I would go home. And I did.

As I drove uptown, I thought to myself that if the *Tribune* and just one of the evening papers were good we would be all right commercially. But commercially successful or not, I was crushed. Pockmarked with flaws though the play may have been, at that moment, on that night, I did not see them. Three months later I would, but there was something about *Camelot*, more than any play I have written, that was too much a part of me to be objective.

On Sunday the rest of the papers trickled in. The *Tribune* was not unlike the *Times*, but Walter Kerr had great respect for the aspiration. Both Taubman and Kerr were critical of the breach in style near the end of the second act, and although the music was praised, the dramaturgy was not. The *Mirror* was disappointed that it was not *My Fair Lady* and the evening papers on the whole were good.

I have always had one way of judging if a play has gotten over or not. If at ten o'clock on the morning after the opening there is a line at the box office window, the play is a hit. If there is not—trouble is afoot. At ten o'clock I called the theatre. Trouble was afoot. But we still had an enormous advance sale and unquestionably the play would have a run. But how long? Nobody knew.

Bill Paley at CBS called in his experts to evaluate for him how long the play would last. The experts consisted of two television lawyers who, finding no previous case in the law library, notified Mr. Paley that their personal Nielsen survey indicated the show could not possibly run past May. My own opinion was that it was too early to judge, and that to a large measure it would depend upon the success of the album.

But on one point I was determined: if *Camelot* was going to die in May, I was not. To that end I packed up and departed for a few weeks of skiing in Switzerland. Two weeks after I arrived, I looked around the hotel and discovered I was the only man not on crutches. The lobby looked like the last scene of *A Farewell to Arms*. Skiing happens to be the one sport where the better you get, the more dangerous it becomes. I decided to stop before I got any better.

I returned in February to a bleak *Camelot*. There was hardly any window sale at all and people were walking out of the theatre not by the dozens, but some nights by as much as two to three hundred. The album was rising slowly in the charts, but the word-of-mouth was not good and the chances of recovering the investment seemed infinitesimal. Moss, at long last, was out of the hospital. He had been to Palm Springs to recuperate and was now back in New York. Fritz, who had also been in Palm Springs, returned with him.

Moss went to see the play and inspired us to go back to work on it—something that is seldom done after a play opens, and certainly never done three months after it opens. Some of the flaws that were so clear to Moss's experienced and objective eye, now became clear to me. I spent a week rewriting and we cut out two songs: one sung by the ensemble and one by Julie, and finally brought the play down to size.

And then came the miracle.

Three weeks before, Ed Sullivan, who then had the most popular variety show on television, had decided to do a full hour devoted to Lerner and Loewe. He had honored other composers and lyricists in the past and, in fact, it was the second time he had so honored us. The occasion was the fifth anniversary of *My Fair Lady*. The program usually consisted of a scene or two from whatever show the authors may have had running at the time, and a medley of their previous hits. When Ed, Fritz, and I were having a meeting to discuss the content of the show, I asked if we might be allowed to routine it ourselves. Ed, one of the most gracious gentlemen in television, gave us carte blanche.

It had always been the custom to do only the briefest possible moments from a current play, in order not to give too much of it away. What I had in mind was to do very little from *My Fair Lady* and then spend the last twenty minutes doing all the best songs and scenes from *Camelot,* much more than had ever been presented before from any play running on Broadway.

The Sullivan Show was Sunday night. During the previous week the cast not only rehearsed the T.V. show but, under Moss's direction, the cuts and changes in the play as well. On the television show, Goulet sang "If Ever I Would Leave You": Julie sang "Where Are the Simple Joys of Maidenhood?": Richard did "Camelot": and he and Julie together did "What Do the Simple Folk Do?" All in costume. And they were a smash.

The following morning I was awakened by a phone call from an excited manager at the Majestic Theatre. "You better come down here," he said, "and look at this." "Look at what?" I asked. He answered, "Just come and see what's going on at this box office." I got to the threatre as quickly as I could. For the first time there was a line halfway down the block.

That night the audience came to the threatre and saw the vastly improved musical that Moss had rehearsed the week before. And at eleven-fifteen the curtain came down! The reaction and the applause were overwhelming. The people came up the aisles raving.

Camelot was finally a hit.

Backstage the cast was stunned by the reception, exhausted, bewildered, and jubilant. The change in audience reaction had gathered momentum as the play progressed, and as the wave of approval came sweeping over the orchestra pit on to the stage it not only raised their spirits, but the level of the performance. As Moss, Fritz, and I edged our way through the dark passage that leads from the orchestra on to the stage, I whispered to Moss: "You son of a bitch! How dare you give me an inferiority complex."

When I left the theatre I was too manic for such sedentary locomotion as an automobile and so I decided to walk home. The evening was still ringing in my ears and I could still hear the echoes of Richard's thunderous last speech. He had just knighted the young boy and commanded him to run home and keep the flame of the Round Table alive. Pellinore says to him: "Who was that, Arthur?" Arthur answers triumphantly: "One of what we all are, Pelly. Less than a drop in the great blue motion of the sunlit sea. But it seems some of the drops sparkle, Pelly. Some of them do sparkle!"

Walking uptown I passed Forty-fifth Street, where *Gigi* had opened; a few blocks further, the Mark Hellinger Theatre where *My Fair Lady* was still running, and the faces of a decade crowded my mind. Fritz, Moss, Herman, Rex, Richard, Julie, Cecil, Abe, Hanya, Oliver, Franz, Vincente, Maurice, Arthur . . .

Oh yes, I thought. Some of the drops sparkle. Some of them do sparkle.

Camelot ran a little over two years on Broadway and an additional two years on the road. Jack Hylton, the eminent British producer, presented it at Drury Lane where it also ran for over two years. It ran even longer in Australia.

It was sold to films for a million dollars and the total profits of the play reached well into the seven figures.

For Tim White, the stage version of *The Once and Future King* proved to be more lucrative than all his previous works. After the play opened in New York he returned to Alderney and I never saw him again. However, he sent me his last book of poetry in which he wrote: "Dear Alan, How extraordinary it is that you, a stranger from a far-off land, should have been responsible for making me my fortune. Affectionately, Tim."

By late spring, the album had become number one in the country and remained there for over sixty weeks. The eventual total cast album sale, meaning the album made by the original Broadway cast, the English company's recording starring Laurence Harvey, that light baritone, and the soundtrack album from the film exceeded two and a half million albums.

Fritz, as I had expected he would, had made up his mind that for him *Camelot* was the end of the line. Only sixty, and a vigorous one at that, both vertically and horizontally, the certainty of struggle far outweighed the uncertainty of success, and even success now seemed superfluous. His health was good and he liked it that way. He loved Palm Springs and he loved the French Riviera. He decided to devote his energies to conserving them.

There were no formal farewells, no goodbyes, nothing to mark the end of the long voyage we had been on together. He went to Palm Springs. I went to Europe. And that was that.

It was not until two years later that I understood for the first time what our partnership had truly meant. I had begun to write a new musical. The discovery that overwhelmed me was less a creative one than a personal one. I realized that over the years, Fritz and I had unconsciously built an invisible fortress around our collaboration. When the drawbridge was up, it protected us against the brickbats of humanity and our personal lives seemed far away and lost the sharp outline of reality. Fritz joked about my problems and I, his. Marital difficulties, for instance, lost a good deal of their anxiety when Fritz would say: "You are a funny little boy. You build a nest and then shit in it." Whether it was true or not was of no consequence. We laughed and were soon feverishly working. And nothing else mattered.

I cannot imagine not writing and I shall undoubtedly go on doing so until there is either no more theatre or no more me. But one thing is certain: there will never be another Fritz. No relationship will ever be as close, both professionally and personally. For me there will never again be exactly the same creative exhileration. Writing will never again be as much fun. A collaboration as intense as ours inescapably had to be complex. But I loved him more than I understood or misunderstood him and I know he loved me more than he understood or misunderstood me.

In 1971, I sent him a motion picture script I had written of Saint-Exupery's *The Little Prince*. He called me, filled with his old excitement, and I went out to see him. Writing a film does not have the sustained rigor of writing a play. There are no endless days of auditioning, no agonizing weeks on the road. Discarding the vows and resolutions, he decided to have one last fling and we went to work again. Eleven years slipped away in a minute and it was "pre-Camelot" again. He wrote the most beautiful score, filled with melody and bubbling with the innocence of youth. Alas, it never was heard on the screen as he had composed it. The director, someone named Stanley Donen, took it upon himself to change every tempo, delete musical phrases at will and distort the intention of every song until the entire score was unrecognizable. Unlike the theatre, where the author is the final authority, in motion pictures it is the director. And if one falls in the hands of some cinematic Bigfoot, one pays the price for someone else's ineptitude. In this case the price was high, because it undoubtedly was Fritz's last score.

When Moss was in Palm Springs recuperating, he, too, fell in love with it and he and Kitty bought a house there. After a summer abroad, I returned to New York to move into my own new digs, and Moss and I were able to spend a little time together before he moved out to Palm Springs for the winter. One evening at their apartment in New York, he and I went into his study to have a "jaw." He asked me if I had any idea what I would do next. I said I did not. He asked me if I had ever thought of writing a play—a play, that is, without music. I said that I had from time to time, but that I knew perfectly well that after four pages I would begin to wonder where the first song would come. Moss then told me that the reason he asked was that he had an idea himself which he rather liked, but he was not certain he wanted to write it. He said he would like to tell it to me, and if it excited my interest he would give it to me as a present. He told me the idea and I did like it, genuinely. However, I told him that not only could I not accept it, but that he could write it far better than I, or, for that matter, far better than anyone.

Everything about this little incident touched me deeply, because it was so typical of everything that was Moss. I knew his offer was sincere. At the same time I knew that one of the reasons he was reluctant to write it was because of the hell of his own insecurity. In spite of all his years of success and the universal recognition of his talents, let alone the extraordinary artistic and commercial success of his book *Act One,* I know of no man so tortured by self-doubt and so nobly gifted at concealing it. I also know that my enthusiastic reaction was therapeutic. When we ended our conversation, I think he had made up his mind to take a crack at it.

A few days later, he and Kitty departed for Palm Springs.

That was the last time I ever saw him.

About eleven o'clock in the morning of December 18, the

telephone rang. It was Kitty. When she said the first word, "Alan. . . .", the blood left my lips. She told me that shortly after seven o'clock that morning, in the driveway of their house, Moss had dropped dead.

I sat in my room too stunned and grief-stricken even for tears. Some time later, I do not know how long, I received a phone call from the *New York Times* asking me to write a piece about Moss for the Sunday edition. I said I would.

I sat down at the typewriter. The moment I wrote the first word I fell apart. The piece took me about two hours to write, and I wrote it with trembling hands and saw the pages through blurred eyes.

What I found myself writing about was Moss's gallantry. Despite the crest of success he was riding, the devils that clawed at him within were so violent that he could not get through the day without a morning visit to the psychiatrist and an evening visit before he went home. Yet I doubt if anyone, other than his beloved Kitty, was aware of it. Certainly no one who met him during the day, no matter how well he knew him, would have suspected. When one is plagued by that kind of emotional anguish there is nothing more difficult than the simple act of listening when others speak. Moss was always able to listen, sympathize, empathize, and comment with perception and wit. Somehow he never allowed his preoccupation with his own pain to remove him from the human race. He never locked himself in, nor locked the world out. He never inflicted his suffering on others. He was the most gallant man I ever knew.

As I said when I first mentioned his name in this book, there will never be another Moss Hart, and no priest, minister, rabbi, or lama can convince me that taking him away at the age of fifty-seven was anything but senseless cruelty. I believe deeply there is a Divine Order and that life is without end, but at times Fate deals with it so frivolously that it seems without meaning.

But the tale of *Camelot* was not over.

On November 22, 1963, at Dealey Plaza, Dallas, Texas, the life of every human being on this planet was suddenly changed. The following week, Theodore H. White went to Hyannis Port and interviewed Jacqueline Kennedy for *Life* magazine. Teddy White, President Kennedy, and I had been classmates together in Harvard, and the President and I had been coeditors of the school yearbook at Choate. The interview occupied the two-page centerfold of *Life* and the second page began as follows:

'When Jack quoted something, it was usually classical,' she said, 'but I'm so ashamed of myself—all I keep thinking of is this line from a musical comedy.

'At night, before we'd go to sleep, Jack liked to play some records; and the song he loved most came at the very end of this record. The lines he loved to hear were: "Don't let it be forgot, that once there was a spot, for one brief shining moment that was known as Camelot." '

She wanted to make sure that the point came clear and went on: 'There'll be great presidents again—and the Johnsons are wonderful, they've been wonderful to me—but there'll never be another Camelot again. Once, the more I read of history the more bitter I got. For a while I thought history was something that bitter old men wrote. But then I realized history made Jack what he was. You must think of him as this little boy, sick so much of the time, reading in bed, reading history, reading the Knights of the Round Table, reading Marlborough. For Jack, history was full of heroes. And if it made him this way—if it made him see the heroes—maybe other little boys will see. Men are such a combination of good and bad. Jack had this hero idea of history, the idealistic view.'

But she came back to the idea that transfixed her: ' "Don't let it be forgot, that once there was a spot, for one brief shining moment that was known as Camelot"—and it will never be that way again.'

The interview then continued for another half-page and ended:

> She said it is time people paid attention to the new pres-ident and the new first lady. But she does not want them to forget John F. Kennedy or read of him only in dusty or bitter histories: For one brief moment there was Camelot.

Once the interview appeared, it immediately became a major news story. At the time, I had offices on the Lexington Avenue side of the Waldorf Astoria. *Life* magazine came out on Tuesday. Wednesday afternoon, I was crossing the lobby of the Waldorf on my way to the Park Avenue side of the hotel, when I passed the news-stand. The *Journal-American,* now defunct, had just been delivered. In headline letters above the title of the newspaper I saw:

> *Don't let it be forgot,*
> *That once there was a spot,*
> *For one brief shining moment*
> *That was known as Camelot.*

The tragedy of the hour, the astonishment of seeing a lyric I had written in headlines, and the shock of recognition of a relationship between the two that extended far beyond the covers of one mag-azine, overloaded me with confused emotions. I was so dazed that I did not even buy the newspaper. I lived on Seventy-first Street at the time and I started to walk home. It was not until Eighty-third Street that I realized I had passed my house.

Camelot was then on the road, playing the Opera House in Chicago, a huge barn of a theatre with over three thousand seats. I was told later what happened that night.

The theatre was packed. The verse quoted above is sung in the last scene. Louis Hayward was playing King Arthur. When he came to those lines, there was a sudden wail from the audience. It was not a muffled sob; it was a loud, almost primitive cry of pain. The play stopped, and for almost five minutes everyone in the theatre—on the stage, in the wings, in the pit, and in the audience—wept without restraint. Then the play continued.

Camelot had suddenly become the symbol of those thousand days when people the world over saw a bright new light of hope shining from the White House. Later, Samuel Eliot Morison wrote his monumental *Oxford History of the American People,* which ends with the death of President Kennedy—the last page of the book is the music and lyrics of *Camelot.*

Ironically enough, also from that moment on the first act became the weak act and the second act, the strong one. God knows I would have preferred that history had not become my collaborator.

For myself, I have never been able to see a performance of *Camelot* again. I was in London when it was playing at Drury Lane, having arrived a few days after the producer, Jack Hylton, suddenly died. But I did not go to the theatre. I could not.

The death of the president opened the door to the chamber of horrors called the 1960s. As the national compass began to go mad and the nation began to lose its sense of direction, no less did the performing arts. The theatre and motion pictures found themselves in the same boat, without a rudder or motor, at the mercy of the currents of fadism, trying to keep afloat until by accident or vision they could see where they were going. Fortunately for motion pictures, the films that were successful were extraordinarily so, and in the theatre the plays that were successful, most of which were musicals—and a mixed bag at that—were profitable enough to keep the "invalid" alive.

Kenneth Tynan once wrote that a critic is a man who knows the direction but does not know how to drive. But the critics live in the same country, and if they have been reduced to personal likes and dislikes, peeves and fancies, they are more to be feared than blamed. Would God I could speak in the past tense, but I cannot. Nothing has changed. The drift continues.

In England, the theatre is alive with despair and bitterness. Playwright after playwright, each in his own way, reflects an awareness of Britain's fall from grace and the inability of anyone to break the fall. Over here there is no such awareness, no expression that indicates where we are and who we are. Every play is about only what it is about.

In the musical theatre there is no trend towards any particular kind of musical. Rock and roll came in like an orangutan and went out like a hyena, as every intelligent composer and lyricist knew it would. Youth has many glories, but judgment is not one of them, and no amount of electronic amplification can turn a belch into an aria.

Since Fritz retired I have written three musicals for the theatre, *On a Clear Day You Can See Forever* with Burton Lane, *Coco* with André Previn, 1600 *Pennsylvania Avenue* with Leonard Bernstein, and, reversing the normal order, adapted *Gigi* for the stage. *On a Clear Day* was modestly received. *Coco* less modestly, but because of the incredible Katharine Hepburn did well. *Gigi,* comme çi comme ça. 1600 *Pennsylvania Avenue,* well, you remember the Titanic.

For films, besides *The Little Prince* I adapted *My Fair Lady, Camelot, On a Clear Day,* and *Paint Your Wagon. My Fair Lady* continued her winning ways. *Camelot* did fairly well in the press, but I have no idea how it fared at the box office— (Miscellaneous: $2 million). *On a Clear Day* did quite well and *Paint Your Wagon* was resoundingly booed at home, with the occasional exception, and resoundingly cheered abroad, and has grossed a startlingly large sum of money. But whatever befell the plays, many of the songs survived, and I have recently been informed by those who record such statistics that Berlin, Gershwin, and I are the most performed lyricists extant.

I have survived the malaise known as male menopause, more popularly called an identity crisis, so common to men as they pass the half century. I have doubted my relevance to the point of paralysis, and although I never reached that time of the soul when Scott Fitzgerald said it was always three o'clock in the morning, I have seen two-thirty.

But in the end I have come to realize that I write not because it is what I do, but because it is what I am; not because it is how I make my living, but how I make my life. And I have traveled the "bumpy road of love" enough to have worn it smooth and I am now happily married.

I miss the three-dimensional excitement of the theatre world I knew and God knows I miss the people with whom I shared it. But I love the theatre no less than I did then and I feel the same sense of coming home every time I begin to write.

Now, if I can only remember everything Moss told me . . .

Lyrics

My Fair Lady

Why Can't The English?

HIGGINS (*To* PICKERING)

Why can't the English teach their children how to speak?
This verbal class distinction by now should be antique.
If you spoke as she does, sir,
Instead of the way you do,
Why, you might be selling flowers, too.

An Englishman's way of speaking absolutely classifies him.
The moment he talks he makes some other Englishman despise
   him.
One common language I'm afraid we'll never get.
Oh, why can't the English learn to set

A good example to people whose English is painful to your ears?
The Scotch[1] and the Irish leave you close to tears.
There even are places where English completely disappears.
In America, they haven't used it for years!

Why can't the English teach their children how to speak?
Norwegians learn Norwegian; the Greeks are taught their Greek.
In France every Frenchman knows his language from "A" to
   "Zed"

(spoken)

The French never care what they do, actually, as long as they
   pronounce it properly.

---

1 Obviously it should be "Scots" not "Scotch." However, whenever I have
completed a lyric, I go over it and try to remove every letter "S" that I can, even at
grammatical expense. "S" is a dangerous consonant. Too many can sound like a tea
kettle, and with the growing shortage of male hormones it is even more precarious.

Arabians learn Arabian with the speed of summer lightning.
The Hebrews learn it backwards, which is absolutely frightening.
But use proper English, you're regarded as a freak.
Why can't the English,
Why can't the English
Learn to speak?!

Wouldn't It Be Loverly?

All I want is a room somewhere,
Far away from the cold night air;
With one enormous chair . . .
Oh, wouldn't it be loverly?

Lots of choc'late for me to eat;
Lots of coal makin' lots of heat;
Warm face, warm hands, warm feet . . . !
Oh, wouldn't it be loverly?

Oh, so loverly sittin' absobloominlutely still!
I would never budge till spring
Crept over me winder sill.

Someone's head restin' on my knee,
Warm and tender as he can be,
Who takes good care of me . . .
Oh, wouldn't it be loverly?
Loverly! Loverly!
Loverly! Loverly!

I'm An Ordinary Man

I'm an ordinary man;
Who desires nothing more
Than just the ordinary chance

To live exactly as he likes
And do precisely what he wants.
An average man am I
Of no eccentric whim;
Who likes to live his life
Free of strife,
Doing whatever he thinks is best for him.
Just an ordinary man.

But let a woman in your life
And your serenity is through!
She'll redecorate your home
From the cellar to the dome;
Then get on to the enthralling
Fun of overhauling
You.

Oh, let a woman in your life
And you are up against the wall!
Make a plan and you will find
She has something else in mind;
And so rather than do either
You do something else that neither
Likes at all.

You want to talk of Keats or Milton;
She only wants to talk of love.
You go to see a play or ballet,
And spend it searching for her glove.

Oh, let a woman in your life
And you invite eternal strife!
Let them buy their wedding bands
For those anxious little hands;
I'd be equally as willing

My Fair Lady

For a dentist to be drilling
Than to ever let a woman in my life!

I'm a very gentle man;
Even-tempered and good-natured,
Whom you never hear complain;
Who has the milk of human kindness
By the quart in ev'ry vein.
A patient man am I
Down to my fingertips;
The sort who never could,
Ever would,
Let an insulting remark escape his lips.
Just a very gentle man.

But let a woman in your life
And patience hasn't got a chance.
She will beg you for advice;
Your reply will be concise.
And she'll listen very nicely
Then go out and do precisely
What she wants!

You were a man of grace and polish
Who never spoke above a hush.
Now all at once you're using language
That would make a sailor blush.

Oh, let a woman in your life
And you are plunging in a knife!
Let the others of my sex
Tie the knot around their necks;
I'd prefer a new edition
Of the Spanish Inquisition
Than to ever let a woman in my life!

I'm a quiet living man
Who prefers to spend his evenings
In the silence of his room;
Who likes an atmosphere as restful
As an undiscovered tomb.
A pensive man am I
Of philosophic joys;
Who likes to meditate,
Contemplate,
Free from humanity's mad, inhuman noise.
Just a quiet living man.

But let a woman in your life
And your sabbatical is through!
In a line that never ends
Come an army of her friends;
Come to jabber and to chatter
And to tell her what the matter
Is with you.

She'll have a booming, boist'rous fam'ly
Who will descend on you en masse.
She'll have a large Wagnerian mother
With a voice that shatters glass!
Oh, let a woman in your life . . .

*(Higgins turns on one of his machines at an accelerated speed so
   the voice approximates
a piercing female babble)*

Let a woman in your life . . .
(He turns on a second machine)
Let a woman in your life . . .
*(And a third. The noise becomes unbearable.
His point made, he turns them all off)*
I shall never let a woman in my life!

With A Little Bit O' Luck

The Lord above gave man an arm of iron
So he could do his job and never shirk.
The Lord above gave man an arm of iron—but
With a little bit o' luck,
With a little bit o' luck,
Someone else'll do the blinkin' work!

With a little bit—
With a little bit—
With a little bit o' luck
You'll never work!

The Lord above made liquor for temptation,
To see if man could turn away from sin.
The Lord above made liquor for temptation—but
With a little bit o'luck,
With a little bit o' luck,
When temptation comes you'll give right in!

With a little bit—
With a little bit—
With a little bit o'luck
You'll give right in.
Oh, you can walk the straight and narrow;
But with a little bit o' luck
You'll run amuck!

The gentle sex was made for man to marry,
To share his nest and see his food is cooked.
The gentle sex was made for man to marry—but
With a little bit o' luck,
With a little bit o' luck
You can have it all and not get hooked.

With a little bit—
With a little bit—
With a little bit o' luck
You won't get hooked.
With a little bit—
With a little bit—
With a little bit o' bloomin' luck!

The Lord above made man to help his neighbor,
No matter where, on land or sea or foam.
The Lord above made man to help his neighbor—but
With a little bit o' luck,
With a little bit o' luck,
When he comes around you won't be home!

With a little bit—
With a little bit—
With a little bit o'luck
You won't be home.

They're always throwin' goodness at you;
But with a little bit o' luck
A man can duck!

Oh, it's a crime for man to go philanderin',
And fill his wife's poor heart with grief and doubt.
Oh, it's a crime for man to go philanderin'—but
With a little bit o' luck,
With a little bit o' luck,
You can see the bloodhound don't find out!

With a little bit—
With a little bit—
With a little bit o' luck
She won't find out!

With a little bit—
With a little bit—
With a little bit o' bloomin' luck!

Just You Wait

Just you wait, 'enry 'iggins, just you wait!
You'll be sorry but your tears'll be too late!
You'll be broke and I'll have money;
Will I help you? Don't be funny!
Just you wait, 'enry 'iggins, just you wait!

Just you wait, 'enry 'iggins, till you're sick,
And you scream to fetch a doctor double-quick.
I'll be off a second later
And go straight to the the-ater!
Oh ho ho, 'enry 'iggins, just you wait!

Ooooooooh 'enry 'iggins!
Just you wait until we're swimmin' in the sea!
Ooooooooh 'enry 'iggins!
And you get a cramp a little ways from me!
When you yell you're going to drown
I'll get dressed and go to town!
Oh ho ho, 'enry 'iggins!
Oh ho ho, 'enry 'iggins!
Just you wait!

One day I'll be famous! I'll be proper and prim;
Go to St. James so often I will call it St. Jim!
One evening the King will say: "Oh, Liza, old thing,
I want all of England your praises to sing.
Next week on the twentieth of May
I proclaim Eliza Doolittle Day!
All the people will celebrate the glory of you,

And whatever you wish and want I gladly will do."
"Thanks a lot, King," says I, in a manner well-bred;
"But all I want is 'enry 'iggins 'ead!"
"Done," says the King, with a stroke.
"Guard, run and bring in the bloke!"

Then they'll march you, 'enry 'iggins, to the wall;
And the King will tell me: "Liza, sound the call."
As they raise their rifles higher,
I'll shout: "Ready! Aim! Fire!"
Oh ho ho, 'enry 'iggins!
Down you'll go! 'enry 'iggins!
Just you wait!!!

The Rain In Spain

ELIZA
  The rain in Spain stays mainly in the plain.
HIGGINS
  What was that?
ELIZA
  The rain in Spain stays mainly in the plain.
HIGGINS
  Again.
ELIZA
  The rain in Spain stays mainly in the plain.
HIGGINS
  I think she's got it! I think she's got it!
ELIZA
  The rain in Spain stays mainly in the plain!
HIGGINS (*TRIUMPHANTLY*)
  By George, she's got it!
  By George, she's got it!
  Now once again, where does it rain?

ELIZA

On the plain! On the plain!

HIGGINS

And where's that soggy plain?

ELIZA

In Spain! In Spain!

ALL

The rain in Spain stays mainly in the plain!

The rain in Spain stays mainly in the plain!

HIGGINS

In Hertford, Hertford, and Hampshire . . . ?

ELIZA

Hurricanes hardly happen.

(Higgins taps out "How kind of you to let me come.")

ELIZA

How kind of you to let me come!

HIGGINS

Now once again, where does it rain?

ELIZA

On the plain! On the plain!

HIGGINS

And where's the blasted plain?

ELIZA

In Spain! In Spain!

ALL

The rain in Spain stays mainly in the plain!

The rain in Spain stays mainly in the plain!

I Could Have Danced All Night

Bed! Bed! I couldn't go to bed!

My head's too light to try to set it down!

Sleep! Sleep! I couldn't sleep tonight!

Not for all the jewels in the crown!

I could have danced all night!
I could have danced all night!
And still have begged for more.
I could have spread my wings
And done a thousand things
I've never done before.

I'll never know
What made it so exciting;
Why all at once
My heart took flight.
I only knew when he
Began to dance with me,
I could have danced, danced, danced all night!

Ascot Gavotte

Ev'ry duke and earl and peer is here.
Ev'ry one who should be here is here.
What a smashing, positively dashing
Spectacle: the Ascot op'ning day.

At the gate are all the horses
Waiting for the cue to fly away.
What a gripping, absolutely ripping
Moment at the Ascot op'ning day.

Pulses rushing!
Faces flushing!
Heartbeats speed up!
I have never been so keyed up!

Any second now
They'll begin to run.
Hark! A bell is ringing,

Forward
Look! It has begun . . . !

(long, expressionless, emotionless pause)

What a frenzied moment that was!
Didn't they maintain an exhausting pace?
'Twas a thrilling, absolutely chilling
Running of the Ascot op'ning race.

On The Street Where You Live

I have often walked down this street before;
But the pavement always stayed beneath my feet before.
All at once am I
Several storeys high.
Knowing I'm on the street where you live.

Are there lilac trees in the heart of town?
Can you hear a lark in any other part of town?
Does enchantment pour
Out of ev'ry door?
No, it's just on the street where you live!

And oh! the towering feeling
Just to know somehow you are near!
The overpowering feeling
That any second you may suddenly appear!

People stop and stare. They don't bother me.
For there's nowhere else on earth that I would rather be.
Let the time go by,
I won't care if I
Can be here on the street where you live.

You Did It

PICKERING
> Tonight, old man, you did it!
> You did it! You did it!
> You said that you would do it,
> And indeed you did.
> I thought that you would rue it;
> I doubted you'd do it.
> But now I must admit it
> That succeed you did.
> You should get a medal
> Or be even made a knight.

HIGGINS
> It was nothing. Really nothing.

PICKERING
> All alone you hurdled
> Ev'ry obstacle in sight.

HIGGINS
> Now, wait! Now, wait!
> Give credit where it's due.
> A lot of the glory goes to you.

PICKERING
> But you're the one who did it,
> Who did it, who did it!
> As sturdy as Gibraltar,
> Not a second did you falter.
> There's no doubt about it,
> You did it!
> I must have aged a year tonight.
> At times I thought I'd die of fright.
> Never was there a momentary lull.

HIGGINS
> Shortly after we came in

I saw at once we'd easily win;
And after that I found it deadly dull.

PICKERING

You should have heard the ooh's and ah's;
Ev'ry one wond'ring who she was.

HIGGINS

You'd think they'd never seen a lady before.

PICKERING

And when the Prince of Transylvania
Asked to meet her,
And gave his arm to lead her to the floor . . . !
I said to him: You did it!
You did it! You did it!
They thought she was ecstatic
And so damned aristocratic,
And they never knew
That you did it!

HIGGINS (*SPEAKING*)

Thanks heavens for Zoltan Karpathy. If it weren't for him I would
have died of boredom.

MRS. PEARCE

Karpathy? That dreadful Hungarian? Was he there?

HIGGINGS

Yes!
That blackguard who uses the science of speech
More to blackmail and swindle than teach;
He made it the devilish business of his
"To find out who this Miss Doolittle is."

Ev'ry time we looked around
There he was, that hairy hound
From Budapest.
Never leaving us alone
Never have I ever known
A ruder pest.

Fin'lly I decided it was foolish
Not to let him have his chance with her.
So I stepped aside and let him dance with her.

Oozing charm from ev'ry pore,
He oiled his way around the floor.
Ev'ry trick that he could play,
He used to strip her mask away.
And when at last the dance was done
He glowed as if he knew he'd won!
And with a voice too eager,
And a smile too broad,
He announced to the hostess
That she was a fraud!

MRS. PEARCE

No!

HIGGINS

Ja wohl!
Her English is too good, he said,
Which clearly indicates that she is foreign.
Whereas others are instructed in their native language
English people aren'.
And although she may have studied with an expert
Di'lectician and grammarian,
I can tell that she was born Hungarian!
Not only Hungarian, but of royal blood. She is a princess!

SERVANTS

Congratulations, Professor Higgins,
For your glorious victory!
Congratulations, Professor Higgins!
You'll be mentioned in history!

SERVANTS
> This evening, sir, you did it!
> You did it! You did it!
> You said that you would do it!
> And indeed you did.
>
> This evening, sir, you did it!
> You did it! You did it!
> We know that we have said it,
> But—you did it and the credit
> For it all belongs to you!

REST OF SERVANTS
> Congratulations,
> Professor Higgins!
> For your glorious
> Victory!
>
> Congratulations,
> Professor Higgins!
> Sing a hail and halleluia
> Ev'ry bit of credit
> For it all belongs to you!

Show Me

ELIZA (*To Freddie*)
> Words! Words! Words! I'm so sick of words!
> I get words all day through;
> First from him, now from you!
> Is that all you blighters can do?
>
> Don't talk of stars
> Burning above;
> If you're in love,
> Show me!
>
> Tell me no dreams
> Filled with desire.
> If you're on fire,
> Show me!
>
> Here we are together in the middle of the night!
> Don't talk of spring! Just hold me tight!
> Anyone who's ever been in love'll tell you that
> This is no time for a chat!

The Street Where I Live

Haven't your lips
Longed for my touch?
Don't say how much,
Show me! Show me!

Don't talk of love lasting through time.
Make me no undying vow.
Show me now!

Sing me no song!
Read me no rhyme!
Don't waste my time,
Show me!

Don't talk of June!
Don't talk of fall!
Don't talk at all!
Show me!

Never do I ever want to hear another word.
There isn't one I haven't heard.
Here we are together in what ought to be a dream;
Say one more word and I'll scream!

Haven't your arms
Hungered for mine?
Please don't "expl'ine,"
Show me! show me!

Don't wait until wrinkles and lines
Pop out all over my brow,
Show me now!

Get Me To The Church On Time

FRIENDS

> There's just a few more hours,
> That's all the time you've got.
> A few more hours
> Before they tie the knot.

DOOLITTLE

> There are drinks and girls all over London,
> and I have to track 'em down in just a few
> more hours.

> I'm getting married in the morning!
> Ding dong! the bells are gonna chime.
> Pull out the stopper!
> Let's have a whopper!
> But get me to the church on time!

> I gotta be there in the mornin'
> Spruced up and lookin' in me prime.
> Girls, come and kiss me;
> Show how you'll miss me.
> But get me to the church on time!

> If I am dancin'
> Roll up the floor.
> If I am whistlin'
> Whewt me out the door!

> For I'm gettin' married in the mornin'
> Ding dong! the bells are gonna chime.
> Kick up a rumpus
> But don't lose the compass;
> And get me to the church,

Get me to the church,
For Gawd's sake, get me to the church on time.

I'm getting married in the morning
Ding dong! the bells are gonna chime.
Drug me or jail me,
Stamp me and mail me.
But get me to the church on time.
I gotta be there in the morning
Spruced up and lookin' in me prime.
Some bloke who's able
Lift up the table,
And get me to the church on time.

If I am flying
Then shoot me down,
If I am wooin'
Get her out of town!

For I'm getting married in the morning!
Ding dong! the bells are gonna chime.
Feather and tar me;
Call out the Army;
But get me to the church,
Get me to the church,
For Gawd's sake, get me to the church on time.

A Hymn To Him

HIGGINS

    What in all of Heaven could have prompted her to go?
    After such a triumph at the ball?
    What could have depressed her?
    What could have possessed her?
    I cannot understand the wretch at all.

My Fair Lady

Women are irrational, that's all there is to that!
Their heads are full of cotton, hay and rags!
They're nothing but exasperating, irritating,
Vacillating, calculating, agitating,
Maddening, and infuriating hags!

Why can't a woman be more like a man?
Men are so honest, so thoroughly square;
Eternally noble, historically fair;
Who when you win will always give your back a pat.
Why can't a woman be like that?
Why does ev'ryone do what the others do?
Can't a woman learn to use her head?
Why do they do everything their mothers do?
Why don't they grow up like their father instead?

Why can't a woman take after a man?
Men are so pleasant, so easy to please;
Whenever you're with them, you're always at ease.
Would you be slighted if I didn't speak for hours?
Would you be livid if I had a drink or two?
Would you be wounded if I never sent you flowers?
Why can't a woman be like you?

One man in a million may shout a bit.
Now and then there's one with slight defects.
One perhaps whose truthfulness you doubt a bit.
But by and large we are a marvelous sex!

Why can't a woman behave like a man?
Men are so friendly, good-natured, and kind;
A better companion you never will find.
If I were hours late for dinner, would you bellow?
If I forgot your silly birthday, would you fuss?
Would you complain if I took out another fellow?
Why can't a woman be like us?

Why can't a woman be more like a man?
Men are so decent, such regular chaps.
Ready to help you through any mishaps.
Ready to buck you up whenever you are glum.
Why can't a woman be a chum?
Why is thinking something women never do?
Why is logic never even tried?
Straightening up their hair is all they ever do.
Why don't they straighten up the mess that's inside?

Why can't a woman be more like a man?
If I were a woman who'd been to a ball,
Been hailed as a princess by one and all;
Would I start weeping like a bathtub overflowing?
And carry on as if my home were in a tree?
Would I run off and never tell me where I'm going?
Why can't a woman be like me?

Without You

ELIZA

What a fool I was! What a dominated fool!
To think you were the earth and sky.
What a fool I was! What an addle-pated fool!
What a mutton-headed dolt was I!
No, my reverberating friend,
You are not the beginning and the end!

There'll be spring ev'ry year without you.
England still will be here without you.
There'll be fruit on the tree,
And a shore by the sea;
There'll be crumpets and tea
Without you.

Art and music will thrive without you.
Somehow Keats will survive without you.
And there still will be rain
On that plain down in Spain,
Even that will remain
Without you.
I can do
Without you.

You, dear friend, who talk so well,
You can go to Hertford, Hereford, and Hampshire!
They can still rule the land without you.
Windsor Castle will stand without you.
And without much ado
We can all muddle through
Without you!
Without your pulling it, the tide comes in,
Without your twirling it, the earth can spin.
Without your pushing them, the clouds roll by.
If they can do without you, ducky, so can I!

I shall not feel alone without you.
I can stand on my own without you.
So go back in your shell,
I can do bloody well
Without . . .

Higgins

By George, I really did it!
I did it! I did it!
I said I'd make a woman
And indeed I did!

I knew that I could do it!
I knew it! I knew it!
I said I'd make a woman
And succeed I did!

I've Grown Accustomed To Her Face

I've grown accustomed to her face!
She almost makes the day begin.
I've grown accustomed to the tune
She whistles night and noon.
Her smiles. Her frowns.
Her ups, her downs,
Are second nature to me now;
Like breathing out and breathing in.
I was serenely independent and content before we met;
Surely I could always
Be that way again—and yet
I've grown accustomed to her looks;
Accustomed to her voice;
Accustomed to her face.

Marry Freddy! What an infantile idea! What
a heartless, wicked, brainless thing to do!
But she'll regret it! She'll regret it. It's
doomed before they even take the vow!

I can see her now;
Mrs. Freddy Eynsford Hill,
In a wretched little flat above a store.
I can see her now:
Not a penny in the till,
And a bill collector beating at the door.

She'll try to teach the things I taught her,
And end up selling flow'rs instead;
Begging for her bread and water,
While her husband has his breakfast in bed!

My Fair Lady

In a year or so
When she's prematurely grey,
And the blossoms in her cheek have turned to chalk,
She'll come home and lo!
He'll have upped and run away
With a social climbing heiress from New York!

(tragically)

Poor Eliza!
How simply frightful!
How humiliating!

(irresistibly)

How delightful.

How poignant it will be on that inevitable night,
When she hammers on my door in tears and rags.
Miserable and lonely, repentant, and contrite.
Will I let her in or hurl her to the wolves?
Give her kindness or the treatment she deserves?
Will I take her back, or throw the baggage out?

(with sudden benevolence)

I'm a most forgiving man;
The sort who never could,
Ever would,
Take a position and staunchly never budge.
Just a most forgiving man.

(with sudden vindictiveness)

But I shall never take her back,
If she were crawling on her knees.

Let her promise to atone!
Let her shiver, let her moan!
I will slam the door and let the hellcat freeze.

Marry Freddy! Ha!

But I'm so used to hear her say:
Good morning every day.
Her joys, her woes,
Her highs, her lows
Are second nature to me now;
Like breathing out and breathing in.
I'm very grateful she's a woman
And so easy to forget;
Rather like a habit
One can always break—and yet
I've grown accustomed to the trace
Of something in the air;
Accustomed to her face.

Gigi

Thank Heaven For Little Girls

Each time I see a little girl
Of five or six or seven,
I can't resist the joyous urge
To smile and say.
               Thank heaven
For little girls!
For little girls get bigger every day.

Thank heaven for little girls.
They grow up in the most delightful way.

Those little eyes so helpless and appealing
One day will flash
And send you crashing through the ceiling!

Thank heaven for little girls!
Thank heaven for them all,
No matter where, no matter who.
Without them what would little boys do?

Thank heaven. . . .
Thank heaven. . . .
Thank heaven for little girls.

It's A Bore

HONORÉ
Look at all the captivating
Fascinating things there are to do!
GASTON
Name two!
HONORÉ
Look at all the pleasures,

All the myriad of treasures we have got!

GASTON

Like what?

HONORÉ

Look at Paris in the spring
When each solitary thing
Is more beautiful than ever before.
You can hear ev'ry tree
Almost saying: Look at me! . . .

GASTON

What color are the trees?

HONORÉ

Green.

GASTON

What color were they last year?

HONORÉ

Green.

GASTON

And next year?

HONORÉ

Green.

GASTON

It's a bore.

HONORÉ

Don't you marvel at the pow'r
Of the mighty Eiffel Tw'r,
Knowing there it will remain evermore?
Climbing up to the sky,
Over ninety stories high. . . .

GASTON

How many stories?

HONORÉ

Ninety.

GASTON

How many yesterday?

HONORÉ
    Ninety.
GASTON
    And tomorrow?
HONORÉ
    Ninety.
GASTON
    It's a bore.
HONORÉ
    The river Seine . . . !
GASTON
    All it can do is flow.
HONORÉ
    But think of wine!
GASTON
    It's red or white.
HONORÉ
    But think of girls.
GASTON
    It's either yes or no.
    And if it's no or if it's yes
    It simply couldn't matter less.
HONORÉ
    But think of a race
    With your horse in seventh place,
    Then he suddenly begins
    And he catches up and wins
    With a roar.
GASTON
    It's a bore!
HONORÉ
    Life is thrilling as can be!
GASTON
    Simply not my cup of tea.
HONORÉ
    It's a gay romantic fling!

GASTON
  If you like that sort of thing!
HONORÉ
  It's intriguing!
GASTON
  It's fatiguing!
HONORÉ
  It's a game!
GASTON
  It's the same
  Dull world whereever you go,
  Whatever place you are at.
  The earth is round
  But ev'rything is flat!
HONORÉ
  Don't tell me Venice has no lure.
GASTON
  Just a town without a sewer.
HONORÉ
  The leaning tower I adore!
GASTON
  Indecision is a bore.
HONORÉ
  But think of the thrill
  Of a bull fight in Seville,
  When the bull is uncontrolled
  And he charges at a bold
  Matador!
GASTON
  It's a bore.
HONORÉ
  Think of lunch beneath the trees!
GASTON
  Stop the carriage, if you please.
HONORÉ
  You mean you don't want to come?

GASTON
The thought of lunch leaves me numb.
HONORÉ
But I implore . . . !
GASTON
Oh no, Uncle. It's a bore!

I Don't Understand The Parisians

A necklace is love.
A ring is love.
A rock from some obnoxious
Little king is love.
A sapphire with a star is love.
An ugly black cigar is love.
Ev'rything you are is love.
You would think it would embarrass
All the people here in Paris
To be thinking ev'ry minute of love!

I don't understand the Parisians
Making love ev'ry time they get a chance.

I don't understand the Parisians
Wasting ev'ry lovely night on romance.

Any time
And under ev'ry tree in town
They're in session two by two.
What a crime
With all there is to see in town
They can't find something else to do!

I don't understand how Parisians
Never tire of walking hand in hand.

But they seem to love it,
And speak highly of it!
I don't understand the Parisians.

I don't understand the Parisians
Making all this to-do about l'amour.

I don't understand the Parisians
All this la-di-da is so immature.

When it's warm
They take a carriage ride at night,
Close their eyes and hug and kiss.
When it's cold
They simply move inside at night.
There must be more to life than this!

I don't understand the Parisians
Thinking love so miraculous and grand.
But they rave about it,
And won't live without it!
I don't understand the Parisians!

She's Not Thinking Of Me

She's so gay tonight!
She's like spring tonight!
She's a rollicking, frolicking thing tonight
So disarming;
Soft and charming;
She is *not* thinking of me!

In her eyes tonight
There's a glow tonight
They're so bright they could light Fontainebleau tonight

She's so gracious
So vivacious;
She is *not* thinking of me!

Bless her little heart . . .
Crooked to the core . . .
Acting out her part . . .
What a rollicking, frolicking bore!

She's such fun tonight!
She's a treat tonight!
You could spread her on bread she's so sweet tonight
So devoted,
Sugar coated,
That it's heart-warming to see
Oh, she's simmering with love!
Oh, she's shimmering with love!
Oh, she's not thinking of me!

Is it that painter from Brussels?
Is it that count with the muscles?
Is it that ice-skating lout?
That long English lord with the gout?
Is it Jacques?
Or Leon?
Oh, she's hot
But it's not for Gaston!

Oh, she's gay tonight!
Oh, so gay tonight!
A gigantic, romantic cliché tonight.
How she blushes!
How she gushes!
How she fills me with ennui!
She's so ooh la-la-la-la!

So untrue la-la-la-la!
Oh, she's not thinking of me!

The Night They Invented Champagne

GIGI

What time tomorrow will we get there?
Can I watch you play roulette there?
May I stay up late for supper?
Is it awf'lly, awf'lly upper?

MAMITA

Gigi! You'll drive us wild.
Stop, you silly child.

GIGI

Is ev'rybody celebrated
Full of sin and dissipated?
Is it hot enough to blister?
Will I be your little sister?

MAMITA

Gigi, you are absurd.
Not another word.

GASTON

Let her gush and jabber,
Let her be enthused.
I cannot remember
When I have been more amused.

GIGI

The night they invented chhchamimpagne
It's plain as it can be
They thought of you and me
The night they invented champagne
They absolutely knew
That all we'd want to do
Is fly to the sky on champagne
And shout to ev'ryone in sight

That since the world began
No woman or a man
Has ever been as happy as we are tonight!

I Remember It Well

HONORÉ
  We met at nine.
GRANDMAMA
  We met at eight.
HONORÉ
  I was on time.
GRANDMAMA
  No, you were late.
HONORÉ
  Ah yes! I remember it well.
  We dined with friends.
GRANDMAMA
  We dined alone.
HONORÉ
  A tenor sang.
GRANDMAMA
  A baritone.
HONORÉ
  Ah yes! I remember it well.
  That dazzling April moon!
GRANDMAMA
  There was none that night.
  And the month was June.
HONORÉ
  That's right! That's right!
GRANDMAMA
  It warms my heart
  To know that you
  Remember still
  The way you do.

HONORÉ

Ah yes! I remember it well

How often I've thought of that Friday——

GRANDMAMA

... Monday

HONORÉ

       ... night,

When we had our last rendez-vous.

And somehow I've foolishly wondered if you might

By some chance be thinking of it, too.

That carriage ride.

GRANDMAMA

You walked me home.

HONORÉ

You lost a glove.

GRANDMAMA

I lost a comb.

HONORÉ

Ah yes! I remember it well.

That brilliant sky.

GRANDMAMA

We had some rain.

HONORÉ

Those Russian songs.

GRANDMAMA

From sunny Spain?

HONORÉ

Ah yes! I remember it well.

You wore a gown of gold.

GRANDMAMA

I was all in blue.

HONORÉ

Am I getting old?

GRANDMAMA
   Oh no! Not you!
   How strong you were,
   How young and gay;
   A prince of love
   In ev'ry way.
HONORÉ
   Ah yes! I remember it well.

Gigi

   She's a babe! Just a babe!
   Still cavorting in her crib;
   Eating breakfast with a bib;
   With her baby teeth and all her baby curls.
   She's a tot! Just a tot!
   Good for bouncing on your knee.
   I am positive that she
   Doesn't even know that boys aren't girls.

   She's a snip! Just a snip!
   Making dreadful baby noise;
   Having fun with all her toys;
   Just a chickadee who needs her mother hen.
   She's a cub! A papoose!
   You could never turn her loose.
   She's too infantile to take her from her pen.

   Of course that weekend in Trouville
   In spite of all her youthful zeal,
   She was exceedingly polite,
   And on the whole a sheer delight.
   And if it wasn't joy galore,
   At least not once was she a bore
   That I recall.
   Not, not at all.

Gigi

Hah!

She's a child! A silly child!
Adolescent to her toes,
And good heaven how it shows.
Sticky thumbs are all the fingers she has got.
She's a child! A clumsy child!
She's as swollen as a grape,
And she doesn't have a shape.
Where the figure ought to be it is not.

Just a child! A growing child!
But so backward for her years
If a boy her age appears
I am certain he will never call again.
She's a scamp and a brat!
Doesn't know where she is at.
Unequipped and undesirable to men.

Of course I must in truth confess
That in that brand new little dress
She looked surprisingly mature
And had a definite allure,
It was a shock, in fact, to me,
A most amazing shock to see
The way it clung
On one so young.

Ah!

She's a girl! A little girl!
Getting older, it is true,
Which is what they always do;
Till that unexpected hour
When they blossom like a flow'r . . . !

The Street Where I Live

Oh, no . . . !
Oh, no . . . !
But. . . . . . . !
But. . . . . . !

There's sweeter music when she speaks,
Isn't there?
A diff'rent bloom about her cheeks,
Isn't there?
Could I be wrong? Could it be so?
Oh where, oh where did Gigi go?

Gigi, am I a fool without a mind
Or have I merely been too blind
To realize?
Oh, Gigi, why you've been growing up before my eyes.
Gigi, you're not at all that funny, awkward little girl I knew!
Oh no! Over night there's been a breathless change in you.
Oh, Gigi, while you were trembling on the brink
Was I out yonder somewhere blinking
At a star?
Oh, Gigi, have I been standing up too too close
Or back too far?
When did your sparkle turn to fire?
And your warmth become desire?
Oh, what miracle has made you the way you are?

Gigi . . . !
Gigi . . . . ! !
Gigi. . . . . . . !!!

Oh no! I was mad not to have seen the change in you!

Oh, Gigi, while you were trembling on the brink
Was I out yonder somewhere blinking
At a star?

Gigi

Oh, Gigi, have I been standing up too close
Or back too far?
When did your sparkle turn to fire?
And your warmth become desire?
Oh, what miracle has made you the way you are?

I'm Glad I'm Not Young Any More

I

Poor boy. Poor boy.
Down-hearted and depressed and in a spin.
Poor boy. Poor boy.
Oh, youth can really do a fellow in.

How lovely to sit here in the shade.
With none of the woes of man and maid.
I'm glad I'm not young anymore.

The rivals that don't exist at all;
The feeling you're only two feet tall;
I'm glad that I'm not young anymore.

No more confusion.
No morning-after surprise.
No self-delusion.
That when you're telling those lies,
She isn't wise.

And even if love comes through the door;
The kind that goes on forevermore;
Forevermore is shorter than before.
Oh, I'm so glad that I'm not young anymore.

II

The tiny remark that tortures you;

The fear that your friends won't like her too;
I'm glad I'm not young anymore.

The longing to end a stale affair
Until you find out she doesn't care.
I'm glad that I'm not young anymore.

No more frustration.
No star-crossed lover am I.
No aggravation.
Just one reluctant reply;
Lady, goodbye.

The fountain of youth is dull as paint.
Methuselah is my patron saint.
I've never been so comfortable before.
Oh, I'm so glad that I'm not young anymore.

Say A Prayer

Say a prayer for me tonight.
I'll need ev'ry prayer
That you can spare
To get me by.

Say a prayer and while you're praying
Keep on saying:
She's much too young to die.

On to your Waterloo, whispers my heart.
Pray I'll be Wellington, not Bonaparte.

Say a prayer for me this evening.
Bow your head and please
Stay on your knees
Tonight.

Camelot

I Wonder What The King Is Doing Tonight

I know what my people are thinking tonight,
As home through the shadows they wander.
Ev'ryone smiling in secret delight,
They stare at the castle and ponder.
Whenever the wind blows this way,
You can almost hear ev'ryone say:

I wonder what the King is doing tonight.
What merriment is the King pursuing tonight?
The candles at the Court, they never burn'd as bright.
I wonder what the King is up to tonight.
How goes the final hour
As he sees the bridal bower
Being legally and regally prepared?
Well, I'll tell you what the King is doing tonight:
He's scared! He's scared!

You mean that a King who fought a dragon,
Whack'd him in two and fix'd his wagon,
Goes to be wed in terror and distress?
Yes!

A warrior who's so calm in battle
Evern his armor doesn't rattle,
Faces a woman petrified with fright?
Right!

You mean that appalling clamoring
That sounds like a blacksmith hammering
Is merely the banging of his royal knees?
Please!

You wonder what the King is wishing tonight. . . .
He's wishing he were in Scotland fishing tonight.
What occupies his time while waiting for the bride?
He's searching high and low for some place to hide.
And oh, the expectation,
The sublime anticipation
He must feel about the wedding night to come!
Well, I'll tell you what the King is feeling tonight:
He's numb!
He shakes! He quails! He quakes!
Oh, that's what the King is doing tonight.

The Simple Joys Of Maidenhood

St. Genevieve! St. Genevieve!
It's Guinevere. Remember me?
St. Genevieve! St. Genevieve!
I'm over here beneath this tree.
You know how faithful and devout I am.
You must admit I've always been a lamb.
But, Genevieve, St. Genevieve,
I won't obey you any more!
You've gone a bit too far.
I won't be bid and bargain'd for
Like beads at a bazaar.

St. Genevieve, I've run away,
Eluded them and fled;
And from now on I intend to pray
To someone else instead.
Oh, Genevieve, St. Genevieve,
Where were you when my youth was sold?
Dear Genevieve, sweet Genevieve,
Shan't I be young before I'm old?

Where are the simple joys of maidenhood?
Where are all those adoring, daring boys?
Where's the knight pining so for me
He leaps to death in woe for me?
Oh, where are a maiden's simple joys?

Shan't I have the normal life a maiden should?
Shall I never be rescued in the wood?
Shall two knights never tilt for me
And let their blood be spilt for me?
Oh, where are the simple joys of maidenhood?

Shall I not be on a pedestal,
Worshipped and competed for?
Not be carried off, or betterst'll,
Cause a little war?
Where are the simple joys of maidenhood?
Are those sweet, gentle pleasures gone for good?
Shall a feud not begin for me?
Shall kith not kill their kin for me?
Oh, where are the trivial joys . . . ?
Harmless, convivial joys . . . ?
Where are the simple joys of maidenhood?

Camelot

It's true! It's true! The crown has made it clear:
The climate must be perfect all the year.

A law was made a distant moon ago here,
July and August cannot be too hot;
And there's a legal limit to the snow here
In Camelot.

Camelot

The winter is forbidden till December,
And exits March the second on the dot.
By order summer lingers through September
In Camelot.

Camelot! Camelot!
I know it sounds a bit bizarre;
But in Camelot, Camelot.
That's how conditions are.

The rain may never fall till after sundown,
By eight the morning fog must disappear.
In short, there's simply not
A more congenial spot
For happ'ly-ever-aftering than here
In Camelot.

Camelot! Camelot!
I know it gives a person pause
But in Camelot, Camelot
Those are the legal laws.

The snow may never slush upon the hillside.
By nine p.m. the moonlight must appear.
In short, there's simply not
A more congenial spot
For happ'ly-ever-aftering than here
In Camelot.

Follow Me

Far from day, far from night . . .
Out of time, out of sight . . .
Follow me . . .

Dry the rain, warm the snow . . .
Where the winds never go . . .
Follow me . . .
Follow me . . .
Follow me . . .

To a cave by a sapphire shore
We shall walk through an em'rald door.
And for thousands of evermores
To come, my life you shall be.

Only you, only I,
World farewell, world goodbye,
To our home 'neath the sea,
We shall fly,
Follow me . . .

C'est Moi

Camelot! Camelot!
In far off France I heard your call.
Camelot! Camelot!
And here am I to give my all.
I know in my soul what you expect of me;
And all that and more I shall be!

A knight of the Table Round should be invincible;
Succeed where a less fantastic man would fail;
Climb a wall no one else can climb;
Cleave a dragon in record time;
Swim a moat in a coat of heavy iron mail.
No matter the pain he ought to be unwinceable,
Impossible deeds should be his daily fare.
But where in the world
Is there in the world
A man so extraordinaire?

C'est moi! C'est moi.
I'm forced to admit!
'Tis I, I humbly reply.
That mortal who
These marvels can do,
C'est moi, c'est moi, 'tis I.
I've never lost
In battle or game.
I'm simply the best by far.
When swords are cross'd
'Tis always the same:
One blow and au revoir!
C'est moi! C'est moi,
So admir'bly fit;
A French Prometheus unbound.
And here I stand with valor untold,
Exception'lly brave, amazingly bold,
To serve at the Table Round!

The soul of a knight should be a thing remarkable:
His heart and his mind as pure as morning dew.
With a will and a self-restraint,
That's the envy of ev'ry saint,
He could easily work a miracle or two!
To love and desire he ought to be unsparkable.
The way of the flesh should offer no allure.
But where in the world
Is there in the world
A man so untouch'd and pure?

C'est moi!

C'est moi! C'est moi,
I blush to disclose,
I'm far too noble to lie.

The man in whom
These qualities bloom,
C'est moi, c'est moi, 'tis I!

I've never stray'd
From all I believe.
I'm bless'd with an iron will.
Had I been made
The partner of Eve,
We'd be in Eden still.
C'est moi! C'est moi,
The angels have chose
To fight their battles below.
And here I stand as pure as a pray'r
Incredibly clean, with virtue to spare,
The godliest man I know....!
C'est moi!

The Lusty Month Of May

Tra la! It's May!
The lusty month of May!
That lovely month when ev'ryone goes
Blissfully astray.

Tra la! It's here!
That shocking time of year!
When tons of wicked little thoughts
Merrily appear.

It's May! It's May!
That gorgeous holiday;
When ev'ry maiden prays that her lad
Will be a cad!

It's mad! It's gay!
A libelous display.
Those dreary vows that ev'ryone takes,
Ev'ryone breaks.
Ev'ryone makes divine mistakes
The lusty month of May!

Whence this fragrance wafting through the air?
What sweet feelings does its scent transmute?
Whence this perfume floating ev'rywhere?
Don't you know it's that dear forbidden fruit!
Tra la tra la. That dear forbidden fruit!
Tra la la la la.

Tra la la la la la la la la la la la
La la! It's May!
The lusty month of May!
That darling month when ev'ryone throws
Self-control away.

It's time to do
A wretched thing or two.
And try to make each precious day
One you'll always rue.

It's May! It's May!
The month of "yes, you may,"
The time for ev'ry frivolous whim,
Proper or "im."

It's wild! It's gay!
A blot in ev'ry way.
The birds and bees with all of their vast
Amorous past
Gaze at the human race aghast
The lusty month of May!

Then You May Take Me To The Fair

Sir Lionel,
>Do you recall the other night
>That I distinctly said you might
>Serve as my escort
>At the next Town Fair?

>Well, I'm afraid there's someone who
>I must invite in place of you.
>Someone who plainly is
>Beyond compare.

>That Frenchman's power is more tremendous
>Than I have e'er seen anywhere
>And when a man is that stupendous
>He by right should take me to the Fair.

LIONEL
>Your Majesty, let me tilt with him and smite him.
>Don't refuse me so abruptly I implore.
>Oh give me the opportunity to fight him
>And Gaul will be divided once more.

GUINEVERE
>You will bash and thrash him?

LIONEL
>I'll smash and mash him.

GUINEVERE
>You'll give him trouble?

LIONEL
>He will be rubble.

GUINEVERE
>A mighty wack?

LIONEL
>His skull will crack.

GUINEVERE
> Well,
>> Then you may take me to the Fair
>> If you do all the things you promise.
>> In fact my heart will break
>> Should you not take me to the Fair.
>> Sir Sagramore,
>> I have some rather painful news
>> Relative to the subject who's
>> To be beside me at the
>> Next Court Ball.
>>
>> You were the chosen one
>> I know
>> But it's tradition
>> It should go
>> To the unquestion'd
>> Champion in the hall.
>>
>> And I'm convinced that splended Frenchman
>> Can eas'ly conquer one and all;
>> And besting all our local henchmen
>> He should sit beside me at the ball.

SAGRAMORE
> I beg of you Ma'am
> Withhold your invitation.
> I swear to you
> This challenge will be met.
> And when I have finished
> Up the operation
> I'll serve them to your Highness,
> En Brochette!

GUINEVERE
> You'll pierce right through him?

SAGRAMORE
  I'll barbecue him.
GUINEVERE
  A wicked thrust?
SAGRAMORE
  'Twill be dust to dust.
GUINEVERE
  From fore to aft?
SAGRAMORE
  He'll feel a draft!
GUINEVERE
  Well then,
          You may sit
  By me at the Ball
  If you demolish him in battle.
  In fact I know I'd cry
  Were you not by
  Me at the ball.

      Sir Dinadan,
      Didn't I promise that you may
      Guide me to London on the day
      That I go up to
      Judge the cattle show?

      As it is quite a nasty ride,
      There must be someone
      At my side
      Who'll be defending me
      From beast and foe.

      So when I choose
      Whom I prefer go
      I take the strongest
      Knight I know.
      And young DuLac seems

Strongest ergo,
He should take me to the
Cattle show.

DINADAN

Your Majesty can't believe
This blust'ring prattle!
Let him prove it
With a sword or lance instead.
I promise you
When I'm done this gory battle
His shoulders will be
Lonesome for his head!

GUINEVERE

You'll disconnect him?

DINADAN

I'll vivisect him.

GUINEVERE

You'll open wide him?

DINADAN

I'll subdivide him!

GUINEVERE

Oh dear, dear dear, dear,
Then you may guide me to the show
If you can carry out your program.
In fact I'd grieve inside
Should you not guide
Me to the show.

KNIGHTS

Milady we shall put an end to
That Gallic bag of noise and nerve.
When we do all that we intend to
He'll be a plate of French Hors d'oeuvres.

GUINEVERE

I do applaud your noble goals
Now let us see if you achieve them.

And if you do then you will be
The three
Who will go
To the Ball
To the Show
And take me to the Fair!

How To Handle A Woman

Merlyn!
You swore that you had taught me ev'rything from *A* to *Zed*,

With nary an omission in between.
Well, I shall tell you what
You obviously forgot:
That's how a ruler rules a Queen!

And what of teaching me by turning me to animal and bird,
From beaver to the smallest bobolink!
I should have had a whirl
At changing to a girl,
To learn the way the creatures think!

But wasn't there a night, on a summer long gone by,
We pass'd a couple wrangling away;
And did I not say, Merlyn: What if that chap were I?
And did he not give counsel and say....
What was it now?...My mind's a wall.
Oh, yes!...By jove, now I recall.

How to handle a woman?
There's a way, said the wise old man;
A way known by ev'ry woman
Since the whole rigm'role began.

Do I flatter her? I begged him answer . . .
Do I threaten or cajole or plead?
Do I brood or play the gay romancer?
Said he, smiling: No indeed.

How to handle a woman?
Mark me well, I will tell you, Sir:
The way to handle a woman
Is to love her . . . simply love her . . .
Merely love her . . . love her . . . love her.

Before I Gaze At You Again

Before I gaze at you again
I'll need a time for tears.
Before I gaze at you again
Let hours turn to years.
I have so much
Forgetting to do
Before I try to gaze again at you.

Stay away until you cross my mind
Barely once a day.
Till the moment I awake and find
I can smile and say

That I can gaze at you again
Without a blush or qualm,
My eyes a-shine like new again,
My manner poised and calm.
Stay far away!
My love, far away!
Till I forget I gazed at you today.

If Ever I Would Leave You

If ever I would leave you
It wouldn't be in summer;
Seeing you in summer, I never would go.
Your hair streaked with sunlight . . .
Your lips red as flame . . .
Your face with a luster
That puts gold to shame.

But if I'd ever leave you,
It couldn't be in autumn.
How I'd leave in autumn, I never would know.
I've seen how you sparkle
When fall nips the air.
I know you in autumn
And I must be there.

And could I leave you running merrily through the snow?
Or on a wintry evening when you catch the fire's glow?

If ever I would leave you,
How could it be in springtime,
Knowing how in spring I'm bewitch'd by you so?
Oh, no, not in springtime!
Summer, winter or fall!
No, never could I leave you at all.

The Seven Deadly Virtues

Virtue and proper deeds, Your Majesty?
Like what?
Courage, Milord?
Purity and Humility, my liege?

Camelot

Diligence? Charity? Honesty? Fidelity?
The seven deadly virtues?
No, thank you, Your Majesty.

The seven deadly virtues,
Those ghastly little traps,
Oh, no, Milord, they weren't meant for me.
Those seven deadly virtues,
They're made for other chaps,
Who love a life of failure and ennui.

Take Courage! Now there's a sport—
An invitation to the state of rigor mort!

And Purity! A noble yen!
And very restful ev'ry now and then.

I find Humility means to be hurt;
It's not the earth the meek inherit, it's the dirt.
Honesty is fatal and should be taboo.
Diligence? A fate I would hate.
If Charity means giving, I give it to you,
And Fidelity is only for your mate.

You'll never find a virtue
Unstatusing my quo,
Or making my Be-elzebubble burst.
Let others take the high road,
I will take the low;
I cannot wait to rush in
Where angels fear to go.
With all those seven deadly virtues,
Free and happly little me has not been cursed.

What Do The Simple Folk DO?

GUINEVERE

> What do the simple folk do
> To help them escape when they're blue?
> The shepherd who is ailing,
> The milkmaid who is glum,
> The cobbler who is wailing
> From nailing
>
> > His thumb?
>
> When they're beset and besieged,
> The folk not noblessely obliged . . .
> However do they manage
> To shed their weary lot?
> Oh, what do simple folk do
> We do not?

ARTHUR

> I have been informed
> By those who know them well,
> They find relief in quite a clever way.
> When they're sorely pressed,
> They whistle for a spell;
> And whistling seems to brighten up their day.
> So they say.

GUINEVERE

> They whistle?

ARTHUR

> So they say.

GUINEVERE

> What else do the simple folk do
> To perk up the heart and get through?
> The wee folk and the grown folk
> Who wander to and fro

Have ways known to their own folk
We throne folk
             Don't know.

When all the doldrums begin,
What keeps each of them in his skin?
What ancient native custom
Provides the needed glow?
Oh, what do simple folk do?
Do you know?

ARTHUR

Once along the road
I came upon a lad
Singing in a voice three times his size.
When I asked him why,
He told me he was sad,
And singing always made his spirits rise.
So that's what simple folk do,
I surmise.

GUINEVERE

They sing?

ARTHUR

I surmise.

GUINEVERE & ARTHUR

Arise, my love! Arise, my love!
Apollo's lighting the skies, my love.
The meadows shine
With columbine
And daffodils blossom away.
Hear Venus call
To one and all:
Come taste delight while you may.
The world is bright,
And all is right,
And life is merry and gay . . . !

GUINEVERE

> What else to the simple folk do?
> They must have a system or two.
> They obviously outshine us
> At turning tears to mirth;
> Have tricks a royal higness
> Is minus
> > From birth.

> What then I wonder do they
> To chase all the goblins away?
> They have some tribal sorc'ry
> You haven't mentioned yet;
> Oh, what do simple folk do
> To forget?'

ARTHUR

> Often I am told
> They dance a firey dance,
> And whirl till they're completely uncontrolled.
> Soon the mind is blank,
> And all are in a trance,
> A vi'lent trance astounding to behold.
> And that's what simple folk do,
> So I'm told.

> *(They dance)*

GUINEVERE

> What else do the simple folk do
> To help them escape when they're blue?

ARTHUR

> They sit around and wonder
> What royal folk would do,
> And that's what simple folk do.

I Loved You Once In Silence

I loved you once in silence,
And mis'ry was all I knew.
Trying so to keep my love from showing,
All the while not knowing
You loved me too.

Yes, loved me in lonesome silence;
Your heart filled with dark despair . . .
Thinking love would flame in you forever,
And I'd never, never
Know the flame was there.

Then one day we cast away our secret longing;
The raging tide we held inside would hold no more.
The silence at last was broken!
We flung wide our prison door.
Ev'ry joyous word of love was spoken . . . !

And now there's twice as much grief,
Twice the strain for us;
Twice the despair,
Twice the pain for us
As we had known before.

Guinevere

Out the room, down the hall;
Through the yard, to the wall;
Slashing fiercely, left and right,
Lance escaped them and took flight.

The Street Where I Live

On a day, dark and drear,
Came to trial Guinevere.
Ruled the jury for her shame
She be sentenced to the flame.

As the dawn filled the sky,
On the day she would die,
There was wonder far and near:
Would the King burn Guinevere?

Would the King let her die?
Would the King let her die?
There was wonder far and near:
Would the King burn Guinevere?

She must burn. She must burn.
Spoke the King: She must burn.
And the moment now was here
For the end of Guinevere.

Then suddenly earth and sky were dazed by a pounding roar.
And suddenly through the dawn an army began to pour.
And lo! Ahead the army, holding aloft his spear,
Came Lancelot to save his dear
Guinevere!

By the score fell the dead,
As the yard turned to red.
Countless numbers felt his spear
As he rescued Guinevere.

In that dawn, in that gloom,
More than love met its doom.
In the dying candles' gleam
Came the sundown of a dream.

Guinevere! Guinevere!
In that dim, mournful year,
Saw the men she held most dear
Go to war for Guinevere.

Guinevere! Guinevere!
Guinevere! Guinevere!
Saw the men she held most dear
Go to war for Guinevere!
Guinevere! Guinevere! Guinevere!

Camelot (Reprise)

ARTHUR

Each evening from December to December
Before you drift to sleep upon your cot,
Think back on all the tales that you remember
Of Camelot.
Ask ev'ry person if he'd heard the story;
And tell it strong and clear if he has not:
That once there was a fleeting wisp of glory
Called Camelot.

Camelot! Camelot!
Now say it out with love and joy!

YOUNG TOM

Camelot! Camelot!

ARTHUR

Yes, Camelot, my boy.

Where once it never rained till after sundown;
By eight a.m. the morning fog had flown.
Don't let it be forgot.
That once there was a spot
For one brief shining moment that was known
As Camelot.

Index

Index

audiences (*continued*)
  writer's relationship with, 50,
    56, 82
  see also Camelot; *My Fair Lady*
auditions, 103–4

Baer, Max, 24
Balanchine, George, 38, 55
Ball, Lucille, 202
ballet, 55–56, 162
Band Wagon, The, 150
Barkleys of Broadway, The, 150
Baruch, Bernard, 58
Baudelaire, Charles, 138
Beaton, Cecil, 62, 76–77, 80, 100–
    101, 103, 104, 109, 123, 124,
    158, 174–75, 185, 259
Beaumont, Hugh "Binkie," 94–95,
    100, 142, 181, 249
"Before I Gaze at You Again," 247,
    327
Belasco, David, 39
Bell, Book and Candle, 63, 74, 80,
    94–95
Bells Are Ringing, The, 187, 201
Bergerac, Jacques, 179–81, 184
Bergman, Ingrid, 249
Berlin, Irving, 53, 69, 88, 92, 152,
    159, 199, 268
Bernstein, Leonard, 267
Beyond the Horizon, 52
Bogarde, Dirk, 167, 173
Bois de Boulogne, 179, 183
Bolshoi Ballet, 137
Bolton, Guy, 52
Borge, Victor, 37, 59
Boy Friend, The, 66, 137
Brecht, Bertolt, 55
Breuer, Bessie, 47
Brigadoon, 26, 31, 36–37, 38, 44, 48,
    56, 61, 70, 95, 96, 119, 243, 253

Brigadoon (film), 41, 45, 153
Broadway Melody, 152
Brooks, Richard, 151–52
Brown, Nacio, 152
Brown and Freed, 152
Buchwald, Art, 183–84
Burton, Philip, 210
Burton, Richard, 234–39, 252,
    253, 258, 259
  drinking capacity of, 222–23
  Harris compared with, 223–24
  personal and star qualities of,
    222–23, 224–25, 235, 246
  signed for *Camelot*, 210–11
Burton, Sybil Williams, 211

Caesar and Cleopatra, 135
Cagney, James, 156–57
Call Me Mister, 51
Camelot, 24, 39, 44, 56, 103, 131,
    201, 203–68
  advance sales for, 217, 250, 256
  audience reaction to, 240–41,
    250–51, 252–54, 258, 266
  Boston preview of, 240
  cast album of, 257, 260
  cast recruitment for, 210–14
  in Chicago, 266
  choreography for, 216, 225
  costumes for, 216–17, 222
  creating music and lyrics for,
    208–9, 226
  cuckoldry in, 205, 206–9
  director of, *see* Hart, Moss
  financing of, 218
  foreign productions of, 259,
    266
  Hart's replacement for, 233–35,
    238
  as hit, 258
  idealism in, 207

338

Index

Index

Index

Index

Index

Index

Index